THE JEWISH COMMUNITIES OF THE WORLD

THE JEWISH COMMUNITIES OF THE WORLD

A Contemporary Guide
Fourth Edition

Edited by
Antony Lerman
Assistant Director, Institute of Jewish Affairs

David M. Jacobs
Research and Writing

Lena Stanley-Clamp
Project Co-ordinator

Anne Frankel and Alan Montague
Editorial and Research Assistants

Facts On File®
New York

Facts On File, Inc.
460 Park Avenue South
New York, New York 10016

First edition (Institute of Jewish Affairs;
   World Jewish Congress, New York) 1959
Second edition (Institute of Jewish Affairs;
   World Jewish Congress, New York) 1963
Third edition (Andre Deutsch for
   Institute of Jewish Affairs) 1971
Fourth edition (Macmillan for
   Institute of Jewish Affairs) 1989

Library of Congress Cataloging-in-Publication Data
The Jewish communities of the world
1. Jews—Politics and government—1948–
I. Lerman, Antony.   II. Jacobs, David M.   III. Stanley-
Clamp, Lena.   IV. Institute of Jewish Affairs.
DS143.J45   1989   909′.04924   88–30991
ISBN 0–8160–2072–8

Facts On File books are available at special
discounts when purchased in bulk quantities
for businesses, associations, institutions,
or sales promotion. Please contact the Special
Sales Department at 212/683–2244.
(Dial 1–800–322–8755, except in NY, AK, HI)

Printed in Hong Kong

10, 9, 8, 7, 6, 5, 3, 2, 1

CONTENTS

PREFACE

The first edition of *The Jewish Communities of the World*, by the late Dr Nehemiah Robinson, was published in 1959. A second edition appeared in 1963 and a third in 1971. A new edition which takes note of the many changes and developments in Jewish communities was therefore long overdue. The opportunity was taken with this volume, however, to completely rewrite the book, providing more historical background and setting out the information on the current state of communities in a more useful manner.

Every effort has been made to ensure that both the historical and contemporary information is accurate. Nevertheless, mistakes are inevitable in a reference work of this kind which relies on such a wide variety of sources, the reliability of which cannot always be taken for granted. Except for a few countries, the Jewish population figures are estimates as no demographic data are available.

The need for careful research, editing, checking of facts and repeated redrafting means that the book is the work of many hands. The foundations were laid by David M. Jacobs, who was commissioned by the Institute of Jewish Affairs to do the original research and writing. He was assisted by Marion Jacobs, who, among other things, typed the original manuscript. Information on the present position of Jewish communities is based on material in the Institute of Jewish Affairs' archives and on questionnaires sent to the communities themselves.

The entire project was co-ordinated by Lena Stanley-Clamp, who organised the sending of entries to the communities for a further check on their accuracy, assisted in editing, research and checking the manuscript for consistency. It was her concentration on final completion of the project, when others were bogged down in distracting detail, which ensured the publication of this volume.

Anne Frankel and I edited the manuscript and Alan Montague conducted additional research to bring the volume up to date. Michael May checked the European entries and provided additional information for them. Parts of the manuscript were read by Dr Stephen J. Roth, Director of the Institute of Jewish Affairs, and additional help was given by Dr Elizabeth Eppler.

The volume would not have appeared without the close co-operation of all the above-mentioned and the additional help provided by Cynthia Shiloh, Patricia Harris and Dr Howard Spier. My own work as general editor was made considerably easier as a result.

The staff of World Jewish Congress offices in New York, Buenos Aires, Paris and Jerusalem also gave their assistance. Finally, special thanks must go to the many individuals in Jewish communities throughout the world who responded to questionnaires and then followed this up by checking the accuracy of the entry for their community.

ANTONY LERMAN
London

AFGHANISTAN

Population: 17 000 000   Jewish population: 50

There was certainly a Jewish community in Afghanistan up to the
twelfth century but the modern community started as an extension of
Persian Jewry, beginning with the flight of Jews from Meshed to Herat
in 1839. They lived mainly in the towns of Herat, Kabul and Balkh. By
the third quarter of the nineteenth century there were some 40 000 Jews
in Afghanistan. However, anti-Jewish repression began in 1870 and the
community started to contract.

In 1948 there were still approximately 4000 Jews in the country, but
some then left for Israel via Iran and India, despite a ban on emigration.
When the ban was lifted in 1951, 3500 left, most going to Israel. Prior to
the Soviet invasion in 1979 there were a few families still left in Herat
and Kabul and a functioning synagogue in Kabul itself.

Afghan Jews started emigrating to Palestine at the end of the First
World War. By 1937 there were 1000 Afghan Jews in the country. By
1967 the number had risen to 7000, half of whom had been born in
Afghanistan and half in Israel. In 1926 an Afghan Jewish Council was
set up in Jerusalem, and in 1943 an organisation of Afghan youth was
founded, also in Jerusalem.

Afghanistan's Communist government does not have relations with
Israel.

ALBANIA

Population: 3 000 000   Jewish population: 200

Jews fleeing after their expulsion from Spain in 1492, and from
Southern Italy slightly later, settled on the coast in Durres (Durazzo)
and Vlore (Valona). There was also a Jewish community in Berat, in
central Albania, in the seventeenth century, and Shabbatai Zvi spent
his last years in the country. Before the Second World War a Jewish
community existed in Shkoder (Scutari) in the North, and a larger one
in Koritza in the South.

In 1938 a number of German Jews fled to Albania, which remained
under the control of Italy until September 1943. In April 1944, the
Germans rounded up 400 Jews and deported them to Pristina in Serbia
before sending them on to Belsen, where more than half died.

1

Today there is no organised community, and the few Jews live in Tirana and Valona.

Religion is officially forbidden in Albania which has no diplomatic relations with Israel.

ALGERIA

Population: 20 500 000   Jewish population: 600

In Roman times converts to Judaism from local Berber tribes established communities in the region. When Christianity became the official religion of the Empire the Jews suffered persecution, but after the seventh-century Arab conquest new Jewish colonies were founded. Although Judaism was banned by the Almohad rule during the twelfth century, an influx of Sephardim from Spain in the fourteenth and fifteenth centuries succeeded in raising the community's cultural level and Algeria became the spiritual centre of Maghreb Jewry. The community flourished under Turkish rule in the sixteenth century but declined after power passed to the local Deys. Two leading families, the Bacri and the Busnach, ran community affairs during this period.

Jews continued to be oppressed under the rule of the Deys until 1830, when France occupied the country. The Crémieux Decree of 24 October 1870 granted French citizenship to all Algerian Jews except those living in the south. Despite official protection antisemitic attacks occurred during 1884–7 and again in 1897–8. A major attack took place on 5 August 1934 in Constantine when rioting Muslims attacked Jews and killed 25. During the Second World War Algeria was governed by the Vichy regime which imposed antisemitic laws and abolished the Crémieux Decree. The German occupation was brief and the arrival of the Allies in November 1942 prevented any deportations. Many Jews were involved in the Resistance and the pre-liberation revolt in Algiers was led by a Jew, José Abulker.

After the war the position of the Jews began to deteriorate; they were attacked in 1956 and the Great Synagogue of Algiers was burnt in a riot in 1960. In 1962 Algeria became independent and most of the Jewish population of around 140 000 emigrated. Between May and July 1962, 125 000 went to France and 10 000 to Israel. Since then most of the remaining Jews have left the country. The few who stayed live mostly in Algiers with others in Blida, Constantine and Oran. In Oran, where 30 000 Jews once lived there are now only about 20. The synagogue closed down some time ago and is used as a mosque. There is still a synagogue and a communal centre in Algiers and the Consistoire, the central body, is at Blida, just outside Algiers. Some 14 000 Algerian Jews have settled in Israel.

Algeria has no diplomatic relations with Israel.

ARGENTINA

Population: 29 627 000   Jewish population: 228 000

History

The Marranos who settled in Argentina in the sixteenth and seventeenth centuries eventually assimilated and the present community dates from French settlers who came in the 1860s. Refugees from Eastern Europe followed after 1889 and in the 1930s Jews from Nazi Germany arrived in the country. After the war there was a further immigration of Jews from Eastern Europe.

From 1892 the Jewish Colonisation Association (JCA), initiated by Baron de Hirsch, established Jewish agricultural settlements mainly in the central eastern provinces of Entre Rios and Santa Fé. A small number of Jews still farm on these lands. During the years of the military regime, from 1976 to 1983, many Argentinian Jews emigrated to Israel, Spain and the USA.

Composition of the Community

Most of the community are Ashkenazim from Eastern and Central Europe; about 15 per cent are Sephardim (mainly from the Middle East). The German community lives in the exclusive suburb of Belgrano in Buenos Aires. The Sephardim include Syrians from Damascus and Aleppo, Ladino-speaking Jews from the Eastern Mediterranean and Spanish-speaking Moroccans from Tetuan and Tangiers.

Most Argentinian Jews are middle class, though a small number are poor. The main centres of Jewish population are: Buenos Aires, 180 000; Rosario, 15 000; Cordoba, 10 000; Santa Fé, 5000; the towns of La Plata, Bahia Blanca, Mendoza and Mar del Plata 4000 each; Parana 3000; Resistencia 2000. A number of Jews live in rural areas and in the former JCA colonies, notably Moiseville in Santa Fé province, Riviera in La Pampa, and General Roca in Rio Negro.

Communal Organisation

The main organisation, Delegación des Asociaciones Israelitas Argentinas (Representative Organisation of Argentine Jewish Associations) known as DAIA, was founded in 1939. Its leaders are elected by a committee of representatives from the main affiliated organisations. The DAIA is recognised by the government as the community's spokesman, it deals with all issues affecting Jewish rights and it represents Argentinian Jewry within the World Jewish Congress.

The largest organisation is the Ashkenazi Kehilla, known as AMIA, Asociación Mutual Israelita Argentina (Jewish Mutual Society of Argentina). Established in 1894, its leaders are elected democratically. The main Sephardi organisations are the Congregación Israelita Latina (Jewish Latin Congregation) founded in 1891 by North Africans; the Asociación Israelita Sefaradí Argentina (Sephardi Jewish Association of Argentina), AISA, founded early this century by Jews from Aleppo and subsequently including Sephardim from Palestine and the Caucasus; the organisation established by the Damascene Jews in 1913; and the largest, the Asociación Comunidad Israelita Sefaradi de Buenos Aires (Association of the Sephardi Jewish Community of Buenos Aires), ACIS, which united Ladino speakers with Jews from Rhodes, Turkey and the Balkans.

Although the Sephardim do not have an all-embracing organisation the Ente Coordinador Sefaradi Argentino (Sephardi Co-ordinating Body of Argentina), ECSA, attends to domestic affairs. The Federación de Comunidades Israelitas (Federation of Jewish Communities), often known by its Hebrew title of Vaad Hakehillot (the Council of the Communities), is the umbrella organisation for the provincial Jewish communities. The Organización Sionista Argentina (OSA) is the national federation of all the country's Zionist parties. The movement is very active with 49 groups in Buenos Aires alone. Zionist politics tend to dominate elections to the local bodies. The Zionist Women's Organisation is the largest WIZO Federation in South America while the Council of Jewish Women is the largest affiliate of the International Council of Jewish Women on the continent.

The offices of the Congreso Judio Latinoamericano, the Latin American Branch of the World Jewish Congress, are in Buenos Aires.

Religious Life
The Buenos Aires-based AMIA supervises the rabbinate and all Ashkenazi religious activity. The Federación Sefaradi Latinoamericana (FESELA) is the Sephardi religious umbrella organisation. The central organisation for Conservative Jews is the Seminario Rabinico Latinoamericano. The main synagogue is the Bet-El community. There is also a Reform congregation, the Emanu-El. There are about 50 synagogues in Buenos Aires and other communal centres, synagogues or prayer rooms in most provincial communities. There are also five kosher restaurants in Buenos Aires and 29 kosher butchers under the supervision of the Chief Rabbi, and a further 17 independent kosher butchers.

Education
Greater Buenos Aires has 71 Jewish primary and secondary schools, incorporating approximately 20 000 pupils, and six *yeshivot* including one Lubavitch. There are a further 27 Jewish schools in the provinces. Most

of the administration of the Jewish educational system is done by the Education Department in the Kehilla building.

Cultural Activities
Buenos Aires has a Jewish museum, three libraries and four bookshops. The two largest cultural institutions are the Sociedad Hebraica with 25 000 members, and the Sephardi CASA, which has fine sports and recreation grounds. Hacoaj and Maccabi also provide excellent sport facilities. Cordoba has a well-equipped community centre administered by a Conservative rabbi.

Press
All the Jewish newspapers are published in Buenos Aires. The fortnightly *La Luz* has a circulation of 12 000. The bi-weekly *Oji* is published by the Latin American Jewish Congress in an edition of 5000. The independent Zionist weekly *Seminario Israelita* has a circulation of 4000 and covers religious affairs and international news. *Coloquio*, published tri-annually by the Latin American Jewish Congress in an edition of 2000, covers politics, Jewish history and Jewish affairs. The quarterly *Maj'shavot*, with a circulation of 1500, is concerned with religious matters and is published by the Latin American Office of the World Council of Synagogues.

Welfare
Welfare activities are co-ordinated by the Ente Coordinador de Entidades Asistenciales, a branch of AMIA, whose many services include a Jewish hospital, two homes for the aged, a community dining room and the Jewish Tuberculosis League.

Relations with Israel
These are on full ambassadorial level.

General Position
Although the disturbed political situation of Argentina inevitably affected the Jews – at least 500 'disappeared' under the military regime – organised Jewish life continued. Today the greatest threat the community faces is that of assimilation.

ARUBA

Population: 65 000   Jewish population: 30

Aruba and Curaçao constitute the Netherlands Antilles. Some Jews came from Curaçao in the nineteenth century but did not stay. The present settlement dates from 1924 and the synagogue and communal centre in Oranjestad were built in 1962. The community is governed

5

by a Board of five elected members. There is no rabbi, but there is an ORT group and a United Jewish Appeal (UJA) group. The Beth Israel Congregation is affiliated to the World Jewish Congress.

AUSTRALIA

Population: 15 369 000   Jewish population: 90 000

History
When Australia was founded as a British penal settlement in 1788, several Jews were amongst the first deported convicts. In 1817 a burial society was founded in New South Wales but it was not until the 1820s that the first free Jewish immigrants arrived in the country. In 1832 Sydney's Jewish congregation was established and its synagogue was opened in 1844. Melbourne's first Jewish Service was held in 1839 and a synagogue was opened in 1848. Further congregations were established at Adelaide in 1848, Ballerat in 1853, Geelong in 1854, Brisbane in 1865 and Perth in 1892, and in Tasmania at Hobart in 1845 and Launceston in 1846.

During the nineteenth-century gold rush Jewish immigration increased and continued steadily until the Second World War. The post-war years brought a further influx of Jews, many of them from Germany and Eastern Europe.

Australian Jews have made important contributions to public life. Two have held the position of Governor General. The Commander in Chief of the Australian Army in the First World War was a Jew.

Composition of the Community
The community is predominantly Ashkenazi and middle class, with most young Jews today receiving higher education. Of the two largest communities, Melbourne is the more traditional with many Yiddish-speaking Jews of Polish origin, whereas the Jews of Sydney (many of German or Hungarian origin) are more assimilated.

The centres of Jewish population are: Melbourne, 35–40 000; Sydney, 28–30 000; Adelaide, 1600; Brisbane, 1500; Gold Coast (Queensland), 1200; Canberra, 300; and Hobart, 50. These figures may be slightly higher as the overall figure for Australian Jewry is now put at 90 000 following research carried out in 1984 by the Australian Institute of Jewish Affairs.

Legal Status
All Australian Jewish organisations have a voluntary status. A constitutional separation of church and state exists.

Communal Organisation

The Executive Council of Australian Jewry (ECAJ) is the central political organisation of Australian Jewry and alternates its headquarters every two years between Sydney and Melbourne. It concentrates on public relations, anti-defamation and foreign relations and is affiliated to the World Jewish Congress. Each state with a Jewish community has its own central body, which sends its representatives to the ECAJ. The two main bodies are the New South Wales Jewish Board of Deputies in Sydney and the Victorian Jewish Board of Deputies in Melbourne. Others include the West Australian Jewish Board of Deputies in Perth, the South Australian Jewish Board of Deputies in Adelaide and the Queensland Jewish Board of Deputies in Brisbane.

The central Zionist organisation, to which all parties and youth movements are affiliated, is the Zionist Federation of Australia which has its headquarters in Sydney. State Zionist Councils exist in New South Wales, Queensland, South Australia, West Australia and Victoria. The JNF, the Federal United Israel Appeal, Magen David Adom and Friends of the Hebrew University have branches throughout the country. WIZO has its central office in Melbourne and state branches in Victoria and New South Wales. The National Council of Jewish Women of Australia has sections in every major city.

Religious Life

The central religious body, the Association of Jewish Ministers of Australia and New Zealand, is based in Sydney. Liberal and Sephardi Jews have their own organisations: the Australian Union for Progressive Judaism and the Sephardi Federation of Australian Jewry. There are approximately 15 synagogues in Sydney, 20 in Melbourne, 3 in Perth and others in Canberra, Newcastle, New South Wales, Brisbane, Gold Coast (Queensland), Adelaide, Ballarat, Geelong and Hobart. There are Batei Din in Sydney and Melbourne. *Shechita* is permitted and there are two kosher restaurants in Sydney and four in Melbourne. Approximately 20 per cent of the Jewish population observe *kashrut*.

Education

Jewish educational institutions exist on all levels. The two main supervisory bodies are the New South Wales Board of Jewish Education in Sydney and the United Jewish Education Board in Melbourne. However, many schools are independent.

Melbourne has eight private day-schools including several hassidic foundations, a Liberal school and a Yiddish school. Mount Scopus College (probably the largest of its type in the Diaspora) has 2300 students between the ages of 4 and 17. Sydney has eight Jewish schools,

7

attended by approximately half of the city's Jewish school-age children. There are also Jewish day-schools in Adelaide and Perth. The Carmel School in Perth has a kindergarten.

The Prahran College of Advanced Education in Melbourne has a Department of Jewish Studies, the universities of Melbourne and Sydney offer Hebrew, Semitic and Middle East Studies and Shalom College at the University of New South Wales concentrates solely on Jewish studies. The Yeshiva Gedolah in Melbourne offers a four-year course for prospective rabbis and a one-year course in rabbinic studies. All the Jewish communities organise educational courses on a part-time basis. An unusual feature of Australian Jewish education is the extensive teaching of Yiddish: full time at one school in Melbourne and part-time elsewhere.

Cultural Activities
Youth activities and sport in Sydney are organised by the Hakoah Club and the Maccabi Sports Centre. Melbourne's Zionist youth groups include Betar, B'nai Akiva, Habonim and Hashomer Hatzair. Sydney's cultural facilities include the A. L. Falk Memorial Library of Judaica, the A. M. Rosenblum Museum and two further Jewish museums. Shalom College also functions as a community cultural centre.

Melbourne has the Southern Jewish Community Centre and a museum built in 1982. There are two Jewish bookshops in Sydney, two in Melbourne and the National Jewish Memorial Centre in Canberra. Two important cultural organisations are the expanding Australian Jewish Historical Society and the Australian Institute of Jewish Affairs (affiliated to the Institute of Jewish Affairs in London) which arranges lectures and seminars and pursues research projects.

Press
The *Australian Jewish News* is published weekly in Melbourne and Sydney in English and Yiddish editions. The *Australian Jewish Times* is published weekly in Sydney. Publications in Yiddish are the quarterly Bundist *Unzer Gedank* and *Melbourner Bletter*, the Yiddish section of the *Melbourne Chronicle*, a quarterly devoted to creative writing and commentary on contemporary Jewish affairs.

The ethnic radio stations in Melbourne and Sydney broadcast regular programmes of Jewish interest in English, Yiddish and Hebrew.

Welfare
Welfare is organised by the Australian Jewish Welfare Society in Sydney and the Jewish Welfare Relief Society in Melbourne. There are Montefiore Homes for the aged in both cities, and the Wolper Jewish Hospital in Sydney.

Relations with Israel
Relations with Israel are on full ambassadorial level. The Israeli Embassy is in Melbourne and there is a Consulate General in Sydney. Australia has a history of pro-Israel sympathies and in 1981 sent troops to participate in the multi-national force and observers (MFO) in Sinai.

Historical Sites
The oldest synagogues are at Hobart and Launceston in Tasmania and were built in the 1840s. However, the Launceston synagogue was closed down in 1960.

General Position
Unlike many other Diaspora communities, the Australian Jewish community shows signs of increase rather than decline, with a rising birth rate and continuing immigration. Communal life is vigorous and the system of Jewish education is exceptionally good.

There are some significant anti-Zionist groups, notably the extreme left of the Australian Labour Party which is pro-PLO and controls a radio station in Melbourne. Some student groups, left-wing trade unions and many of the approximately 10 000 Arab Muslims are also anti-Zionist. On the right the only antisemitic organisation of any significance is the Australian League of Rights.

AUSTRIA

Population: 7 552 000   Jewish population: 12 000

History
There may have been a Jewish community in Austria during the Roman era, but first reference to Jews is in 906 CE. A charter granted to the Jews in 1238 was followed by the Privilegium Fredericianum, given by Frederick the Quarrelsome in 1244. In the thirteenth and fourteenth centuries Vienna was considered one of the leading Jewish communities, but the next four centuries were mainly characterised by persecutions. In 1420 the community experienced expulsion, conversion and murder. This was followed by a very slow return but in 1670 Emperor Leopold I expelled Jews from the Austrian territories. They were eventually allowed to return, but restrictions on residence and other difficulties remained until the Edict of Toleration of 1782. Full rights were granted in 1867.

In the fifty years before the Second World War the culture of German-speaking Jewry reached its peak, making incomparable contributions to science, music, art and literature. Amongst the major figures of Viennese Jewry were Sigmund Freud, Gustav Mahler, Alfred Adler,

Karl Kraus, Arnold Schoenberg, Arthur Schnitzler and Stefan Zweig.

After the Anschluss on 13 March 1938, the activity of all Jewish organisations was forbidden, the Great Synagogue of Vienna was desecrated and occupied by the German army, and 500 Jews committed suicide. However, out of a community of 183 000, about 120 000 Austrian Jews managed to emigrate during the next two years. Almost all the remaining 60–70 000 were murdered.

Composition of the Community

The majority of Austria's Jews live in Vienna (11 000), with small communities in Graz, Salzburg, Linz and Innsbruck. The community is primarily Ashkenazi (8–9 000) but there are about 900 Georgian Jews from Bokhara, and 25 to 30 families from Iran. Twenty per cent of the 6300 registered Jews are of pre-1938 Austrian origin. The rest are from Eastern Europe (mainly Hungarian, Czech and Polish refugees from Communist purges). Between 3000 and 4000 are emigrants from the USSR who came to Austria after a brief stay in Israel.

The community is mostly middle class. More than half the population is aged over 60.

Legal Status

The Israelitische Kultusgemeinde (Jewish Community) has the same status in public law as the various churches, with the right to public performance of religion and internal autonomy, including the right to impose taxation on its members. The 1890 Israelitengesetz, which was partly repealed in September 1981, allowed the existence of one, undivided community in each locality: the Israelitische Kultusgemeinde. However, from May 1982, independent communities have been permitted, based on individual congregations, though none have yet been established.

Communal Organisation

The various Jewish communities in the country are represented in the umbrella organisation, the Bundesverband der Israelitischen Kultusgemeinden Osterreichs (Federation of Jewish Communities of Austria) which is affiliated to the World Jewish Congress. Dominant among these communities is the Israelitische Kultusgemeinde of Vienna which has a governing board (Kultus Vorstand) elected by the members of the community, and a President who is also the head of the Bundesverband. The Zionist groups are organised in the Zionist Federation of Austria, which consists of the Allgemeine Zionisten, Hashomer Hatzair, Mizrahi and Herut. The Jewish Agency and Jewish National Fund have offices in Vienna where there is also a WIZO (which has several working groups) and a B'nai B'rith Lodge. A second B'nai B'rith Lodge, composed mostly of younger members, has recently been granted a charter.

Religious Life
The community has a Chief Rabbi but no Beth Din. The Chief Rabbi is not recognised by the ultra-Orthodox. The principal synagogue in Vienna is the Stadt Tempel, and there are several ultra-Orthodox prayer rooms, and a Sephardi prayer room. Synagogues exist in the towns of Eisenstadt (now a museum), Baden, Linz and Salzburg. Recently, the synagogue in St. Polten was rebuilt as a museum by the state. There are 2 kosher restaurants and 2 kosher butchers in Vienna and a kosher hotel in Bad Gastein. About 25 per cent of the population keep *kashrut*. *Shechita* is permitted.

Education
Vienna has two Jewish kindergartens, a primary school and an evening school for Russian immigrants. There is also an ultra-Orthodox school for children from the age of 4 to 16 with a *cheder*, primary school and high school. In 1984 the once famous Chajes Gymnasium was reopened after 46 years' closure. Vienna University has a department of Jewish studies (Institut fur Judaistik). Some 35 per cent of young Jews attend university.

Cultural Activities
Vienna, Graz, Innsbruck, Linz and Salzburg have community centres. Youth organisations include B'nai Akiva, Hashomer Hatzair and a Hakoah sports club. The Chief Rabbi gives talks on the radio four to five times a year on the eve of Jewish holidays.

Press
The community issues a monthly publication, *Die Gemeinde*, with a circulation of 4500. The *Illustrierte Neue Welt*, a Zionist-orientated monthly periodical, is the direct successor to *Die Welt*, founded by Theodor Herzl in 1897. The Association of Jewish Students publishes the annual *Jüdisches Echo* and a bi-monthly bulletin, *Noodnik*.

Welfare
Vienna has a home for the aged with a geriatric clinic attached to it.

Relations with Israel
Austria has full diplomatic relations with Israel but following the election of Kurt Waldheim to the presidency in 1986, Israel is only represented in Vienna by a chargé d'affaires while the Austrian ambassador remains in Tel Aviv.

Historical Sites
The synagogue in Vienna's Seitenstattengasse was founded in 1826. Edlach has a memorial to Theodor Herzl. In Eisenstadt the house of the Wertheimer family, who played such an important part in eighteenth-century Jewish history, is now converted into a Jewish Museum. Since

1982 an important Jewish collection from Vienna has been on display in the Eisenstadt Austrian Jewish Museum. One of the largest private Judaica collections with over 2500 exhibits is in the home of Mr Max Berger. Also of Jewish interest is the Sigmund Freud house in Vienna.

The Road Chain, which was once used to prevent traffic entering the Jewish Quarter during the sabbath and on festivals, still exists in the Unterbergstrasse.

General Position
Jews enjoy equal rights and some hold important positions. The post-war period produced the first Jewish Chancellor, Dr Bruno Kreisky, who, though not a professing Jew, was recognised as such and has never denied his Jewish origins. Austria was of paramount importance to the Jewish world as the transit country for Soviet Jewish emigrants. The former Chancellor, Dr Kreisky, gave full support to this cause. Jewish emigration from the USSR declined drastically in the 1980s making this aspect of Austrian policy much less relevant.

Surveys show that antisemitism still exists. Spokesmen for the Jewish community maintain that the revelations about Dr Kurt Waldheim's Nazi past, which surfaced during his presidential election campaign in the spring of 1986 and continued after his election to the presidency, have led to open expressions of antisemitism. The Waldheim affair has certainly damaged relations between Jews and non-Jews in Austria as well as relations between the Austrian government on the one hand, and Jewish diaspora organisations and the State of Israel on the other.

Of some concern is the Aktion Neue Rechte which enjoys a certain popularity among students. Simon Wiesenthal's Documentation Centre on war criminals is in Vienna and a Jewish-Christian interfaith organisation is active.

BAHAMAS

Population: 250 000   Jewish population: 200

There are Jews resident in Nassau and at Freeport on Grand Bahama, where there is a synagogue named after the first Jew to set foot in the Bahamas, Luis de Torres, Columbus' interpreter. A Marano, who continued to practise his religion in secret, he was also one of the first Europeans to live in the West Indies.

The Bahamas were first settled by the British in 1620. In the eighteenth century a Jew, Moses Franks, was Attorney General and Chief Justice of the islands. After the First World War some ten families from Poland, Russia and the United Kingdom came to live in Nassau. During the 1980s some 40 families have been resident in the Bahamas and Jewish visitors from abroad come to stay there during the tourist season.

The Nassau Hebrew Congregation and the Freeport Congregation have united to form the United Bahamas Hebrew Congregation.

Israel has a consulate with an honorary consul general in Nassau.

BARBADOS

Population: 270 000   Jewish population: 50

Jewish settlement dates back over 300 years, as Barbados was one of the places where Jewish refugees fled after the Portuguese re-conquest of north-east Brazil. (See under Brazil and USA.) The first community was established in Bridgetown in 1656. Brazilian Jews were largely responsible for the introduction of sugar into the island and most of the sugar industry was in their hands until 1666 when they were prohibited from retailing goods and trading with the indigenous population. These discriminatory measures were repealed in 1761.

Barbados granted emancipation to Jews in 1802, one of the first parts of the British Empire to do so. This act was subsequently confirmed by the British Parliament in 1820. However, due to the economic decline of Barbados, the old community gradually disappeared. The synagogue, which is still standing, was sold in 1920. It is now to be restored together with the old cemetery with the support of the government. Most of the present community are refugees or children of refugees who settled after 1933. Their numbers are augmented throughout most of the year by hundreds of Jewish visitors from abroad.

The central body is the Jewish Community Council in Bridgetown which is affiliated to the World Jewish Congress. Services are held on Friday evenings in the community centre. The Israeli ambassador in Jamaica, resident in Kingston, is also accredited to Barbados.

BELGIUM

Population: 9 863 000   Jewish population: 30 000

History
Some Jewish settlement is known to have existed in Roman times, but the communities were destroyed, through massacre and expulsion, at the time of the Great Plague of 1348. In the early sixteenth century Marranos began to settle in Bruges and Antwerp and a semi-overt synagogue in Antwerp

was established in the seventeenth century. The Ashkenazis settled in the eighteenth century under Austrian rule. In 1794, the French occupied Belgium and Jews were given the right to settle freely in Brussels and Antwerp. Under the 1831 constitution of independent Belgium Jewish equality was finally established.

By 1940 there were an estimated 100 000 Jews living in Belgium, including 20 000 refugees from Germany. Only 5–10 per cent of the Jewish population had Belgian nationality because of the Belgian government's restrictive naturalisation policies. Large numbers of Jews fled the country before the German invasion.

Deportation started on 4 August 1942 and an internment camp for deportation to Auschwitz was set up at Dossin near Malines. Of the 25 631 Jews deported, only 1244 survived. Twenty-five thousand Jews were hidden by the Belgians; 1000 Belgian Jews fought with the partisans and 242 were killed in action.

Composition of the Community

The Belgian Jewish community is primarily Ashkenazi, with a strong ultra-Orthodox element in Antwerp. There are also small Sephardi communities in Antwerp and Brussels. The main concentrations of Jews are in Brussels and Antwerp. Much smaller communities can be found in Liège, Charleroi, Ghent, Ostend, Knokke, Arlon and Mons.

The majority of Belgian Jews are middle class, working in wholesale and retail trades, and in the professions. There is a strong concentration of Jews in the Antwerp diamond industry.

Legal Status

The Belgian Constitution established freedom of religion in 1831, and under a Royal Decree of February 1876 the Jewish religion and its central organisation, the Consistoire Central, was granted the same status and rights as are available to other religions.

Communal Organisation

The umbrella organisation of the Belgian Jewish community is the Comité de Coordination des Organisations Juives de Belgique (Co-ordinating Committee of Jewish Organisations of Belgium), which was founded in 1970. In 1977 it was incorporated with the Belgian section of the World Jewish Congress and became the Belgian affiliate to the WJC. The Zionist Federation has 5000 members, and there are active WIZO groups in Brussels, Antwerp, Charleroi, Ghent, Liège and Mons. The Fédération des Organisations Feminines Juives de Belgique co-ordinates the work of the various women's groups. B'nai B'rith has an active organisation in the country.

Youth movements include the youth branches of the Agudat Israel,

Betar, B'nai Akiva, Dror, Hashomer Hatzair, Hanoar Hatzioni, the Federation of Jewish Youth, Maccabi and the Jewish Youth Centre.

Religious Life

The Consistoire Central Israélite de Belgique acts as the representative and unifying body of all the individual communities. There are several synagogues in both Antwerp and Brussels. Antwerp has 3 Jewish congregations and Brussels 6 and both cities have Sephardi and Liberal synagogues. Synagogues also exist in Arlon, Knokke, Liège and Ostend. Antwerp itself is a major centre of Hassidism and the following hassidic movements have *shtiblach* in the city: Belz, Gur, Lubavitch, Satmar, Chortkow and Wischnitz.

Antwerp is well supplied with kosher butchers, bakers and restaurants and Brussels has a kosher butcher and a kosher baker. There is a Beth Din of the Orthodox (Machsike Hadass) in Brussels.

Education

Belgium has a well-developed Jewish school system. Schools in Antwerp include the Yessodei Hatorah (1100 pupils), which concentrates on Talmud studies, the Tachkemoni School (780 pupils), an Orthodox school and several *yeshivot*. Ninety per cent of Jewish children in Antwerp attend these schools.

Brussels has three schools: the Athénée Maimonide primary and secondary with 410 children; the Ganenou primary and secondary with 562 children; and the Beth Aviv primary with 150 children. The Martin Buber Institute, linked to the Free University of Brussels, teaches Jewish courses at university level.

Cultural Activities

A variety of cultural activities are conducted, particularly at the community centres, including the Centre Communautaire Laïque Juif, the Centre des Jeunes and the Centre Ben Gurion in Brussels, the Romi Goldmuntz Centre in Antwerp and community centres in Charleroi, Liège and Ostend.

There is no Jewish museum in the country but the Plantin-Moretus Museum in Antwerp has early examples of Jewish printing, including the Polyglot Bible.

Press

The main Flemish language paper is the *Belgisch Israelitisch* which is a weekly published in Antwerp. The weekly *Israël d'aujourdhui* and the monthly papers *Centrale*, *Kehilatenou*, and *Magazine J* are published in Brussels. A Zionist paper, *La Tribune Sioniste*, is published fortnightly as is *Regards*, which takes a left-wing Zionist view. The Anti-Defamation

League publishes a monthly *In de naam van de Vrijheid* (In the Name of Freedom). There are four Jewish bookshops in Antwerp and one in Brussels. A private radio station, Radio Judaica, broadcasts for several hours daily except Saturdays.

Welfare
The Central Organisation for Jewish Social Work operates from both Brussels and Antwerp, organises fund-raising and owns a holiday camp at Koksijde-on-Sea. Brussels has a Jewish social service office and a geriatric centre. The United HIAS has offices in the city. Colonie Amitié organises holiday camps for children.

The Antwerp offices of the Centrale run a club for the aged and a medico-psychiatric centre. There is also a home for the aged and a geriatric centre.

Relations with Israel
Diplomatic relations are on full ambassadorial level and the Israel Ambassador also represents his country at the European Economic Community.

Historical Sites
In the Anderlecht district of Brussels a monument to the Jews killed by the Nazis and Jewish resistance fighters has 25 838 names engraved on it. The memorial square has been renamed by the city council as the Square of the Jewish Martyrs.

General Position
The Belgian community is very vigorous, with a flourishing ultra-Orthodox and hassidic section in Antwerp. There is little antisemitism and in 1981 strong laws against racial discrimination and incitement to racial hatred were introduced. Small, fringe Flemish and Walloon antisemitic groups exist on the ultra-right.

BERMUDA

Population: 68 000   Jewish population: 50

Although there have been reports of Jews, mainly merchants, on Bermuda since the seventeenth century, no organised community took root. The island played a brief role in Jewish history between 19 and 30 April 1943 when President Franklin D. Roosevelt called a conference to consider ways of rescuing Jews from the Nazis. The Bermuda Conference, as it is known, reached no effective conclusions, and was subsequently described by the leading British delegate as 'a façade for inaction'.

The few Jews living on the island have no communal organisation. However, an Oneg Shabbat is held on the first Friday of every month and there are services on High Holy Days although there is no synagogue. The community exists because the country is a major holiday resort for United States, Canadian and British Jews, and because there are some Jews attached to the United States military base. The few Jewish permanent residents play a leading role in the island's life.

BOLIVIA

Population: 6 252 000   Jewish population: 600

History
The most Catholic of all the South American countries, Bolivia only became receptive to Jewish immigration at the beginning of this century. The first Jews arrived in 1905 and were followed in the 1920s and early 1930s by refugees from Russia and Eastern Europe, many of whom moved on later. A large number of Germans and Austrians arrived in the early war years but immigration was stopped in 1940. At its peak, the Jewish population numbered approximately 10 000.

Composition of the Community
Most Bolivian Jews are Ashkenazim from either Eastern Europe or Germany and Central Europe. There are few Sephardim. The largest community in La Paz numbers approximately 520. One hundred and eighty Jews live in Cochabamba, roughly 60 or 70 in Santa Cruz and less than 10 in Tarija. Most Bolivian Jews are middle class and in commerce with a few working in light industry.

Legal Status
The Circulo Israelita de Bolivia, the community's central body is recognised by the government.

Communal Organisation
The Circulo Israelita de la Paz, which is affiliated to the World Jewish Congress, was merged in 1980 with the Comunidad Israelita. Originally the Circulo represented East European Jewry and the Comunidad the German. The Circulo maintains the Chevra Kadisha, a cemetery, the Bikur Cholim, two synagogues and an old-age home. Cochabamba has an Asociación Israelita de Cochabamba, a WIZO group and a Magbit. Santa Cruz also has its own Circulo Israelita.

17

Religious Life

There are two synagogues in La Paz and one in Cochabamba. The Ashkenazi synagogue of the Circulo Israelita in La Paz employs a rabbi from Israel who also acts as *shochet* and *mohel*, La Paz's other synagogue performs services in accordance with the German Jewish ritual.

Education

The Colegio Boliviano Israelita (Bolivian Jewish College) in La Paz comprises a kindergarten, primary and secondary schools. Of its 600 pupils only 10 per cent are Jewish, but its teachers of Hebrew, Jewish history and religion are Jews. The college is administered by a council of representatives of the Circulo Israelita and other institutions.

Recently, many Jewish parents have been sending their children abroad – particularly to Israel – for secondary and higher education. Many of them do not return.

Cultural Activities

B'nai B'rith, known here as the Asociación Benefactora Israelita Boliviana, has an active branch, with its own library in La Paz. Dor Hemshech arranges social and cultural activities for young couples. Social activities also take place in the large building owned by the Circulo Israelita in the centre of La Paz. This building also houses the offices of B'nai B'rith, WIZO and Maccabi. In the La Paz suburb of Obrajes, the community owns a recreation centre (with a garden) used mainly at weekends. Club Maccabi runs youth activities in La Paz and in Cochabamba.

Welfare

There are homes for the aged in both La Paz and Cochabamba. The home in La Paz is also used as a Jewish youth hostel. The home is owned by SOPRO (Sociedad por la Protección a los Immigrantes Israelies) which aided Jewish immigrants between 1940 and 1950 and still gives help to the needy.

Relations with Israel

There are close relations between the two countries, with Israel maintaining an embassy in La Paz and Bolivia one of the few states retaining its embassy in Jerusalem. Bolivia has benefited from Israeli expertise in the fields of management and agriculture. The Bolivia–Israel Cultural Institute organises various activities including talks by visiting lecturers.

General Position
In October 1982, telephone threats and raids on the Cochabamba synagogue indicated that antisemitism is still alive in Bolivia. The Jewish community as a whole is threatened by further decline as a result of its young members choosing to emigrate.

BRAZIL

Population: 130 000 000   Jewish population: 150 000

History
Jewish converts to Christianity, led by Fernão de Noronha, were amongst the first Portuguese settlers in Brazil in the early sixteenth century and were instrumental in developing the production of cotton, rice, sugar and tobacco.

With the seventeenth-century Dutch conquest of north-east Brazil (including the towns of Bahia, Recife and Pernambuco), many Jews ceased practising their religion in secret and in 1642 the first rabbi in all the Americas, Isaac de Fonseca Aboab, was appointed in Recife. However, when Recife was reoccupied by Portugal in 1654, many Jews, including Rabbi Aboab, fled to Amsterdam. (Another small group fled to North America, so laying the foundations of that country's Jewish community.)

The Inquisition, under Portuguese direction, continued until 1769. Although many Jews had converted, they were persecuted as heretics. A particularly tragic case was that of the promising young playwright, Antonio José da Silva, born in Rio de Janeiro in 1705, who was arrested and burnt at the stake at a Lisbon auto-da-fé in 1739. A Portuguese Royal Decree ending persecution of 'New Christians' by the Inquisition was passed in 1773. Brazil became independent in 1822 and religious liberty was decreed in the Imperial Constitution of 1824. Some of the remaining converts thereupon openly reverted to Judaism and Moroccan Sephardim soon began to arrive in the country, eventually founding the first Brazilian synagogue in Belém do Para in 1824.

The ruler of Brazil between 1841 and 1889 was Dom Pedro II, a philosemite who studied Hebrew under a Swedish professor and, when exiled, published his own French translations of Hebrew literature.

By 1856 Alsatian Jews had come to dominate trade in precious stones in Rio de Janeiro. European Jewish immigration steadily increased, and after 1871 there was a further influx of French and Alsatian Jews, particularly to São Paulo. However, many Jews assimilated. By 1901, the nominal Jewish population had only reached 1021. In the early years of this century there was further immigration of East European Jews and, in 1903, the first Jewish agricultural settlement, Colonia Filipson, was created. However, neither this nor the Qautro Irmaos settlement set up in 1910, lasted long and most of the original colonists eventually settled in Pôrto Alegre. A Jewish school was founded in Rio in 1916 and by 1917 the Jewish population had risen to 5000. Immigration increased in the 1920s and after 1933 the country received refugees from Germany. Although community structures had been established at the beginning of the century, a central communal organisation of Brazilian Jewry was not created until 1951.

Composition of the Community
Brazilian Jewry is 80 per cent Ashkenazi and 20 per cent Sephardi. The principal communities are in São Paulo (75 000), Rio de Janeiro (55 000) and Pôrto Alegre (15 000) with smaller communities in Belo Horizonte, Salvador (the former Bahia), Belém, Curitiba and Recife. At Manaus, more than 700 miles up the Amazon, are two synagogues and a Jewish social centre.

According to the Brazilian National Institute of Statistics, in 1980 there were 91 795 Jews in Brazil with 44 569 in São Paulo and 29 157 in Rio. However, these figures were not accepted by the Brazilian Jewish community, as they are based only on the number of people who gave their religion as Jewish in the official census.

The Jewish community is largely affluent although some have been affected by the deterioration in the Brazilian economy. Many hold positions in industry, commerce, journalism and the professions. Although Jews participate in cultural life, they tend not to be involved in politics.

Legal Status
The Imperial Constitution of 1824 designated Roman Catholicism as the official religion of the country with other religious groups having the right to practise in private. Since Brazil became a republic in 1889, church and state have been completely separate.

Communal Organisation
The central organisation, the Confederaçao Israelita do Brasil (CIB) was founded in 1951. It is situated in São Paulo and is affiliated to the World Jewish Congress. The CIB unites the various local community federations and is headed by a president. The local federations, including the Jewish Federation of the State of Rio Janeiro, co-ordinate the activities of all their local bodies. The umbrella Zionist organisation is the Organizaçao Sionista Unificada do Brasil (United Zionist Organization of Brazil) and is based in São Paulo. Other Israel and Hebrew-oriented organisations include the Brit Ivrit Olamit, the Dor Hemshech Institute and the KKL

in Rio and Dror in São Paulo. WIZO has headquarters in São Paulo and ten other centres throughout the country. The Liga Feminina Israelita do Brasil is active both in Rio and São Paulo.

Religious Life
Brazilian Jewry is divided into various religious congregations, the largest, with 2500 families, being the Liberal Congregaçao Israelita Paulista (founded in 1936 by German refugees) in São Paulo. There are two hassidic congregations, a Machsike Hadass synagogue and other Orthodox groups, the main one being the Centro Judaico Religioso de São Paulo. There are several Sephardi congregations, a Syrian and Lebanese Synagogue, the Beth Yaacov Synagogue and a Hungarian synagogue.

Rio has 3 Conservative synagogues, 4 Sephardi (one Moroccan and two Eastern Mediterranean), 1 Reform and 1 Orthodox. There is also a Council of Sephardi Congregations.

There are a number of synagogues catering to various trends in Porto Alegre and most of the smaller communities have a synagogue. São Paulo has 4 kosher restaurants, 3 butchers and 2 bakers. Rio has 2 kosher restaurants and Pôrto Alegre has a kosher butcher.

Education
The Jewish school system in Brazil maintains standards well above the average. There are 7 schools and a yeshiva in São Paulo and Rio's educational institutions include 6 combined elementary and secondary day-schools, an ORT school and a teachers' seminary. There are 2 Jewish schools in Belo Horizonte and schools in Belém, Recife, Pôrto Alegre, Mogi das Cruzes and Santo Andre. The main *yeshiva* is at Petropolis near Rio. A Jewish Study Centre has been established in the University of São Paulo.

Cultural Activities
All towns where there are communities have active community centres. B'nai B'rith operates in São Paulo, Rio and Pôrto Alegre. The Brazilian Jewish clubs maintain sports schools all year round for approximately 2500 students. There are three Jewish libraries in Rio and a Jewish bookshop in São Paulo.

A Yiddish cultural organisation, the Sociedad pro-Idiche, operates in Rio.

Press
Jewish newspapers in São Paulo include the monthlies *O Hebreu* and *Revista Shalom* and the fortnightly *Resenna Judaica. Diario Israelita, Jornal Israelita* and the weekly Yiddish language *Imprensa Israelita* are published in Rio. There is also a Jewish magazine for children aged between seven and thirteen called *Shalom Infantil.*

There are two weekly Jewish broadcasts: a radio programme *A Voz*

21

Israelita in Rio, and a television programme in São Paulo. Jewish books in Portuguese are published by the São Paulo University and B'nai B'rith, which has its own publishing house. The São Paulo Jewish University Council also issues occasional pamphlets.

Welfare

The Jewish hospitals in Brazil are the Albert Einstein and the Linat Hatzedek in São Paulo and the Hospital Policlinica Israelita in Rio. There are homes for the aged in São Paulo, Pôrto Alegre and Rio, and a children's home in Rio. In the mid-1970s, São Paulo's welfare organisations united under an umbrella organisation, the Brasileiro-Israelita do Bem Estar Social (UNIBES). The services provided include ambulances, psychiatric care, dental care and a general auxiliary service. The Albert Einstein Hospital is open to the general public.

Relations with Israel

Full diplomatic relations exist between the two countries. Israel has an embassy in Brasilia, a consulate general in São Paulo and in Rio. Relations between the two countries have been cool on occasions, particularly when Brazil supported the UN 'Zionism is Racism' resolution in 1975. Between 1948 and 1968, 3400 Brazilian Jews emigrated to Israel. Some were involved in the establishment of several kibbutzim including Ga'ash and B'ror Hayil.

General Position

Brazilian Jewry is an affluent, flourishing community, providing excellent welfare and educational services. It noticeably lacks the integration problems of the Spanish-speaking republics. Rather, intermarriage has become common and the level of assimilation is a cause for worry. There is a tendency, as in much of Latin America, for the Jews to be more of a secular ethnic community than a religious one. The different communities have not yet fused and still remain to some extent divided: the Ashkenazim into German, Hungarian and East European, and the Sephardim into Ladino speakers and people of Eastern Mediterranean origin.

BULGARIA

Population: 8 949 300   Jewish population: 5000

History

Small groups of Jews lived in Bulgaria during the Roman era. In the eighth and ninth centuries Jewish refugees from Byzantine persecution established a flourishing Romaniot community using Greek in the synagogue. Their number was increased by Jews fleeing from the Crusades in Central Europe. Interestingly, the Bulgar Tsar Ivan Aleksander (1331–71) had a Jewish queen, Sarah, who changed her name to Theodora on her marriage. After 1396 Bulgaria became part of the Ottoman Empire, and a refuge for Jewish fugitives from the Spanish Inquisition, particularly in the cities of Sofia, Nicopolis and Plevna. In 1640 the various sections of Bulgarian Jewry united into one community, the Romaniots and the Ashkenazim adopting Ladino, although the Ashkenazim mainly used their own ritual in the synagogue.

When Bulgaria attained independence, the Congress of Berlin (1878) granted equal rights to all national minorities, including Jews. Despite a certain amount of antisemitism the Jewish community was free to develop in its own way. Various Zionist groups were formed in the 1880s and the combined Zionist Society, Ezrat Achim, established in 1894, bought land at Hartuv in Palestine in the following year where the first ten families of Bulgarian *olim* settled in 1896. By the early twentieth century most of Bulgarian Jewry had embraced Zionism, but in the 1930s antisemitism became an increasing problem.

In 1940 Bulgaria allied herself with Nazi Germany and in December 1940 the Sobranie (Parliament) passed a Law for the Protection of the Nation, based on the German Nuremberg Laws. In April 1941 Bulgaria acquired Thrace and Macedonia, whose 12 000 Jews were the first of 20 000 arranged to be deported by an agreement made between Germany and the newly-established Commissariat for Jewish Affairs. However, after the deportation of the Thracian and Macedonian Jews church leaders protested and the deportations ceased. The King subsequently allowed 20 000 Jews to be deported to Bulgarian camps but the war was nearing its end and the Jewish community was saved.

After the end of the war emigration to Israel became the objective of Bulgarian Jewry. Between 1948 and 1951, 44 267 Bulgarian Jews managed to reach Israel, before the Communist regime stopped emigration.

Composition of the Community
The community is largely Sephardi, with about two-thirds living in Sofia. Very few still speak Ladino. The majority are artisans or well-educated professionals and many are engaged in the arts.

Legal Status
Jews have equal rights and discrimination is punishable by law. Two central communal bodies were established in 1957: the secular Obstestvenna Kulturno-Prosvetna Organizatsiya na Evreite v NRB (Social, Cultural and Educational Organisation of Jews in the People's Republic of Bulgaria), known as OKPOE, and the Duchoven Izrailtjanski Savet (the Jewish Religious Council). The state supports the synagogues.

Communal Organisation

The Social, Cultural and Educational Organisation of Jews in the People's Republic of Bulgaria (OKPOE) is based in Sofia and has nine branches, the largest in Burgas, Plevni, Yambol and Varna. Recently the Community has been allowed to send observers to meetings of the World Jewish Congress.

Religious Life

The central religious organisation is the Jewish Religious Council. Synagogues are functioning in Sofia (the Central) and in Samokov and Vidin. There are no rabbis but the state pays the cantor's salary at the Sofia synagogue. Kosher food is difficult to obtain in Bulgaria and there are very few religious marriages.

Education

There are no Jewish schools and no educational programme for children.

Cultural Activities

Sofia has a Jewish Cultural Centre run by the OKPOE. The OKPOE also organises a programme of lectures, concerts and meetings, some dealing with specific Jewish cultural matters, whilst others publicise the government and party policies.

Press

Evrejski Vesti (Jewish News) is published fortnightly and a yearbook, *Godishnik*, appears regularly. Both publications are issued by OKPOE and follow the official political line.

Welfare

There are no separate Jewish welfare facilities.

Relations with Israel

Since 1967 Bulgaria and Israel have had no diplomatic relations as Bulgaria follows Moscow's foreign policy guidelines.

After 1948, 90 per cent of Bulgarian Jews emigrated to Israel where they have integrated very successfully. The Association of Immigrants from Bulgaria runs a home for the aged and deals with matters concerning the restitution of Bulgarian property. A Bulgarian language daily *Far Tribuna* is published in Israel.

Historical Sites

The Sofia Central Synagogue is one of the largest and most beautiful in the Balkans, and with the synagogues in Vidin and Samokov has been officially declared a 'cultural monument'. Maintenance and restoration are financed by the state. In Burgas the synagogue is now an art gallery and in Parzardzik it is the municipal museum.

General Position
The Jews who remained in Bulgaria are well established but Bulgarian Jewry is threatened with extinction through total assimilation. There is no open antisemitism and the intermarriage rate is reported to be 80 per cent.

BURMA

Population: 35 314 000   Jewish population: 20

A Jewish congregation was founded in Rangoon in 1857 by Sephardi Jews of Baghdadi origin. By 1930 the community had grown to about 3000 and groups with their own synagogues had been established in Mandalay, Bassein and Moulmein. However, as the Second World War approached many left the country and by the time of the Japanese invasion the majority had fled.

After the war a few hundred returned and the US army rebuilt the Musmeah Yeshua Synagogue in Rangoon. Since then numbers have declined due to departures, assimilation and conversions to Islam and Buddhism. Today the remainder are mostly elderly and indigent. Communal life is organised around the Rangoon synagogue but only on High Holy Days, when Israeli Embassy staff attend, can a *minyan* be obtained. The Musmeah Yeshua Synagogue Committee is affiliated to the World Jewish Congress.

The Israeli Embassy is located in Rangoon and has a resident ambassador. Burma has an embassy in Ramat Gan.

CANADA

Population: 25 358 500   Jewish population: 325 000

History
Jews were banned from living in Canada during the period of French rule. The first congregation was set up in Montreal in 1768. It followed the Sephardi rite but Ashkenazi Jews were among its founders and members. A second synagogue was chartered in Montreal in 1846, and an Ashkenazi synagogue was established in Toronto in 1856. In 1807 Ezekiel Hart was elected to the Quebec Assembly, but was not allowed to take his seat. In 1832 full civil rights were finally granted.

The big wave of immigration followed the pogroms in Russia in the late nineteenth century. In 1892 the Jewish Colonisation Association set up farming settlements in Saskatchewan. There were further waves of Jewish immigration after the two world wars, and some 67 000 Jews entered Canada between 1946 and 1967, including many from Israel and North Africa.

Composition of the Community

The core of the community is Ashkenazi, but the French-speaking Morrocan Jews in Montreal are Sephardi. The two main centres are Montreal and Toronto. In recent years many Jews have migrated from Montreal to Toronto, which now has the largest community in Canada, with 125 000; Montreal has dropped to 115 000. The next largest communities are: Vancouver, 20 000; Winnipeg, 15 000; Ottawa, 15 000; Calgary, Alberta 7500. Other centres are Hamilton, Ontario 5000; Edmonton, Alberta 5000; Windsor, Ontario 2000.

Communal Organisation

Canadian Jewry's main representative body, recognised by the government, is the Canadian Jewish Congress, founded in 1919 and reorganised in 1934. It is affiliated to the World Jewish Congress. Based at Samuel Bronfman House in Montreal, it has 27 departments with a staff of 130, and six regional divisions. Every Jewish community in Canada has its own Congress committee.

The main Zionist body is the Canadian Zionist Federation to which all Zionist groupings are affiliated (Labour, Mizrahi, Revisionist, the Zionist Organisation of Canada), as well as the women's organisation, the Haddasah-WIZO, which is one of the major WIZO federations in the world.

Religious Life

Toronto has some 35 Orthodox synagogues, 8 Conservative, 4 Reform and 3 Sephardi. In Montreal there are nearly as many, including the famous Sephardi Synagogue Shearith Israel, the oldest congregation in Canada. There are synagogues in most small communities. Kosher food is available in Toronto (6 restaurants), Montreal (5 restaurants), Vancouver (1 bakery), Winnipeg (1 restaurant), Ottawa (1 restaurant, 1 butcher, 1 baker).

Education

Toronto and Montreal have twelve Jewish schools and two yeshivot. Jewish schools can also be found in Calgary, 3; Vancouver, 2; Winnipeg, 5; Ottawa, 3.

Press

The most important of the 20 or so publications of the Canadian community is the *Canadian Jewish News*, which is a weekly newspaper published in an edition of 55 000 from Toronto. Interestingly the paper with the second largest circulation (30 000) is written in Hungarian: the weekly *Menora* which is also disttributed in the USA. The *Jewish Star* is published every two weeks in separate editions in Edmonton and Calgary. *Der Kanader Adler*, once a daily, is now published as a weekly in Montreal.

On the Zionist and Israel side are the *Canadian Zionist* published seven times a year from Toronto in an edition of 35 000, and the more academic Canadian *Middle East Digest* which appears ten times a year. The *Jewish Standard* is a semi-monthly unaffiliated Zionist paper with a circulation of 9000.

More specialist journals are *Orah* published monthly in an edition of 16 000 from Montreal by Hadassah-WIZO for its members, and the *Covenant* issued by B'nai B'rith quarterly in an edition of 12 000, also for its members. This last is published in both English and French.

Appearing every month during the academic year is *Images*, published by the Jewish Federations of York University and Toronto University in a very large edition of 30 000 copies. Of a more esoteric nature is the scholarly *Journal of Psychology and Judaism*, which has a small circulation of 1000 and is published in Ottawa.

Two significant papers appear in French only in Montreal. These are *Kol Yaakov* (circulation 6000) which is a general Sephardi quarterly, and *Jonathan*, issued by the Quebec-Israel Committee in an edition of 5000 it deals with Jewish affairs on a fairly intellectual level. An important, highly specialist paper is *Ethiopian Jewry Report* published by the Canadian Association for Ethiopian Jews. Probably the best periodical on its subject, it appears quarterly and has a circulation of 10 000.

Welfare

In Montreal there are 4 Jewish hospitals and a home for the aged. Toronto has 1 hospital, 2 nursing homes and a home for the aged, and there are homes for the aged in Vancouver, Winnipeg and Hamilton.

Cultural Activities

Both Montreal and Toronto have Holocaust Museums, and the main Jewish centres have a considerable number of libraries and bookshops. There are as many as seven Jewish bookshops in Toronto as well as a library. Montreal has three bookshops, and the Montreal Jewish Public Library is an outstanding institution, unique in North America. The smaller community of Winnipeg also has its own library.

In both the academic and literary life of Canada Jews play a major role. Canadian Jewish writers have been referred to as the third group alongside the French and the English.

Relations with Israel
Full diplomatic relations exist between the two countries. In recent years, particularly after Israel's 1982 invasion of Lebanon, there has been a shift towards a more even-handed approach.

General Position
In recent years there have been isolated cases of neo-Nazi activity and antisemitism but these have not affected the life of the community. The community is very prominent in the country's economic life and there is a considerable Jewish presence in the academic world, the professions and the civil service.

CHANNEL ISLANDS

Population: 133 000   Jewish population: 140

The first reference to Jews in the Channel Islands was in the middle of the eighteenth century when they seem to have been itinerant pedlars from Cornwall and Southern England. In 1836 land was purchased on St. Helier for a Jewish cemetery and in 1842 a synagogue was built, remaining in use until the virtual disappearance of the community in 1870. A small number of Polish immigrants settled in the early years of the twentieth century and in 1920 the Cemetery Trust was reconstituted.

In 1940 the islands were occupied by the Germans, but most Jews had already escaped or remained safely hidden. After the war Jews gradually returned with immigration increasing after 1960. The congregation was formally established in 1962 and the new synagogue opened in 1972.

Of a total Jewish population of 140, the great majority live on Jersey. The St. Helier community has a Ladies' Guild, a WIZO group and a JIA committee. There is no resident rabbi, but a minister from the United Kingdom visits from time to time. Sunday Hebrew classes are held for the Jewish children living on Jersey.

The community divides into two age-groups: mainly retired people and young couples in their thirties.

CHILE

Population: 11 900 000   Jewish population: 17 000

History

A Jewish convert, or 'New Christian', is thought to have been amongst the Spanish officers who discovered Chile in 1535. Later, Marranos settled in the country but in 1639, and again in 1644, some were taken to Peru to be burnt at the stake. Other Marranos from Santiago suffered a similar fate. It was not until Chile became independent of Spain in 1810 that religious liberty was proclaimed, and Jews were allowed into the country. Immigration remained slow, however, and even by 1914 there were only about 500 Jews in Santiago.

The first time the nascent community met to pray as a group was to celebrate Rosh Hashana in 1906, and the first organisation was set up three years later. This was the Sociedad La Unión Israelita en Chile, which met on 9 August 1909, and was subsequently known as La Unión Israelita de Chile.

In 1919, after the first congress of Chilean Jewry, the Federación Sionista de Chile was formed. In 1920 the Ashkenazi organisations united to form the Circulo Israelita and in 1935 the Sephardi bodies established the Comunidad Israelita Sephardi. The next few years saw the arrival of large numbers of Jews from Germany (despite immigration restrictions) and the increase of antisemitism. In 1940 all Chilean Jewish organisations united to form the Comité Representativo de la Collectividad Israelita de Chile (now the Comité Representativo de las Entidades Judias de Chile).

Composition of the Community

The community is mostly of Ashkenazi origin and is now beginning to fuse with the small group of Sephardis. Approximately 90 per cent of the Jewish population live in the capital Santiago with roughly 1700 Jews in Valparaiso, including Viña del Mar, and smaller communities in Concepción, Arica, La Serena and Valdivia.

Although the first immigrants were mainly pedlars, Jews are now mostly middle class, working in industry and the professions with many contributing to academic, cultural and artistic life.

Legal Status

The statutes and legal personality of the Unión Israelita de Chile were officially recognised by the Ministry of Justice on 7 December 1909. Members of the government officially attend the High Holiday services as a sign of respect for the Jewish community.

Communal Organisation
The Comité Representativo de las Entidades Judias de Chile represents all Jewish bodies and is led by a president. It is affiliated to the World Jewish Congress. The Federación Sionista de Chile remains the major Zionist organisation with local Zionist groups being the Centro Sionista Dr Epstein in Concepción, the Centro Sionista Dr Herzl in Valdivia, and the Zionist department of Valparaiso's Jewish community. Zionist political parties with separate organisations include Mapam, Poale Zion, Sionistas Generales Klalim (General Zionists), and the Unión Sionista Revisionista. Other groups include the OSI, an independent Zionist movement, WIZO and Friends of the Hebrew University.

Religious Life
Chilean Jewry is divided into various religious groupings with a single chief rabbi. The main religious bodies are the Comunidad Israelita Ashkenazi (Orthodox); the Circulo Israelita (Orthodox and Conservative); the Comunidad Israelita Sefaradi de Santiago (Sephardi and Conservative); the MAZsE (Hungarian Conservative); and the Sociedad Cultural Israelita B'nei Jisroel (German Conservative). There are 12 synagogues in Santiago and 1 each in Viña del Mar (Valparaiso), Concepción and Temuco.

Education
The Vaad Hahinuch (the Education Committee, to which are affiliated all communal bodies) organises Jewish education. Approximately 40 per cent of all Jewish children attend a Jewish day school. The school complex in Santiago has a Centre for Jewish Studies offering a degree course in Jewish culture.

Cultural Activities
There are community centres in Arica, Concepción, La Serena, Temuco, Valdivia and Viña del Mar. In Santiago the various communal organisations are also social centres and there is a club for Sephardi Jews. The largest individual organisation, the Estadio Israelito Maccabi, with a membership of approximately 2500 families, provides both cultural and sporting activities. The main Zionist youth organisation is the Federación Juvenil Sionista; others include Betar, Hashomer Hatzair and Ijud Habonim.

Press
Weekly papers include *La Palabra Israelita*, in both Spanish and Yiddish, the Spanish-language Zionist *Mundo Judio* and *El Vocero* published by the Comunidad Israelita and the Vaad Hahinuch.

Welfare
The two homes for the aged in Santiago are the Villa Israel (Orthodox) and Cisroco (Orthodox and catering for elderly German Jews).

Relations with Israel
Israel has a resident ambassador in Santiago and Chile an ambassador in Tel Aviv. Several hundred Chilean Jews have settled in Israel. The Chilean Jewish community has planted a forest in Israel named after the Chilean Jewish poetess, Gabriela Mistral.

General Position
Without being strongly religious, the community retains a firm Jewish identity and at the same time involves itself in the life of the country.

CHINA, PEOPLE'S REPUBLIC OF

Population: 1 031 883 000   Jewish population: 5

History
The origins of the Jewish community of China can be traced back to the ninth and tenth centuries when about 1000 Jews settled in Kaifeng in Honan Province. They probably came overland from India and Persia, taking advantage of the development of the Silk Road during the late Tang period. The first synagogue was built at Kaifeng in 1163 and for 600 years the community were able to practise Judaism without restriction. During the eighteenth century the community assimilated almost entirely and the synagogue was eventually dismantled.

When Hong Kong became a British colony in the 1840s many Jews from Iraq came to China as merchants. Jews escaping Russia after the October 1917 Revolution also settled in China and German Jews fled to Shanghai and Harbin after Hitler's rise to power. By 1941 30 000 Jews were living in China, principally in Hongkew, the American section of the International Settlement in Shanghai. Several synagogues and a flourishing Jewish press existed at this time. When the Japanese occupied Shanghai Jews were interned but not ill-treated. There was no antisemitic persecution.

The vast majority of the community left China after the Communist take-over in 1949.

Present Position
There are very few Jews, if any, remaining in China. In 1985 the American Joint Distribution Committee was sending aid to a small number of Jews in Shanghai but it is doubtful whether any remain.

Some of the population of Kaifeng claim Jewish descent but none of them maintain Jewish practices. There is no evidence of any organised community.

Historical Sites
The museum in Kaifeng intends to develop a Judaica section chronicling the history of the old community. The Beth Hatefutzot museum has provided photographic materials to assist Chinese scholars in this purpose. Recently there have been reports that the Chinese government has appointed a senior official to document the history of former Jewish communities in China and publicise the sites where they lived, for the benefit of Jewish and other visitors. Also, a Sino-Judaic institute was founded in the United States in July 1985 with the aim of fostering good relations between Jews and the Chinese, and the Jewish Historical Society in Hong Kong has established links with the Chinese representatives there in order to promote interest in the past Jewish presence in China.

Relations with Israel
China does not recognise the State of Israel and there are no diplomatic relations between the two countries. However, there are trade links and a treaty establishing agricultural cooperation has recently been signed.

COLOMBIA

Population: 27 515 000   Jewish population: 7000

The Marranos who settled in the country in the sixteenth century were wiped out by the Inquisition and it was not until the nineteenth century that a few Jews entered the country. Serious immigration started after the First World War with the arrival of Sephardi Jews followed by refugees from Germany and Eastern Europe. Many of these immigrants initially earned their living as pedlars. The 1934 ban on Jewish immigration was lifted in 1945 when permission was given for the settlement of 300 Jews a year for the next five years.

Colombia has a mixed Ashkenazi-Sephardi community, with the majority living in Bogota and smaller communities in Cali, Medellin and Barranquilla. Many Jews today work in the professions.

The Confederación de Asociaciones Judias de Colombia (COAJ) in Bogota is the central communal organisation and is affiliated to the World Jewish Congress. Bogota has a communal centre, the Centro Israelita, and the German-speaking Jews and the Sephardim have their own organisations: the Asociación Israelita Montefiore and the Comunidad Hebrea Sefaradi. There is a youth club organisation and the Centro Universitario Hebreo. Zionist and Israel-oriented groups include WIZO, Friends of the Magen David Adom, the JNF and the Zionist Federation of Colombia. Both Medellin and Barranquilla have community centres and Cali has a combined centre and synagogue, a welfare organisation and a cultural society. The Federation of Jewish Women based in Barranquilla is very active in social work.

Israel maintains an embassy in Bogota, and Colombia has an embassy in Israel.

COSTA RICA

Population: 2 655 000   Jewish population: 2500

History
The first Jewish immigrants were Sephardim from Curaçao and Aruba who arrived in the late eighteenth and early nineteenth centuries and subsequently assimilated. After the First World War the present community came into being with the arrival of Turkish and Polish Jews who were followed by German and Austrian refugees in the 1930s. Seventy families of Holocaust survivors arrived after 1945. In 1952 Jewish homes in San José were attacked during agitation for a law restricting commerce to Costa Ricans. Otherwise there has been little overt antisemitism. Small numbers of Jewish immigrants from other Latin American countries have settled in Costa Rica in the 1980s.

Composition of the Community
The Costa Rican community is mostly Ashkenazi of Polish origin and is concentrated in the capital, San José.

Legal Status
Immediately before and after the Second World War various laws limited the rights of Jews, notably the prevention of land purchase by foreign companies and the 1948 immigration acts. All such restrictions have since been lifted.

Communal Organisation
The main Jewish organisation is the Centro Israelita Sionista de Costa Rica which was founded in 1930 and is affiliated to the World Jewish Congress. WIZO, which runs six groups, is one of the strongest organisations; it sets guidelines for the activities of the community. Other Zionist groups include the Asociación Sionista Unida, the Zionist Revisionist Organisation and the JNF.

Religious Life
San José has one synagogue, the Shaarei Zion, with a resident rabbi. There is also a cemetery and a Chevra Kadisha in the city.

Education
The Chaim Weizmann Institute, San José's Jewish school, maintains high educational standards, has a large staff, teaches Hebrew and Jewish culture along with general studies and has a number of non-Jewish pupils. It also arranges for most of its graduates to spend a year on a kibbutz.

Cultural Activities
The Jewish Sports Centre provides social and sports facilities. Other organisations include B'nai B'rith and the Zionist youth movements, Hanoar Hatzioni and Atid.

Press
The Centro Israelita Sionista publishes a monthly, *Hayom*, in Spanish.

Welfare
The Jewish Women's Welfare Association, which is affiliated to the International Council of Jewish Women (ICJW), organises charitable work and provides a variety of social services throughout the country.

Relations with Israel
Relations between the two countries are very good. Israel has an embassy and a resident ambassador in San José, and Costa Rica moved its embassy back to Jerusalem in 1982. Costa Rica has always given Israel strong diplomatic and political support. Cultural goodwill is promoted by the Israeli-Costa Rican Cultural Institute and recently the country has benefited from Israeli technical and scientific expertise.

General Position
This stable yet energetic community has good relations with the government and does not experience religious or racial discrimination. Harmony is promoted by the Confraternidad Judio-Cristiana which publishes a bulletin called *Shalom* and arranges various courses and meetings.
    There is little assimilation or intermarriage. This is largely due to

the quality of the Jewish day school in San José which inculcates a strong spirit of Jewish commitment.

CUBA

Population: 10 300 000   Jewish population: 1000

History
Small groups of Marranos probably accompanied the Spanish explorers to Cuba in the fifteenth century. Modern settlement, however, began with the Cuban War of Independence at the end of the nineteenth century. Cuba's first finance minister, General Carlos Roloff, was the most famous of these Jewish settlers. Born as Akiva Holland, he was an emigrant from the Ukraine.

The Jewish population grew and by 1900 numbered 300 families. Between 1902 and 1914 some 5700 Sephardi Jews immigrated from Syria and Turkey. The United Hebrew Congregation was founded in 1904 and the Union Hebrea Chevet Ahim was founded in 1914 by the 4000 Sephardim then living in Havana. By this time Cuba had received Jewish immigrants from strife-torn Mexico. Migration from Eastern Europe affected Cuba to the extent that many Jews passed through the country on their way to America. But only a few remained and by 1919 the total Jewish population had fallen to 2000.

The 'Law of 50 per cent', passed in 1933, ruled that at least 50 per cent of all manufacturing employees had to be Cuban citizens. Many Jews found difficulty obtaining citizenship and the resources of the United States charity organisations were severely stretched. By the end of the Second World War, however, the Jewish community had revived and by 1948 numbered 12 000. In that year the magnificent community centre in Havana was built – the Patronato de la Casa de la Comunidad Hebrea de Cuba.

With the accession to power of Fidel Castro in 1959 about 85 per cent of the Jewish community fled, fearing for their economic position. The present regime is not antisemitic but has become virulently anti-Zionist. There has been some improvement in the position of the community with the liberalisation of the government's policy towards Cuba's Jews since 1985. A further hopeful sign was the permission granted in January 1987 to a few Cuban Jews to leave the country to reunite with their families in Venezuela.

Composition of the Community
There are roughly equal numbers of Ashkenazim and Sephardim and most of them live in Havana.

Communal Organisation

The central organisation is the Comisión Coordinadora de las Sociedades Hebreas de Cuba (Co-ordinating Committee of Cuban Jewish Societies) in Havana. It remains affiliated to the World Jewish Congress. The Zionist Union of Cuba was dismantled in 1978 by order of Castro, prior to Havana's hosting of the Eleventh World Festival of Youth and Students. A B'nai B'rith Lodge, Maimonides 1516, has been in existence since 1943 and meets once a month. There is also a Jewish women's organisation and a Chevra Kadisha.

Religious Life

There are still five synagogues in Havana but they have fallen into a state of disrepair and are barely used, but the government has promised aid for their maintenance. They include the Conservative Patronato de la Casa de la Comunidad Hebrea de Cuba, the Reform United Hebrew Congregation, two Orthodox synagogues, Adat Israel and Chevet Ahim, and the Centro Hebreo Sefaradi.

There is no rabbi, cantor or professional leader but visiting rabbis are allowed to conduct services on major Holy Days. Jewish students have also recently been allowed to receive religious instruction abroad and a visiting *mohel* can carry out circumcision. The community owns a kosher butcher shop and pays for the services of a *shochet*. The Canadian Jewish Congress supplies kosher meat, matzot and other religious requisites.

Cultural Activities

The Patronato still functions and maintains its library. It also provides children's Sunday school classes in Hebrew, houses conferences and organises youth activities.

Relations with Israel

Cuba was the last Soviet ally to sever relations with Israel. The move was made in September 1973. Cuba supports the PLO which has diplomatic headquarters in Havana and her political attitude to Israel is similar to that of Eastern European countries.

General Position

Cuba's remaining Jewish population is poor and finds it difficult to maintain its religious identity in an atheistic society. The fact that there are no relations with Israel or the United States is clearly detrimental but there is some compensation in the help offered by the Canadian Jewish Congress and the World Jewish Congress.

CURAÇAO

Population: 260 000   Jewish population: 600

History
In 1652 the Dutch West India Company granted a charter and a tract of land for Jewish settlement. A hundred years later a Jewish community was flourishing with a synagogue, America's oldest, built in 1732. Curaçao, being under the tolerant rule of Dutch Protestants, also acted as a refuge and transit point for refugees fleeing from persecution on the South American mainland.

Composition of the Community
The largest group are twentieth-century Ashkenazi immigrants. The smaller group include descendants of the seventeenth-century Sephardi settlers. Most of the community are affluent and self-employed.

Legal Status
The Jewish community has legal status, but only civil marriages are recognised.

Communal Organisation
There is a Jewish Community Council and a synagogue board headed by an elected president. The Mikveh Israel-Emmanuel congregation is affiliated to the World Jewish Congress. The WIZO Federation is active.

Religious Life
Willemstad's two Sephardi synagogues – Mikveh-Israel Emmanuel, the United Netherlands Portuguese Congregation, founded in the seventeenth century, and the Liberal Temple Emmanuel, established in 1864 – were united in 1964. The congregation now uses the Reconstructionist prayerbook. The Orthodox Ashkenazi synagogue, the Shaare Tsedek, has a resident minister. *Kashrut* is not observed.

Education
There is a Hebrew Sunday school.

Relations with Israel
Willemstad has an Israeli consulate.

Press
The monthly *Mikveh Israel* is published in Dutch. There is also
a radio programme of Jewish interest sponsored by the Israeli consulate.

Historical Sites
The Mikveh Israel synagogue, originally built in 1654, and whose
present building on the same site dates from 1732, houses a Jewish
museum. The Temple Emmanuel Synagogue, built in 1864, is no longer
in use. The seventeenth-century cemetery at Blenheim is the oldest in
the Americas.

General Position
This, the oldest Jewish congregation of the Americas, still continues
to maintain itself and there are no unaffiliated Jews. Relations with the
non-Jewish population are good and the government struck coins and
special commemorative stamps for the 250th anniversary of the Mikveh
Israel synagogue in 1982.

CYPRUS

Population: 648 600   Jewish population: 25

The first mention of Cyprus (referred to as Kittim) is in the book
of Isaiah. By the first century CE a substantial Jewish population
had established itself on the island. The Cyprus community fought in
the Jewish revolt against the Romans but after their defeat Jews were
banned from the island. In the late Middle Ages communities grew up
in Nicosia, Paphos and Famagusta. Few records exist of Jews during the
Ottoman period. After the establishment of British rule in the nineteenth
century there were attempts to found Jewish agricultural settlements but
they met with little success.

After the Second World War Britain established internment camps
for Jews caught trying to enter Palestine 'illegally'. Between 1945 and
1949 approximately 11 000 Jews were interned.

By 1963 approximately 130 Jews were living in Cyprus. The number
has dwindled to its present figure of 25 because of emigration, mostly
to Britain or Israel.

The central body, the Committee of the Jewish Community of
Cyprus, which is affiliated to the World Jewish Congress, is based in
Nicosia. The island has no synagogue or rabbi, but there is a cemetery
at Margo. Despite its proximity to Nicosia, it is in the Turkish sector so

cannot be visited by residents of the Greek sector. A cemetery at Larnaca is not in use.

Full diplomatic relations exist between Cyprus and Israel which has an embassy in Nicosia.

CZECHOSLOVAKIA

Population: 15 437 000   Jewish population: 12 000

History

Jews are recorded as having lived in Moravia in the ninth century and in Bohemia in the tenth. The First Crusade in 1096, brought persecution and forced baptism. The later Middle Ages saw an improvement in the situation of the Jews and, despite several expulsions, by the end of the sixteenth century Prague had become an important Jewish community. In the seventeenth century Jewish refugees fled to Bohemia to escape from the Cossack massacres led by Chmielnicki.

Between 1726 and 1849, and 1853 and 1859, the Familiantengesetz was imposed on Prague Jewry, restricting the number of Jewish families permitted to marry. In 1744, during the first of these periods, the Empress Maria Theresa ordered the expulsion of the Jews of Prague. They were subsequently allowed to return after they promised to pay high taxes. In the following years limitations upon the Jews were gradually removed and by 1867 the process of legal emancipation had been completed. Jews subsequently contributed to the economic progress of the city and became increasingly secularised and assimilated into the general community. The new independent Czech Republic, established after the fall of the Austro-Hungarian Empire, recognised Jewish nationality in 1919 and by 1935 the community numbered 357 000. Germany occupied the highly populated Jewish area of the Sudetenland in September 1938 and Czechoslovakia in March 1939, dividing the country into the Protectorate of Bohemia and Moravia and the Republic of Slovakia. Many Czech Jews managed to leave the country before deportation started but those who remained were sent to the camp at Theresienstadt (Terezin) where few survived. There were only 42 000 Jews left in Czechoslovakia at the end of the war.

After the war, the new Communist regime had many prominent Jewish members. However, the first East European 'anti-Zionist' trials (of Rudolf Slansky and his associates) took place in 1952, followed by a wave of anti-Jewish and anti-Zionist activities, and many Jews emigrated. In 1968, after the Soviets overthrew the Dubček regime, a further Jewish emigration occurred.

Composition of the Community
The community is entirely Ashkenazi, composed mainly of survivors of the Holocaust, including those who returned after the war. In addition to the 6000 registered Jews, a further 6–8000 unidentified Jews are estimated to be living in the country.

Legal Status
Jews have equal citizenship rights and freedom to practise their religion. There are laws against discrimination. However, in practice all communal activities are under strict government control.

Communal Organisation
The Council of Jewish Communities of the Bohemia and Moravia Socialist Republic is based in Prague. The Federation of Jewish Communities in the Slovak Socialist Republic is based in Bratislava and controls Slovakia's 13 communities. The Zionist organisation was closed down in 1951. However, contacts have been maintained with other Jewish organisations abroad and for several years the community has been permitted to send observers to World Jewish Congress meetings.

Religious Life
The Council of Jewish Communities for Bohemia and Moravia, including the rabbinate, is based in Prague's old Jewish Town Hall. After a very long interval Prague now has a rabbi who studied at the seminary in Budapest.

Bohemia and Moravia have synagogues in Prague, Brno, Karlovy Vary (Karlsbad), Mikulov (Nikolsburg), Olomouc (Olmutz), Ostrava and Plzeň (Pilsen). A further ten congregations are affiliated to the Central Council. Slovakia has synagogues in Bratislava, Galanta, Košice, Piestany and Trnava. A further eight congregations are in existence. Prague, Bratislava and Košice all have kosher restaurants.

Education
There are no Jewish schools.

Cultural Activities
The Jewish Town Hall in the old Jewish quarter of Prague is the centre of all communal activities, including the Hebrew youth choir, which is run by the Chief Cantor. There are also communal centres in Brno, Karlovy Vary, Olomouc, Ostrava, Plzeň, Bratislava and Košice.

Press
Vestnik, a monthly, publishes news of community activities and educational articles on Judaism. There is also a communal yearbook.

Welfare

The American Joint Distribution Committee, banned in 1950, renewed contacts in 1981 and has subsequently helped in welfare work and the modernisation of the community. It also runs the kosher restaurants.

The Council of the Jewish Community is in contact with the Zentralwohlfahrtstelle der Juden in Deutschland in Frankfurt on Main (Central Welfare Board of the Jews in Germany), which arranges rest cures for the aged at West German spa resorts. The Council gives financial help to people on low pensions.

Relations with Israel

Czechoslovakia supported Israel in 1948 by sending arms. The anti-Zionist accusations of the 1952 Slansky trial began a change of policy and in 1967 diplomatic relations with Israel were severed.

Historical Sites

Prague is one of the most important Jewish historical sites in Europe. Although the community has declined, the relics of its glorious past remain. The Jewish Town Hall with its old Hebrew clock intact still stands in the ancient Judenstadt. A statue of Rabbi Yehuda Loew ben Bezalel (the Maharal), the rabbi associated with the famous Golem of Prague, stands in the new Town Hall Square and a Hebrew inscription forms part of the design on Charles Bridge. The famous State Jewish Museum in Prague was ironically created by the Nazis who gathered there all Jewish treasures in Czechoslovakia.

Synagogues include the Altneuschul, one of the oldest synagogues in Europe, founded in the eleventh century, with its present building restored in 1883 but dating from the fourteenth century (today it functions as the communal synagogue); the High Synagogue which contains an exhibition of 1000 years of Bohemian Jewish history; the Spanish Synagogue which has an exhibition of Jewish textiles; the Pinkas Synagogue which is now a memorial to the Holocaust victims of Prague, with their 77 297 names inscribed on its walls; the Maisl Synagogue which has an exhibition of Jewish silver and the Klaus Synagogue which has an exhibition on Jewish customs and festivals.

Cemeteries include the Old Cemetery which is the oldest Jewish cemetery in Europe, and contains the graves of famous rabbis, including Avigdor Karo and Yehuda Loew ben Bezalel, and the New Cemetery which contains the grave of Franz Kafka. The old cemeteries have generally deteriorated and, in some cases, the bodies have been removed to new burial places to make way for housing projects. However, several have been restored with the financial help of the state.

Outside of Prague interesting sites are in Boskovice where there is a medieval ghetto and Jewish cemetery; in Holešov, which has the

Schach Synagogue; in Mikulov, where there are the remains of many old synagogues, and a cemetery containing the graves of famous rabbis; in Trnava, whose synagogue courtyard has a monument to Czech Jews deported in the war, and at Terezin, where there is also a memorial to concentration camp victims. The state has given financial help for the restoration of several old Jewish cemeteries.

General Position
The small Jewish community maintains a religious life and has re-established contact with world Jewry. The state has recently begun to take an interest in Jewish history by restoring ancient cemeteries and synagogues and helping to establish museums.

DENMARK

Population: 5 116 000   Jewish population: 9000

History
Jews first settled in Denmark in the seventeenth century when Jewish manpower was recruited in Gluckstadt on the Elbe estuary (then in Danish hands). A small number of Jews had already been living in Copenhagen and in 1657 King Frederick III gave Sephardi Jews permission to settle anywhere in the country. Ashkenazi Jews, however, still needed a special dispensation. Civic equality was granted to Jews in 1814 and political equality followed in 1849. The Jewish population increased steadily until, in the middle of the nineteenth century, there were about 4200 Jews living in Denmark. The number subsequently declined to 3500 in 1901 because of intermarriage and a low birth rate. However it was greatly increased at the beginning of this century by refugees from the Russian pogroms, reaching a pre-war peak of 7500.

Crisis followed in the Second World War when the occupying Germans abrogated an agreement they had with the Danes to protect the Jews. The Danes then undertook what must have been one of the most remarkable rescue operations of the war: 5191 Jews, 1301 people of part Jewish parentage and 686 Christians married to Jews were transported by sea to Sweden. The remaining 472 Jews were captured and deported to Theresienstadt where 423 of them survived.

In 1969 Denmark received about 2500 Jewish refugees from Poland. Most of them settled in the Copenhagen area.

Composition of the Community
Today the community is primarily Ashkenazi descending from the Russian Jews who immigrated at the beginning of the century. The

largest concentration of Jews is in greater Copenhagen (8000) but there is a small Polish Jewish community in Aarhus, and another small community in Odense. Jews are to be found in middle class professions, as lawyers and civil servants, and in business.

Legal Status
The reforms of 1814 and 1849 gave Jews full legal rights. At the same time rabbis were granted the same status as priests of the Lutheran Church, and are still today responsible for the registration of births and deaths.

Communal Organisation
The central body is the Mosaiske Troessamfund i Kobenhavn (Jewish Congregation in Copenhagen). Its 20-member Assembly of Delegates is elected by the community every four years. The Delegates, in turn, elect a seven-member governing body. The Congregation is affiliated to the World Jewish Congress.

The main Zionist organisation is the Dansk Zionistforbund (Danish Zionist Federation), whose office in Copenhagen is in the same building as the Congregation. Other groups include the Keren Hayesod, the Dor Hemshech Institute, WIZO, B'nai Akiva, Hakoah, Danish Zionist Union, Mizrahi, Jewish National Fund and Agudat Israel. The Friends of the Hebrew University are also active. The Polish Jews have their own Federation in Copenhagen. The B'nai B'rith has existed in Denmark since 1912. The Jewish Youth Federation has its own club. Other youth organisations include the Scandinavian Jewish Youth Federation, B'nai Akiva and the Maccabi group Hakoah.

Religious Life
Denmark has a Chief Rabbi and an assistant rabbi. The main synagogue in Copenhagen was built in 1833 and its services are conducted in accordance with Orthodox tradition. There is also an Orthodox Machsike Hadass Synagogue in Copenhagen.

In Copenhagen there are two kosher butchers, a kosher grocery and a catering firm. One of the butchers supplies kosher food for the Swedish and Norwegian communities where *shechita* is not allowed.

Education
Copenhagen has three kindergartens and a day school. The latter was founded in 1805 and was originally divided into single sex schools. In 1945 the two sections were combined and renamed the Caroline School, after Denmark's reigning Queen. The school caters for some 300 pupils, about half the Jewish children in the 6 to 16 years age range. The Machsike Hadass Synagogue provides its own Hebrew classes. Other

Hebrew classes for children and adults are provided by the Congregation which also publishes Danish translations of religious literature. About 20 per cent of Danish Jewish children spend some time studying in Israel.

Cultural Activities

The Royal Library in Copenhagen has a Jewish Department, with a very important collection of Judaica (about 80 000 volumes). It includes the Bibliotheca Simonseniana, named after the late Chief Rabbi David Simonsen. The Liberty Museum in Copenhagen has a section on the persecution of the Jews on its Wartime Resistance shelves.

Specialist interests are catered for by a Jewish Craftsmen's Society and a Jewish Folk Society.

Press

A Jewish newspaper, *Jodisk Orientering*, is published monthly in Copenhagen and a quarterly, *Israel*, is published by the Danish Zionist Organisation.

Welfare

There are two homes for the aged, run in co-operation with the Copenhagen Municipality. One of them, Meyers Minde, was founded in 1805.

Relations with Israel

Relations are at ambassadorial level. Israel's embassy is in Copenhagen; the Danish embassy is in Tel Aviv with a consulate in Jerusalem. In 1952 the King Christian X Tuberculosis Hospital was opened at Etanim near Jerusalem. The money was raised by both Jews and Gentiles in Denmark. Half of this money was contributed by the Danish state.

Historical Sites

The central Copenhagen Synagogue was designed by one of Denmark's leading architects, Gustav Friedrich Hechst. The community centre in Copenhagen is housed on premises built in 1754. The building was bought by the community in 1902. It was extensively restored after the war and re-opened in 1968.

In the Israelplads in Copenhagen a large memorial stone from Eilat stands as tribute to the Danes who helped in the Jewish rescue operations of 1943. A gift from Israel, it was erected in 1975 and is inscribed in both Hebrew and Danish. Further up the North East coast of Zealand are two villages which were used as ports from which Jews sailed to safety during the war. At one of them, Gilleleje, visitors can still see the church which was used as a hiding place for Jewish fugitives, and at

Snekkersten a memorial marks the rescue work of the Danish innkeeper H. C. Thomsen, who died in a concentration camp.

There are two Jewish cemeteries in Copenhagen, the old cemetery established in 1693 and the new one founded in 1886. The latter contains a monument to the 49 Danish Jews who died in Theresienstadt.

General Position
The relations between Jews and Gentiles have always been exceptionally good in Denmark, and this led in the past to a certain amount of assimilation and intermarriage. Danish Jews have made important contributions to both cultural and political life. The rescue of Denmark's Jewish community is unique in the annals of the Holocaust period.

DOMINICAN REPUBLIC

Population: 6 416 000   Jewish population: 150

History
Sephardi Jews, mainly from Curaçao, settled on the island of Hispaniola during the eighteenth century. They supported the Dominicans, particularly in the 1844 War of Independence against Haiti. Easily adapting to Dominican society they eventually assimilated, though many of today's upper class Dominicans still boast a Jewish ancestry.

The Dominican Republic was the only country of the 32 present at the 1938 Evian Conference on Jewish Refugees that agreed to accept a substantial number of refugees (100 000). Although only approximately 600 actually arrived, as many as 5000 others were saved by having Dominican visas.

In January 1940 an agreement was reached between the government of the Dominican Republic and the Dominican Republic Settlement Association of New York (DORSA), arranging for refugees to be settled at Sosua on the north coast, on land donated by President Trujillo himself. After overcoming many difficulties, those who stayed in Sosua established a successful dairy industry, which now supplies the whole country. Over the years many Jews left for Santo Domingo or abroad.

Composition of the Community
The major elements are the German and Austrian Ashkenazim, who came in the 1930s, and their descendants. The community is divided between Santo Domingo and Sosua. The local community maintains the dairy farms at Sosua and is developing tourist facilities in nearby Sosumar.

Legal Status
The 1940 agreement between the government and DORSA included a bill of rights guaranteeing freedom of religion.

Communal Organisation
The Parroquia Israelita de la Republica Dominicana is the central communal body with the Unión Sionista de la Republica Dominicana being the Zionist organisation. The Parroquia Israelita is affiliated to the World Jewish Congress. A branch of the JNF exists as well as a WIZO Federation. All of these are based in Santo Domingo.

Religious Life
There is a synagogue in Santo Domingo and in Sosua. The latter is a small clapboard building, whilst the Santo Domingo synagogue was built in 1956 with an endowment from President Trujillo. There is no rabbi on the island. The cheese produced at the Sosua dairies is kosher and the few people who observe strict *kashrut* obtain their meat from Miami.

Cultural Activities
The social and cultural life of the community is centred on the Centro Israelita de la Republica Dominicana in Santo Domingo.

Relations with Israel
Israel maintains an embassy with a resident ambassador in Santo Domingo and the Dominican Republic has an embassy in Israel. In 1963 a Treaty of Friendship was signed between the two countries.

General Position
Assimilation similar to that which caused the total absorption of the original Sephardi settlers now faces the newer Ashkenazi immigrants. There is no antisemitism but intermarriage is widespread and many emigrate mainly to the USA, Canada and Israel.

ECUADOR

Population: 8 880 000   Jewish population: 1000

History
The history of the Jews in Ecuador belongs exclusively to the twentieth century. Between 1924 and 1947 3500 Jews came to Ecuador, mainly from Germany. Many left after 1945. More recently immigration has come from other Latin American countries, particularly Argentina and Chile.

Composition of the Community
The community centred in Quito is mainly of German Ashkenazi origin. Jews also live in Guayaquil, Riobaba, Ambato and Cuenca.

Communal Organisation
The central body, the Asociación Israelita de Quito, is affiliated to the World Jewish Congress. A similar organisation, the Comunidad de Culto Israelita, exists in the smaller community of Guayaquil. The two organisations are independent. The Zionist organisation, the Federación Sionista del Ecuador is in Quito. Both WIZO and the Jewish Women's Society are active in Ecuador.

Religious Life
There is a synagogue and a rabbi in Quito.

Cultural Activities
Both Quito and Guayaquil have community centres. B'nai B'rith is based in Quito.

Press
Quito has a Jewish newspaper *Informemonos*, published in both German and Spanish.

Relations with Israel
There are full diplomatic relations between the two countries.

General Position
In 1982 there were some antisemitic manifestations in Quito, but these were strongly opposed by the government which at the same time expressed support for Israel.

EGYPT

Population: 49 000 000　　　　　　　　　　Jewish population: 240

History
A Jewish, or to be more correct Israelite, connection with Egypt goes back to the dawn of Jewish history. The historical facts are not unequivocally established but it is generally considered that much of Canaan was under the control of the Egyptians at the time of Amenhotep IV (1375–58 BCE), when the Israelite tribes were starting

to emerge. A number of Israelites moved into the North Eastern edge of the Nile Delta: the Land of Goshen. During the nineteenth dynasty, the Pharoah, Ramses II (1298–32 BCE), began to exploit the Jews as forced labour for his building projects, the ruins of many of which are still extant. But it was under his successor, Merneptah, probably in 1220 BCE, that the Jews revolted and fled across the Sinai to Canaan. For 3000 years this escape from Egyptian bondage has been celebrated every spring as one of the most important of all Jewish family ceremonies.

Relations with Egypt were not always hostile: King Solomon married an Egyptian princess. Serious Jewish settlement began in the late fourth century BCE when under Greek rule a Jewish community gradually evolved in Alexandria. The Hellenised Greek-speaking community produced a number of important writers, notably the philosopher Philo (c.20 BCE to 40 CE), and a Greek translation of the Bible, the Septuagint. During this period anti-Jewish feeling amongst the local Greeks caused a number of serious riots. After the Christianisation of the Roman empire the situation deteriorated still further culminating in a mass baptism at Alexandria in 415 CE. By the time of the Arab Conquest of 640 the community had ceased to be of significance.

A new community slowly emerged in Cairo in the tenth century. It was there that the title of Nagid as the head of the community originated. Moses Maimonides (1135–1204) settled in Cairo in 1165 and wrote most of his work there. He was appointed Nagid of Egyptian Jewry by the Vizier, an office which was then passed down through his family until the fourteenth century. His son, who also lived in Cairo, was a scholar of note.

In subsequent centuries Egyptian Jewry led a quiet existence only becoming politically significant in the nineteenth century. The twentieth century saw a growth of anti-Western and anti-Zionist feeling and on Balfour Day, 22 November 1945, 10 Jews were killed, 350 injured and much Jewish property destroyed in severe rioting. On 15 May 1948 after the outbreak of war with Israel 2000 Jews were arrested and their property confiscated. In the following two months there were further riots in which 50 Jews were killed. There was a steady decline in the population which by 1956 had fallen to 40 000 (1948: 75 000) and by the middle of 1957, after Suez, to 15 000. By 1967 it had dropped to 2500. By this time the Jewish population was concentrated in the cities of Cairo and Alexandria.

Present Position

After President Sadat visited Israel in 1977 and the peace treaty was signed in 1979 Jewish rights were restored. The Jewish community was then allowed to establish full contact with the State of Israel and with world Jewry. Today the Jewish community of Cairo is affiliated to the World Jewish Congress and there is a central Jewish organisation in

Cairo. Cairo has four functioning synagogues and Alexandria has one, the Great Synagogue.

Israel and Egypt have full diplomatic relations. There is an Israeli embassy in Cairo and a consulate general in Alexandria. There is an Israeli government tourist office and an Academic Mission in Cairo. There is also a small American-Israeli community living in the Maadi district of Cairo.

EL SALVADOR

Population: 5 480 000   Jewish population: 100

The first Jewish settlers were French Sephardim who came to El Salvador at the beginning of the nineteenth century. These were followed after 1850 by Jews from Alsace and in the 1920s by Jews from Eastern Europe and the Orient. After the Second World War a number of Jewish refugees arrived from Germany.

The Comunidad Israelita de El Salvador was established in 1944, followed in 1950 by a synagogue and social centre and the appointment of a rabbi. The Convention of the Federación de Comunidades Judias de Centro America y Panama, known as FEDECO, was held in San Salvador in 1966 and 1974. By 1976 there were approximately 370 Jews (120 Jewish families) living in the country. Ninety per cent of these were Ashkenazim. The Comunidad Israelita de El Salvador represents the community in the World Jewish Congress.

Since 1980 continuing civil war has resulted in steady Jewish emigration; the synagogue is no longer in use and there is no rabbi. Services are held on Friday nights in a private house rented for that purpose.

Relations with Israel are good. Since 1984 Israel has had an embassy in El Salvador which is one of the two Latin American countries to retain its embassy in Jerusalem.

ETHIOPIA

Population: 42 000 000   Jewish population: 15 000

History
The origins of the Falashas are obscure. They are members of a Hamitic tribe known as the Agau and call themselves Beta Israel (House of Israel). They were probably introduced to elements of Judaism in the second or third century CE as a result of a wave of Semitic influence that passed over the region.

During the Middle Ages an isolated kingdom was established in north-west Ethiopia. This was destroyed in 1616 after a period of warfare and the Jews lost their independence, becoming part of Christian Abyssinia. In the nineteenth century European missionaries became active in the area and a considerable number of Falashas were converted to Christianity.

Contact with world Jewry only began in 1867 when Joseph Halévy was sent to investigate the community by the Alliance Israélite Universelle. Halévy was convinced that the Falashas were authentic Jews but no action was taken. A student of Halévy, Jacques Faitlovich, visited Ethiopia in 1904 where he saw the community's need for both education and contact with other Jews. Over the next fifty years Faitlovich worked to achieve these ends, establishing schools and sending young Falashas to Europe for training. He persuaded the Jewish Agency to help in this work but when he died in 1955 this support was reduced. At this time the Falashas were facing increasing hostility from the Ethiopian government. In response to their appeals for help Professor Norman Bentwich came to the country in 1961. As a result of his visit the Falasha Welfare Association was founded which aimed to provide immediate aid to the community. Simultaneously the American Association for Ethiopian Jews was promoting the idea that only wholesale emigration to Israel would solve the Falashas' problems. The efforts of these and other organisations succeeded in arousing concern in Israel and in 1975 the Falashas were officially recognised as Jews by the Chief Rabbinate.

A Marxist coup deposed Haile Salassie's government in 1974. During the following decade the new regime increased suppression of the Falashas and in the early 1980s measures were passed forbidding religious practice and the teaching of Hebrew. This period also saw the community caught in the middle of the civil war being fought in the North-East of the country. Under these conditions Falashas began leaving their homes in Gondar and Tigre provinces and by the beginning of 1984 5000 had reached Israel. At this point the position of the community rapidly worsened. The onset of severe famine and the escalation of the civil war caused the Falashas to flee in unprecedented numbers to refugee camps across the Sudanese border. When it became clear that many in these camps were dying from starvation and disease, the Israeli government decided to mount a rescue mission, Operation Moses. The airlift of Falashas to Israel began in late November 1984. It was co-ordinated by the Jewish Agency and funded by Jewish communal organisations, particularly in America. Tacit co-operation was gained from the Ethiopian and Sudanese governments after negotiations involving the United States and Egypt, and the entire exercise was conducted in complete secrecy. Operation Moses lasted until 6 January 1985. It was ended one month prematurely when details of the mission were leaked to the press and the Sudanese government withdrew its co-operation. By this time over 7000 Falashas had been transported to Israel. It is thought that up to 15 000 were left behind in Ethiopia.

Composition of the Community

The Falasha community is split between Ethiopia and Israel with many stranded in the refugee camps in Sudan.

The Falashas in Ethiopia are mostly too old or infirm to have survived the journey to Sudan. Their main area of settlement is in Gondar province around Lake Tana and particularly in the township of Ambober. They continue their involvement in farming and handicrafts, but still suffer the effects of the famine and have lost some of their villages to refugees escaping the civil war in the north of the country.

The new immigrants in Israel undergo a three-year absorption programme organised by the Jewish Agency. After spending their first year in special centres learning Hebrew and receiving vocational training, families have been rehoused in towns throughout the country, including the West Bank.

Legal Status

In 1983 the Marxist government in Ethiopia softened its approach to the Falashas. Schools and synagogues were re-opened and freedom to practise religion granted again. As far as can be gathered these reforms are still in operation, although some restrictions may continue to be imposed. The Falashas in Israel have been granted full Israeli citizenship under the Law of Return.

Communal Organisation

There is no formal communal organisation in Ethiopia and no proper leadership. In each settlement there may be one or two elders who act as spokesmen. The Asmara Jewish Community is affiliated to the World Jewish Congress.

In Israel the organisation of the community is confused. Some religious figures, Rabbi Hadani being the most prominent, attempt to act as leaders but they do not have the community's full support. Dissension is particularly obvious among the younger Falashas.

Religious Life

As far as can be known religious life in Ethiopia continues in the same way as before Operation Moses, and in greater freedom since the reforms of 1983. The form of religion practised is a development of pre-Talmudic Judaism and the Bible used is a translation of the Septuagint into Ge'ez, the Hamitic language.

In Israel religious questions have caused difficulties. At first the Orthodox Rabbinate queried whether the Falashas were fully Jewish.

They required them to undergo a 'conversion in doubt' involving symbolic circumcision, ritual immersion and a declaration of willingness to keep the commandments. The Falashas protested against this and in July 1985 these protests together with pressure from government and public opinion forced the Orthodox Rabbinate to drop their demands. In doubtful cases ritual immersion before marriage is still required. Although this has brought renewed protests from the younger members of the community, in general both sides accepted it as a workable compromise. As yet the Falashas do not have their own synagogues, but there are some ordained Falasha rabbis and services are held in a mixture of Hebrew and Ge'ez.

General Position
The community remaining in Ethiopia is now very much in decline and the main concern is over their emigration to Israel. There is little prospect of this happening on any large scale although 800 Falashas were airlifted to Israel in March 1985 by the United States airforce and small groups continue to make their own way to the camps in the Sudan. The government, embarrassed by Operation Moses, has increased its efforts to stop Falashas leaving the country and has adopted a strong anti-Israel position. It must not be forgotten that 400–1000 Falashas remain in the Sudan, still suffering the effects of the famine and disease. The prospect of their reaching Israel is equally bleak. The new regime that came to power in April 1985 has put on trial those in the previous Sudanese government who co-operated with Operation Moses and is determined to prevent further emigration.

The Falashas in Israel are in a far better position although they still face problems. Only a minority have found jobs and those employed often encounter exploitation. Children have adapted more quickly than their parents and traditional family structures have been disrupted. There are fears that the younger Falashas are too eager to abandon their own culture while the older immigrants do not make sufficient efforts to adjust. There have also been isolated cases of racism.

FINLAND

Population: 4 894 000   Jewish population: 1 200

History
Finland was under Swedish rule until 1809 and during this period Jews were banned from living in the country. After Russia occupied the country small numbers of Jews who had previously served in the Russian army were allowed to settle but their freedom was severely limited. It was not until 1889 that civilian Jews were permitted to settle and not till

Finland became an independent country in 1918 that they were given full citizenship rights. The Jewish population subsequently rose to an inter-war peak of 2000.

During the Second World War the Finns, though allied to Germany, refused to enforce antisemitic legislation. Initially they agreed to the deportation of 50 Austrian Jews, but refused to continue this practice after hearing that the first 11 had been massacred at their destination. The Jewish population has decreased since the end of the war because of emigration and assimilation.

Composition of the Community
The community is Ashkenazi and mostly upper-middle and middle class. Eight hundred Jews live in Helsinki, 200 in Turku and 20 in Tampere.

Legal Status
The Jewish community has legal status and the right to levy taxes on its members. Marriages can be either religious or civil.

Communal Organisation
The Suomen Juutalaisten Seurakuntien Keskusneuvosto (Central Council of Jewish Communities in Finland) is a consultative body based in Helsinki dealing with general matters. It is affiliated to the World Jewish Congress. The communities of Helsinki and Turku are members of the Central Council. The representative body for the Helsinki community is the Community Council, consisting of 32 members elected for a three-year term. They in turn elect the 7–9 members of the executive Community Board for the same period. The Zionist movement is represented by Keren Kayemet and WIZO. The Council of Jewish Women is also active.

Religious Life
There is a rabbi in Helsinki and synagogues in Helsinki and Turku. Some 30 per cent of the Jewish population keep *kashrut*. *Shechita* is permitted and there is a kosher butcher as well as a kosher sausage factory in Helsinki. The Chevra Kadisha, founded in 1864, looks after Helsinki's two cemeteries.

Education
Helsinki has a kindergarten and a Jewish Comprehensive School with 3 preparatory and 6 secondary school classes, recognised by the Ministry of Education. Turku also has a kindergarten and afternoon classes for children under 15. Some 70 per cent of young Jews go to universities.

Cultural Activities
Jewish cultural organisations in Helsinki include a Jewish choral society
founded in 1917 and a youth club. Cultural activities are conducted by
a Chug Ivri, a B'nai Akiva group and a Jewish students' association.
There is also a community library with 5000 volumes of Judaica. Finnish
youth participate in camps organised by the Scandinavian Jewish Youth
Association.

Press
A periodical, *Shalom*, appears ten times a year. It is published by
the Friends of Israel Association. *Ha-Kehila*, published by the Jewish
community of Helsinki, appears 4–6 times a year, and *Shofar*, published
by the Jewish Youth Club of Helsinki, appears 4 times a year.

Welfare
Helsinki's 16-bed Jewish hospital was founded in 1962. The Bikur
Cholim, founded in 1879, gives aid to the needy and arranges for free
treatment. The Lechem Anijim, founded in 1898, helps the poor. The
Gemilus Chasodim v'Hachnosas Kalo, founded in 1904, grants loans to
members of the community and gives financial aid to brides.

Relations with Israel
Relations are at full ambassadorial level.

General Position
Finnish Jews are well integrated into the general community. There
is little antisemitism, but there is a steady decline in numbers and a
certain amount of intermarriage, with many having emigrated to Israel.

FRANCE

Population: 54 832 000   Jewish population: 535 000

History
Jews may have lived in France during the pre-Roman period. Earliest
records are of settlements in the South of France after the destruction of
the Second Temple and of Jews occupying prominent positions under the
Merovingians. In the Middle Ages France was the home of Jewish scholars
including Rashi, Rabbenu Tam and the Tosaphists. During the Crusades
Jews were expelled from the Kingdom of France though some remained
in Provence and the South East, and in Alsace Lorraine. There were also
Marrano communities in Bayonne and Bordeaux. Laws promulgated in

1790 and 1791, following the French Revolution, gave Jews equal rights. Napoleon organised the Jews into Consistories, and set up the Sanhedrin in 1807. By the middle of the nineteenth century, French Jewry had become an international centre of Jewish philanthropy through such organisations as the Alliance Israélite Universelle. Individual Jews continued to play an increasingly prominent part in French life, despite the antisemitism revealed in the Dreyfus Case. A steady flow of East European Jews entered France at the turn of the century and German Jews followed in the early 1930s. In the late 1950s and early 1960s France received a quarter of a million Jews from North Africa and a sizable number from Egypt.

The pre-war community numbered about 300 000. During the German occupation approximately 80 000 Jews were deported from the centre at Drancy and only 2000 returned. Antisemitic legislation was passed by the Vichy regime as early as October 1940, long before the area was occupied by the Germans in November 1943.

Composition of the Community
The community comprises an old – mainly Alsatian – French Ashkenazi element, families of Eastern European descent who settled at the turn of the century and Sephardi Jews from Egypt and North Africa who constitute 54 per cent of the community. The total number of Jews living in France is 535 000. The main concentrations are in: Paris and suburbs, 270 000; Marseilles, 70 000; Lyons, 30 000; Nice, 20 000; Toulouse, 25 000; Strasbourg, 15 000. There are Jewish communities in many smaller French towns. The socio-economic structure of French Jewry is as follows: professional and managerial 21 per cent; middle management and clerical 47 per cent; merchants 16 per cent; manual workers and service industry 10 per cent.

Legal Status
The law of 9 September 1905 separating church and state abolished the hundred-year-old consistorial system. Since then the Jewish community has had the non-official status which applies to all recognised religions (Alsace-Lorraine is an exception since it was never under the Consistorial system). There is no obligatory community tax, but there is a voluntary fee which gives entitlement to a seat in a synagogue. The tax on kosher meat and other kosher products goes indirectly to the Consistoire. Religious marriage is not recognised by the state, thus civil marriage is a necessary prerequisite.

Communal Organisation
The overall body is the Conseil Représentatif des Institutions Juives de France (Representative Council of French Jewish Institutions), commonly known as CRIF. Its president is regarded as political head of the

community and usually negotiates with the government on Jewish communal matters. CRIF is affliated to the World Jewish Congress.

The Fonds Social Juif Unifié (FSJU) dispenses funds collected by the Appel Unifié Juif de France (AUJF) for domestic purposes and for Israel. The headquarters of the European Jewish Congress is in Paris. The Alliance Israélite Universelle organises schools abroad. Zionist groups include the Mouvement Sioniste de France, WIZO and Pioneer Women and the Renouveau Juif. The Coopération Feminine concerns itself with social and cultural work. B'nai B'rith is well established in France.

The Education Department of Jewish Youth (DEJJ) organises youth activities at community centres. A wide range of youth movements operate throughout the country.

Religious Life
The Consistoire Central Israélite de France (usually abbreviated as the Consistoire) is the central religious body. Its Chief Rabbi and Beth Din have national recognition. The local Consistoires in every city are members of the Consistoire Central. However, the Alsace-Lorraine communities remain independent of the Consistoire Central for historical reasons. The Conseil Représentatif du Judaisme Traditionaliste represents ultra-Orthodox Jews while the Union Libérale Israélite and the Mouvement Libéral Juif de France represent Liberal Jews. Neither of these groups recognises the Chief Rabbi or Beth Din.

French Jewry is composed of the ultra-Orthodox and very strict Orthodox (about 7 per cent with 10 synagogues and 7 rabbis), the moderate Orthodox, including the Sephardim, organised in the Consistoires (48 per cent with 20 synagogues, 80 rabbis and 100 ministers) and Reform and Liberal (5 per cent, with 3 synagogues and 3 rabbis). Approximately 40 per cent of French Jewry are non-practising. Many synagogues exist throughout France, with a large number in Paris.

There are numerous kosher butchers in Paris and others in Caen, Grenoble, Lyons, Marseilles, Montpellier, Nancy, Nice, Perigueux, Perpignan, Toulon and Toulouse. There are kosher restaurants in Paris, Grenoble, Lyons, Marseilles, Nancy, Nice and Strasbourg. Approximately one quarter of French Jewry keep *kashrut*.

Education
In the Paris region are 24 full-time Jewish schools, including secondary and primary schools, kindergartens, and religious seminaries. There are also Jewish schools in Strasbourg, Nice and Toulouse. The Séminaire Israélite de France trains rabbis for the French-speaking world, including Switzerland, Luxembourg, Belgium and Canada.

Most French universities have courses in biblical or modern Hebrew. By law, Hebrew education can also be given in lycées, if demanded by at least ten parents under the authority of an inspector general of the Ministry of Education. Yiddish is taught at Paris University and the Rashi Centre in Paris contains the University Centre for Jewish Studies, which gives courses at university level. Interest in Jewish education is clearly growing as, in 1984, there were throughout France more than 250 classes teaching modern Hebrew, which was a 20 per cent increase on 1983.

Cultural Activities

Museums: in Paris there is a museum of Jewish art and the Cluny Museum houses the Strauss Rothschild Collection. There are museums attached to the Carpentras and Cavaillon Synagogues in the Vaucluse area. The Arles Museum houses the Lunel Collection and the Museum of the History of France at Bayonne has a Jewish room. Two important collections are in Alsace-Lorraine: the Réné Wiener Collection at the Lorraine Museum in Nancy and the History of the Jews of Alsace-Lorraine Collection at the Alsatian Museum in Strasbourg.

Libraries: Paris has the library of the Alliance Israélite Universelle, the Medem Yiddish Library, and the libraries of the Séminaire Israélite de France and the Centre de Documentation Juive Contemporaine. Archive collections are at the Consistoire Central, the Consistoire de Paris, the Alliance Israélite Universelle and the Centre de Documentation Juive Contemporaine. Strasbourg has a communal library.

The FSJU funds cultural activities and the DEJJ organises the annual Jewish Book Week and a Jewish Music Week. The Colloque des Intellectuels Juifs de Langue Française, organised by the French Section of the World Jewish Congress, is held annually. There are a number of Jewish dance and theatre companies, and many community centres, linked to the various synagogues, run cultural activities.

Research

The Centre de Documentation Juive Contemporaine conducts research into the Holocaust period in France and the Centre d'Etudes et de Recherche sur l'Antisémitisme Contemporain (CERAC – affiliated to the Institute of Jewish Affairs in London) studies present-day antisemitism, while CIDIP (Centre d'Information et de Documentation sur Israël et le Proche-Orient) provides information on Israel and the Middle East.

Press

Three Jewish daily papers are published in France: the bulletin of the Agence Télégraphique Juive and two Yiddish newspapers, the Socialist-Zionist *Unzer Wort*, and the extreme left-wing *Naie Presse*. There are three weekly publications: *Tribune Juive* and the Yiddish papers *Unzer*

Weg, published by the Mizrachi, and *Unzer Stimme*, which is Bundist.

Monthly magazines include *L'Arche*, which has a national circulation and a number of local editions, *Information Juive*, *La Terre Retrouvée*, *Amitié France-Israël* and *Hamore*, which is an educational publication. Published quarterly are the academic journal *Nouveaux Cahiers*, produced by the Alliance Israélite Universelle, and *AMIF*, published by the Association Médicale Israélite de France.

Other publications nclude: the twice-yearly *Revue des Etudes Juives*; the left-wing Zionist bi-monthly *Les Cahiers Bernard Lazare*; *Conversations avec les Jeunes*, issued fortnightly by the Lubavitch Movement; *Le Messager*, published by the Liberals; the bi-monthly *Revue de la WIZO*; an economic monthly on Israel published by the JTA. The Consistoire Central has its own yearbook and the Consistoire de Paris issues an annual calendar.

There are Jewish booksellers in Paris, Lyons, Marseilles and Strasbourg. Fondation Sefer publishes translations of the Talmud and prayer books. A number of general publishers produce collections of books on Jewish subjects.

Since 1930 (except for the Nazi period), a weekly programme *Ecoute Israël* has been broadcast on the radio. Television broadcasts the weekly *La Source de la Vie*, and several local Jewish radio stations in Paris and other large cities have opened in recent years.

Welfare

There has been no Jewish hospital since the Rothschild Hospital was nationalised. There is an orphanage at Haguenau, and homes for the aged in Paris, Nice and Aix-les-Bains. Retirement homes exist in Nancy, Bayonne, Strasbourg and Colmar.

Jewish welfare organisations in Paris include: the American Joint Distribution Committee; the Paris Jewish Committee for Social Welfare Action (CASIP); the Jewish Committee for Social Welfare Action and Reconstruction (COJASOR); the Operation for the Protection of Jewish Children (OPEJ) and a child welfare organization, Oeuvres au Secours des Enfants (OSE).

Relations with Israel

Because of its Arab connections France did not recognise the State of Israel until 1949. The Algerian conflict and the Suez crisis brought an improvement in French-Israeli relations but in the Six-Day War France displayed pro-Arab sympathies.

Diplomatic relations are on full ambassadorial level. There are French consulates in several Israeli towns (including Jerusalem). Active cultural relations exist, backed up by an official agreement between the two countries.

Historical Sites

The old synagogues at Carpentras (1367, rebuilt 1741) and Cavaillon (1774) are classified as French national monuments. There are ancient Jewish cemeteries in the Landes (Peyrehorade and Bastide-Clarence) and in Alsace at Jurgholtz and Rosenwiller. The memorial to the Unknown Jewish Martyr in Paris is of architectural interest and contains the reading-room of the Centre de Documentation.

General Position

Jews have traditionally been active in French public life. There have been several Jewish Prime Ministers, and a recent cabinet had four Jewish ministers. There are also numerous Jewish deputies. The community has produced a number of important Jewish writers and scholars including Nobel prize winners. Jews hold high office in the law and other professions.

Antisemitism still exists in France. The attack against the synagogue in Rue Copernic in 1980 was followed by several similar bomb outrages, which, however, turned out to be mainly Arab in origin. There are laws punishing antisemitic or racist acts. The International League Against Antisemitism and Racism (LICRA) and the Movement against Racism for Friendship between Peoples (MRAP) are organisations which can institute legal proceedings. Antisemitic organisations which violate the law have on occasion been banned (for example, FANE – Fédération d'Action Nationale et Européenne – in September 1980, and the successor organisation, FNE, in January 1985). The rise of the Front National led by Jean-Marie Le Pen has caused anxiety to French Jewry, particularly as it gained 10 per cent of the total vote in the parliamentary elections in 1986. The party claims not to be antisemitic, merely nationalistic. The trial in 1986 of Klaus Barbie on a charge of crimes against humanity has revived interest in the fate of French Jewry during the Nazi occupation, especially among the young French people.

GERMAN DEMOCRATIC REPUBLIC

Population: 16 640 000   Jewish population: 400

History

(See Federal Republic of Germany for history and for Holocaust period.) Following the Second World War the GDR, unlike the Federal Republic, refused to pay its share of indemnification to victims of Nazi persecution.

Composition of the Community

The community is purely Ashkenazi. In 1981 the number of registered Jews was 448. A smaller number was reported in 1985 – 197 in Berlin, 60 in Dresden, 47 in Leipzig, 24 in Halle, 22 in Magdeburg, 36 in Erfurt, 8 in Schwerin and some in Karl Marx Stadt (Chemnitz). The community is composed mainly of old people, though Berlin records 85 persons under the age of 55.

Legal Status

The community has an official status with the right to levy taxes on members. There are laws against racial discrimination.

Communal Organisation

The central organisation is the Verband der Jüdischen Gemeinden in der Deutschen Demokratischen Republik (Union of Jewish Communities in the GDR) based in Dresden. There are organised communities in East Berlin and the other locccallities mentioned above. For a number of years the Union has been allowed to send observers to World Jewish Congress meetings.

Religious Life

Following an agreement between the American Jewish Congress and the East German authorities, the Jewish community of East Berlin acquired a resident rabbi in 1987. Until then religious affairs were run by a few volunteers. There are synagogues in Berlin, Dresden, Halle, Magdeburg, Erfurt and Leipzig. Sabbath services are conducted in Berlin but in Leipzig, Dresden and Erfurt religious services only take place on high holidays. On such occasions a famous choir composed of non-Jews performs in the Leipzig synagogue. The other communities are mostly too small to form a *minyan*. Approximately 50 per cent of East Berlin's registered Jews keep *kashrut* and there is a kosher butcher. A *shochet* comes fortnightly from Hungary to perform *shechita*.

Education

The University in East Berlin has a department of Jewish studies.

Cultural Activities

The Jewish Community Library in Berlin has 4500 volumes and a collection of books from Israel supplied at the community's request in 1984. The community centre organises regular cultural activities, clubs for children and young people and a women's group. Smaller community centres are at Erfurt, Halle, Karl Marx Stadt, Leipzig, Magdeburg and Schwerin.

Press
The community publishes a quarterly called *Nachrichtenblatt*.

Welfare
There is a home for the aged in East Berlin (Niederschönhausen).

Relations with Israel
The GDR and Israel have no diplomatic relations, the GDR having followed a particularly anti-Israel foreign policy. However, a small number of Jews have emigrated to Israel.

Historical Sites
The Holocaust Memorial is on the site of the Dresden Synagogue destroyed by the Nazis in 1938. In Berlin the Rykerstrasse Synagogue was renovated in 1978, and the ruins of the Oranienburgerstrasse Synagogue are still standing. The Grosse Hamburgerstrasse Cemetery contains the grave of Moses Mendelsohn.

General Position
The small and ageing community receives support from the GDR authorities. It is believed that many more Jews live in East Germany but have never associated themselves in any way with the community. Christian-Jewish understanding is actively promoted by a number of groups.

GERMANY, FEDERAL REPUBLIC OF

Population: 61 035 000   Jewish population: 28 000

History
Jewish settlement in Germany goes back at least to the fourth century CE. In the eighth and ninth centuries, the Carolingians encouraged Jewish settlement, resulting in flourishing communities by the tenth century. The eleventh century saw an active intellectual life, particularly in the Rhine Valley (Rashi himself studied in Worms). However, the peaceful period for German Jewry came to an end with the beginning of the First Crusade in 1096.

The next few centuries saw many massacres and expulsions, and the flight of German Jews into Eastern Europe, where their German dialect was gradually transformed into Yiddish. However, the division of Germany into small principalities and city states helped to protect the remaining Jews during this period. In the seventeenth century, after the Thirty Years War, the situation improved and German Jewry began to flourish again. At the beginning of the nineteenth century, full emancipation was granted to Jews in the areas under French occupation. The withdrawal of the French produced a setback, and in 1819 the Hep! Hep! riots broke out.

By 1869 emancipation had been achieved and was ratified with the new constitution of 1871. This marked a turning point not only in the history of Germany but of world Jewry. The cultural life of the community had developed rapidly since Moses Mendelssohn had started to modernise the community as part of the Enlightenment (*Aufklärung*, or in Hebrew, *Haskalah*) in the eighteenth century and Jews began to replace Yiddish with German and to study German and Western culture. From the end of the nineteenth century until 1933, this movement was to produce the most extraordinary cultural flowering in every field of intellectual and artistic life. It also saw the development of Jewish culture and religion, Wissenschaft des Judentum (the Science of Judaism) and the development of Reform Judaism, started by Geiger in 1840.

Full emancipation was not achieved, however, until after the First World War. Before that, there was discrimination in certain areas: it was not possible, for instance, for a Jew to become an army officer, a diplomat or a university professor. Thus in many cases Jews abandoned their faith and converted to Christianity, or were converted in childhood by their parents.

With the coming to power of the Nazis in 1933, the then 503 000-strong community was gradually excluded from German life. On 15 September 1935 the Nuremberg Laws were passed, prohibiting marital or extra-marital relations between Jews and Gentiles, as well as forbidding Jews from employing Gentile domestic servants. Various decrees banned Jews from economic life and placed them outside German law. On the night of 10 November 1938 (Kristallnacht), most of the synagogues were burnt and much Jewish property was destroyed in organised riots.

Between 1933 and 1938, some quarter of a million German Jews, about half the community, fled abroad (the USA took 102 200, Great Britain 52 000, Argentina 63 500 and Palestine 33 400). This emigration, particularly of so many leading intellectuals, was to have a major cultural impact on the countries where they settled. By 1938, however, immigration to many countries had become more difficult and, after the outbreak of the Second World War, impossible. Jews were forced to wear the 'Jew-badge' from September 1941 and deportations began in October 1941.

By the end of 1942 the number of Jews in Germany had been reduced to 51 000 and by the beginning of April the following year to 32 000. The number of Jews who remained in hiding in Germany has been estimated at 19 000 and those who returned from the concentration camps after the war at 8000. About 160–180 000 German Jews are estimated to have been murdered by the Nazis in Germany, or to have died as a result of persecution.

After the war, many Jewish refugees congregated in Germany in Displaced Persons camps before moving on, mostly to Israel. In 1952 the new Federal Republic agreed to pay a sum in compensation for the re-settlement in Israel of Jews from Nazi-occupied Europe, for the destroyed Jewish cultural property and for personal damage to individuals. A number of Jews returned to Germany and many Eastern European refugees also settled in the country.

Composition of the Community

The community is overwhelmingly Ashkenazi. Most members are not descendents of the old German community. Sixty-six local Jewish communities are organised in 14 regional or town federations. the major centres are West Berlin (6500), Frankfurt-am-Main (5000), Munich (4000), Düsseldorf (1700), Hamburg (1400) and Cologne (1300). The community is basically middle-class, with a large number of pensioners. There is a high average age of 45 years, and more than 4000 persons are over 70. In addition to the registered community, it is estimated that up to a furtheer 25 000 unregistered Jews live in the Federal Republic and West Berlin.

Legal Status

The Jewish communities are corporations under public law. There is a religious tax in Germany, levied together with income tax, which is then distributed to all religious communities. This helps fund the communities' work.

Communal Organisation

The central body is the Zentralrat der Juden in Deutschland (Central Council of Jews in Germany) in Düsseldorf. This Council represents all German Jews. It operates through the various provincial associations of communities (Landesverbande) and the local communities and looks after Jewish political interests, matters of restitution and indemnification, and similar issues. It keeps a vigilant eye on any signs of Nazi revival. The Zentralrat is affiliated to the World Jewish Congress.

The Zionist Organisation of Germany has its headquarters in Frankfurt where the Jewish Agency also has an office. The main fund-raising organisation is the United Jewish Appeal with offices in Frankfurt, Berlin and Munich. The B'nai B'rith is also active: lodges are to be found in Berlin, Düsseldorf, Frankfurt, Hamburg, Munich and Saarbrücken. Women's organisations are represented by WIZO and the Jüdischer Frauenbund.

Apart from the students' unions, the major youth organisations include the Zionist Youth Movement in Frankfurt and, on the sporting side, Maccabi which has centres in Berlin (head office), Düsseldorf and Frankfurt, where there is also a youth centre.

Religious Life
All the larger communities have their own rabbis, who are organised in the Conference of West German Rabbis with the presiding rabbi in office in Dortmund. There are synagogues in Aachen, Baden-Baden, Bad Nauheim, West Berlin (3), Bonn, Bremen, Cologne, Dortmund, Düsseldorf, Frankfurt (3), Fürth, Hamburg, Hanover, Munich (4), Wiesbaden, Würzburg and many other towns. It is possible to obtain kosher meals in Bad Nauheim, West Berlin, Cologne, Frankfurt, Munich, Stuttgart and Würzburg.

Education
With relatively few children, there are only two elementary Talmud Torah schools which have a total of just over 300 pupils. However, a number of teachers of religion travel between the smaller communities and teach mostly on the various synagogue premises. There is a Jüdische Volkshochschule in West Berlin and a Hochschule (Institute of Higher Learning) for Jewish Studies attached to the University at Heidelberg. The Jewish Student Union, with headquarters in Munich and branches in Frankfurt, Aachen, Heidelberg, Berlin, Cologne, Stuttgart, Hanover and Hamburg, organises seminars.

Cultural Activities
Cologne has a Jewish museum and library attached to the synagogue and community centre.

Press
The principal weekly paper is the *Allgemeine Jüdische Wochenzeitung*, published in Düsseldorf. Other weeklies are the *Münchener Jüdische Nachrichten* and the Yiddish language *Neue Jüdische Zeitung*, both published in Munich. The Central Council also has its own organ, the *Jüdische Presse Dienst*, and several of the larger communities publish news sheets.

Welfare
The overall welfare body is the Zentralwohlfahrtstelle der Juden in Deutschland (Central Welfare Board of the Jews in Germany), whose headquarters is in Frankfurt. All 14 regional federations and communities are affiliated to it.

West Berlin has five homes for old people and a Jewish hospital. There are homes for the aged in Cologne, Düsseldorf, Frankfurt, Munich and Würzburg.

Relations with Israel

The Israeli embassy is in Bonn and the embassy of the Federal Republic is in Tel Aviv. However, it was not until 1965 that Israel agreed to open proper diplomatic relations with Germany, a decision which resulted in a number of Arab states temporarily breaking off diplomatic relations with Bonn. Prior to the actual exchange of diplomatic representatives, the Luxembourg Agreement was ratified between the two countries in 1953, by which the Federal Republic granted Israel the sum of $822 000 000 over 12–14 years as reparation. ($107 000 000 of this was allocated to the Conference on Jewish Material Claims against Germany, a body representing 23 major Jewish organisations around the world for the purpose of relief and rehabilitation of victims of Nazism outside Israel.) President von Weizsäcker made the first official German state visit to Israel in October 1985 and President Herzog came to West Germany in January 1987. These exchanges marked significant steps in the continued normalisation of relations between the two countries.

During the inter-war period many German Jews emigrated to what was then Palestine. There are a number of Israelis living and working in Germany.

Historical Sites

Of the many important Jewish historical sites in West Germany, the most significant is the synagogue in Worms. Originally built in 1034, and faithfully reconstructed after being bombed during the Second World War, it is one of the oldest synagogues in Europe. The adjoining *mikveh* (1186) and the Rashi Chapel (1624) were destroyed by the Nazis in 1938, but have been reconstructed and were re-consecrated in 1961. In the small town of Friedberg in Hessen there is a *mikveh* dating from 1260. The old synagogue at Fürth has also been restored. There are ancient cemeteries at Würzburg and at Heidengsfeld and Hochburg nearby.

Modern memorials to Jews include those at the sites of Dachau and Bergen-Belsen concentration camps. There are others throughout Germany, including two in Munich: one marks the destruction of the city's synagogue on Kristallnacht, 1938; the other commemorates the murder of Israeli athletes by the PLO during the 1972 Olympics.

General Position

The community today is widely distributed across the country with many Jews living in small towns. There is a good relationship with the churches. The International Council of Christians and Jews has its headquarters at Heppenheim.

A number of studies, based on representative opinion polls, have confirmed the existence of marked latent antisemitic prejudices among

Germans. The disturbing results of the Silbermann study of the mid-1970s were partly confirmed in a later investigation (Badi Panahi) which suggested that between 8 and 27 per cent of the population do harbour a marked prejudice against Jews. Overt antisemitism, such as desecration of Jewish cemeteries, daubings of swastikas, threats and violence is kept under surveillance through the instrument of the Agencies for the Protection of the Constitution.

There are about 20 000 members of extreme right-wing groups in Germany. Many prosecutions take place and the courts deal severely with such infringements. In the Bundestag elections of 1987 the extreme right-wing parties, including the NPD (National Democrats), polled only one per cent of the vote and failed to win a seat. The Central Council of Jews in Germany believes that the authorities have contained the problem of antisemitism so that it is no more than a constant irritation which has to be carefully watched.

GIBRALTAR

Population: 28 843   Jewish population: 600

History

Although Jews lived in Gibraltar during the Middle Ages, the present community dates from the British occupation of the country in 1704. Jews were granted legal rights of residence in 1749 when their population of 600 already constituted one third of the total community. In the siege of 1779–83 many Jews fled to England but the community was gradually rebuilt and by the mid-nineteenth century reached a population peak of 2000. During these years a large part of the retail trade was in Jewish hands. Along with many other Gibraltarians the Jews left the country during the Second World War and many did not return.

In the 1960s the first mayor to be appointed in the colony was a Jew, Sir Joshua Hassan. He later became Gibraltar's first Chief Minister. In general Jews have been very active in civic and political life.

Composition of the Community

The community is exclusively Sephardi. Jews are employed in either the retail trades or in the professions.

Legal Status

The Jewish benevolent organisations and synagogues are recognised charities.

Communal Organisation

The Managing Board of the Jewish Community has 11 members elected triennially. It is recognised by all sections and organises fund-raising. The community is affiliated to the World Jewish Congress.

Zionist activity is covered by a Zionist representative, who also acts for the Jewish National Fund, a Jewish Agency representative, a WIZO group and the Israel Appeal Committee.

Religious Life

Gibraltar has four synagogues but only one rabbi, known as the Communal Rabbi. During the academic year a shabbat service is conducted entirely by young people and Talmud Torah pupils. If a *mohel* is required he is flown in from abroad. There is no Beth Din. Three shops sell kosher products and kosher meals are served at the Social and Cultural Club. Kosher meat is imported from abroad.

Education

There is a kindergarten, a primary school, a Sunday school and evening classes for children at comprehensive school. All these are the responsibility of the Talmud Torah Committee of the Managing Board.

Cultural Activities

No library exists, but there is a community archive and a cultural club. The Jewish youth of Gibraltar have their own group.

Press

Although there is no Gibraltarian newspaper a regular radio programme entitled *Pause for Reflection* is given alternately by the Communal Rabbi and clergy of other denominations.

Welfare

The Jewish home for the aged can take up to 15 people. General welfare is organised through the Hebrew Poor Fund, Maternity Relief, Circumcision Society, Malbish Arumim and Ozer Dalim.

Relations with Israel

As Gibraltar is not an independent state its foreign affairs are handled by Great Britain. However, Israel maintains a consulate with an honorary consul and honorary vice-consul.

Historical Sites

The Shaar Hashamayim Synagogue built in 1768 is Gibraltar's most historic building. The house of the eighteenth-century diplomat and community leader, Aaron Nunes Cardozo, still stands, and is now used as the city hall. Gibraltar has a Jewish cemetery, dating back to the beginning of the eighteenth century.

The Jewish population of Gibraltar has remained static at approximately 600 for the last 40 years. There are no signs of a decline. Gibraltarian Jewry is actively Jewish and Zionist. The community is exceptionally active in public life.

GREECE

Population: 9 970 000   Jewish population: 4875

History
Jewish communities existed in Greece as early as the third century BCE. By the first century CE there were flourishing communities with synagogues in all principal cities. Under the Byzantine emperors, Jews were persecuted but a new community arose in 1492 with the influx of refugees from the Spanish Inquisition. Many settled in Salonica, which eventually became an important centre of Jewish culture and was granted autonomy in 1568. Jews continued to prosper under Turkish rule in Greece until the Greek revolt in 1821, when many lost their lives for supporting the Ottoman Empire. Nevertheless over the next 150 years the Jewish communities rebuilt themselves and at the outbreak of the Second World War the number of Jews living in Greece was 77 000.

Between 15 March and 7 August 1943, under the German occupation, the Salonican community was deported to Auschwitz where 43 850 of its 56 000 Jews were killed. On 15 March 1944, the Nazis sought out the 1000 remaining Jews, eventually capturing and deporting half of them. The other half managed to escape, many through the aid of Archbishop Damaskinos of Athens, who called on all monasteries to offer sanctuary to the fugitives. Some of the Jews who remained joined the partisans and the resistance forces. By the end of the war the Jewish population of Greece had dwindled to a mere 11 000. The population further declined by over 4000 with post-war Jewish emigration – mostly to Israel and the USA.

Composition of the Community
Greek Jewry, a Sephardi community, is mainly situated in Athens where 2800 Jews live. Salonica has only 1100 with smaller congregations in Larisa (400), Chalkis, Corfu, Joannina, Trikkala and Florina. Small numbers of Jews live in Veroia, Cavalla, Didimoticho, Rhodes, Karditsa and Patras.

Legal Status
Greece's Jewish communities are described as 'legal bodies of public utility'. The central Jewish organisation, recognised under Law No.

1657/51, is under the jurisdiction of the Ministry of Education and Religion. The community has the right to levy taxes on its members.

Communal Organisation
The umbrella organisation is the Kentriko Israelitiko Symvoulio Ellados (Central Board of Jewish Communities in Greece) known as KIS. This is a 12-member body elected by the general assembly of representatives of all the various communities. It also represents Greek Jewry in the World Jewish Congress.

The Zionist movement is represented by the Zionist Union, which has branches in Athens and Salonica. The Zionist Centre and the Keren Kayemet share the same premises where there is also a Jewish Agency office and a B'nai B'rith lodge.

Women's groups are represented by WIZO, Aviv and B'not B'rit. Athens, Salonica and Larisa all have their own youth groups. The Salonica community runs a summer camp for youth from all over Greece.

Religious Life
No central ecclesiastical authority exists, and each community is autonomous, though the Athens community's Beth Din serves the other communities. There are three rabbis (two in Athens and a peripatetic rabbi for the provinces) and eight synagogues. All hold services according to Sephardic practice. *Shechita* is permitted.

Education
Both Athens and Salonica have kindergartens, catering for 110 children between them. Primary schools exist in Athens (120 pupils, founded in 1946), Salonica (40 pupils for the first three grades only, founded in 1978) and Larisa. Virtually all young Jews attend institutions of higher education.

Cultural Activities
The Jewish Museum of Greece in Athens, founded in 1977, houses a fine collection of Judaica, including Greek Jewish religious items and traditional costumes. The premises of the Central Board in Athens house a small Jewish library. Communal centres providing facilities for talks, discussions and social activities exist in all communities.

Athens has a Jewish youth centre with its own kosher restaurant. Sporting activities are centred around the Maccabi Sports Club in Athens.

Press
The Central Board publishes a literary monthly called *Chronika*, as well as a fortnightly news bulletin. It also issues an annual *luah*.

The Jewish youth of Athens have their own monthly, *Nea Yenia* (New

Generation). A monthly magazine, *Israelina Nea* (Israel News), is published by the friendship league Hellas-Israel.

Welfare
The OPAIE (Foundation for the Administration of Heirless Property and Jewish Rehabilitation Fund) is based in Athens. Otherwise there are no specialist welfare organisations. Each community has its own welfare committee to cater for the needs of the poor.

Relations with Israel
Greece has had strained relations with Israel in the past. The two countries have diplomatic delegations in Tel Aviv and Athens rather than full embassies, and Greece still only gives *de facto* recognition to Israel. However, there has recently been a move towards closer ties, with the two countries signing new co-operation agreements in the fields of tourism, science and culture.

A Hellas-Israel Friendship League exists in Athens with a branch in Salonica. Many Greek Jews have emigrated to Israel.

Historical Sites
The oldest Jewish community in Europe was founded in Chalkis around 20 BCE. The site of the original synagogue still exists and has been built on many times. In the cemetery gravestones can be found with inscriptions dating as far back as 1500 CE. Historic synagogues also exist at Corfu, Joannina and on the island of Crete at Canea. The synagogue at Rhodes was built in 1731.

At Chalkis a statue has been erected in memory of Colonel Mordehai Frizis, a Jewish war hero. He was the first Greek officer to be killed by the Germans and the site where he fell is also marked by a memorial. Monuments to Jewish war victims can also be found in the cemeteries at Athens and Salonica.

General Position
Greek Jews have equal rights and freedom of religious practice. In February 1984 an amendment to the Penal Code was approved making the incitement to religious discrimination a punishable crime with up to two years' imprisonment.

Antisemitism is by no means absent. Periodicals with antisemitic tendencies include the Fascist monthly *Kinema* (Movement) the Arab-financed *Mesogiaki Alilegie* (Mediterranean Solidarity) and the weekly *Stohos* (Target).

The twentieth century has witnessed a significant decline in Greek Jewry. Although the present community is vigorous, intermarriage is increasing.

GUATEMALA

Population: 7 956 000   Jewish population: 800

German Jews began to arrive in Guatemala in 1848, and the first communal group was established in 1870. A number of Sephardim then came to the country. European Jews came in the 1920s and the first synagogue, the Sephardi, was constructed in 1924/5. Refugees from Nazi Germany arrived in the 1930s and Jews began to play a considerable role in the economic development of the country. The Ashkenazi Hebrew Centre, which includes a synagogue, was built in 1965. In recent years many Jews have emigrated and the community has dwindled in spite of a number of Jewish refugees arriving from Cuba.

The central body is the Consejo Central de la Comunidad Judia de Guatemala which is affiliated to the World Jewish Congress. The WIZO Federation is active in the community.

There are three synagogues (Sephardi, Ashkenazi and German), but no ordained rabbi, a Jewish sports centre and a Jewish school, the Institute Einstein. The overwhelming majority of Jews live in Guatemala City. A few live in Quetzaltenango and San Marcos.

Israel has an embassy in Guatemala City and there is a Guatemalan embassy in Israel. Relations between the two countries have been good ever since the Guatemalan UN representative, Dr Jorge Garciá Granados, voted for the Spanish Partition Resolution in 1947.

The 11th Convention of FEDECO was held in 1948 in Antigua near Guatemala City and addressed by the Agriculture and Foreign Ministers of Guatemala.

HAITI

Population: 5 272 000   Jewish population: 150

The first European in Haiti was Luis de Torres, Columbus's interpreter, a Jew who had been baptised before sailing. There were three waves of Jewish immigration: some Marranos settled in the early seventeenth century but they were either killed or expelled with all other whites during the revolt of Toussaint L'Ouverture at the beginning of the nineteenth century. The very small twentieth-century influx included Syrian and Egyptian Jews, followed in the 1930s by a few German refugees.

There is no communal organisation, but religious services are organised by the Israeli embassy and occasionally in a private home. Relations with Israel are good with a resident ambassador in Port-au-Prince.

HONDURAS

Population: 4 092 000   Jewish population: 150

Marranos are believed to have lived in the country in the Colonial period. The modern community dates from the nineteenth century with early settlers followed by immigrants from Central Europe in the 1920s and from Poland a few years later. From 1935 to 1939 German Jews were offered refuge in the country and during the war years Honduran Consulates in many European countries issued visas to Jews who would have otherwise lost their lives.

The largely Ashkenazi community is concentrated in Tegucigalpa with similar communities in San Pedro Sula and the towns of Choluteca, Comayague and Tela. Although there is no resident rabbi there, there is a synagogue in San Pedro Sula and services are held in private homes in Tegucigalpa. The Comunidad Hebrea de Tegucigalpa is affiliated to the World Jewish Congress.

Relations between Honduras and Israel are good. The Israeli Embassy in Guatemala also serves Honduras. There is an Israeli honorary consul in Tegucigalpa.

HONG KONG

Population: 5 420 000   Jewish population: 700

History
The first Jews came to Hong Kong in 1842 after the Treaty of Nanking had opened Chinese ports to foreign settlement. They were mostly of Iraqi origin and many had previously lived in India. By 1882 approximately 60 Jewish families were living in the colony including the famous philanthropic trading and banking families, the Kadoories and Sassoons. Sir Jacob Sassoon was responsible for the building of the Ohel Leah synagogue in 1902 and the adjoining Jewish Recreation club was presented by Sir Elly Kadoorie in 1909. Some Ashkenazi Jews also settled in Hong Kong around this time.

Between 1904 and 1907 the governor of Hong Kong was a Jew, Sir Matthew Nathan. He promoted the development of the territories of Kowloon and in particular the building of the Kowloon–Canton Railway. Nathan Road, Kowloon's main thoroughfare, is named after him.

Before the Second World War Hong Kong received Jewish refugees from Germany and Eastern Europe but many left as war with Japan approached. With the Japanese occupation of the colony in 1941 Jewish communal life virtually ceased – the community centre was destroyed, the synagogue was used to store armaments and most of the Jews who remained were interned. The synagogue and Sifrei Torah, however, came to no harm, thanks to the efforts of an elderly French Jewish resident.

After the war many Jewish survivors emigrated – to Australia, Brazil or Europe. However when mainland China established a Communist regime many of its Jews came to Hong Kong, some settling permanently. The Kadoorie Agricultural Aid Association provided help for many of these refugees.

Composition of the Community
The community is concentrated in urban areas of Hong Kong and Kowloon. The majority of its members are not Hong Kong British citizens but expatriate business people representing approximately 18 nationalities in a mixture of Sephardi and Ashkenazi Jews. There are also a few wealthy residents and others working in the professions – education, medicine and the law.

Legal Status
The community's present status is that of a private voluntary organisation but measures are being taken to ensure its recognition as a legal entity. The community does not have the right to levy taxes. *Shechita* is permitted.

Communal Organisation
The Ohel Leah Synagogue Executive Committee is the central communal organisation and is affiliated to the World Jewish Congress. Zionist groups include the United Israel Appeal Committee and the JNF. The Jewish Women's Association supports WIZO and there is a very active branch of the International Council of Jewish Women.

Religious Life
Religious life is centred around the Ohel Leah synagogue. Services follow Ashkenazi practice and are presided over by an Israeli rabbi. Membership encompasses a wide range of religious stances, from ultra-Orthodox to Reform. Otherwise there are few religious facilities – there is no Beth Din and no *shochet* and the kosher meat – eaten by only a small proportion of the community – is imported from the United States. There is no *mohel* so circumcision is performed by a local Jewish doctor.

The synagogue will probably have to be demolished – perhaps for redevelopment – and already its details are being recorded for posterity by specialists from the Museum of the Diaspora in Tel Aviv. A Jewish cemetery still stands, dating from 1852.

Education
The community holds Sunday Hebrew classes attended by approximately 60 children. Its curriculum covers the Hebrew language, Jewish history, tradition and culture.

Cultural Activities
Social and cultural activities centre around the Recreation Club rebuilt after the war by the Kadoorie family and opened in 1949. It is adjacent to the synagogue. The Jewish Historical Society established in 1984 aims to provide a research centre to further the understanding of Jewish history in Hong Kong and China.

Press
The Hong Kong *Jewish Chronicle* which contains community and local news is published eight times a year and distributed free to all members of the congregation.

Welfare
The Jewish Benevolent Society caters for the needs of the elderly and infirm.

Relations with Israel
As a British Crown Colony, Hong Kong's foreign policy is governed by Great Britain. However Israel has a Consulate-General and an Honorary Consul-General in the colony.

Most families in Hong Kong have Israeli relatives, so close connections are maintained with Israel. Fund-raising for Israel is vigorous, following the example of the Kadoorie family amongst whose benefactions was the Kadoorie Agricultural School in Lower Galilee, established in 1931.

General Position
Although the community is active, and antisemitism is unknown, the future of Hong Kong's Jews is uncertain since the colony is due to be returned to China in 1997. The agreement between Great Britain and China was signed in September 1984 and provides for Hong Kong to handle its own internal affairs after the 1997 Chinese takeover. The survival of the Jewish community will depend on China's willingness to tolerate Hong Kong's capitalist way of life. In the People's Republic of China there is no Jewish community at all.

HUNGARY

Population: 10 658 000   Jewish population: 80 000

History

Jews were already living in Hungary in Roman time, before the coming of the Magyars. The earliest known Jewish graves date from the second century CE. Early Hungarian kings issued anti-Jewish edicts but under Bela IV (1235–70) Jews settled in the country, many of them working as moneylenders. Coins with Hebrew inscriptions from this period still exist.

Jews were expelled from the country in 1349 and then again in 1360 but when this second edict was revoked in 1364, many Jews returned to Hungary. The Ottoman rule of the sixteenth and seventeenth centuries saw the settlement of Sephardi Jewish communities. Jews from Bohemia and Moravia arrived in the eighteenth century and from Poland in the nineteenth and twentieth centuries. These immigrants, versed in Talmudic scholarship, established centres of study in Hungary. Jews were finally emancipated in 1867 despite increasing antisemitism culminating in an incident at Tiszaeszlar and anti-Jewish demonstrations. A relatively peaceful period under the Communist rule of the Jew, Bela Kun, came to an end at his death in 1919.

Between 1938 and 1940, as part of Hitler's and Mussolini's policies, Hungarian territories were increased with the addition of Slovakia, Carpatho-Ruthenia, Transylvania and the Southern Territories. Since large numbers of Jews lived in these areas, the Jewish population grew from 400 000 to 725 000 (plus another 100 000 baptised or of part Jewish background). After Hungary allied itself to Nazi Germany, restrictions against Jews eventually led to racial legislation. Jews were excluded from military service and instead were recruited for labour service under military command which resulted in many deaths.

On 19 March 1944, Germany occupied Hungary. Until that date, the Hungarian government had refused to deport Jews, except for a small number of foreign nationals or people of disputed nationality. But after the occupation, the Jews were forced into ghetto areas and on 15 May deportation to Auschwitz began. All provincial Jews and half the Jewish population of Budapest were deported to concentration camps. About 600 000 Hungarian Jews (including those from the 'new' territories which were again detached after the war) perished in the Holocaust.

Composition of the Community

There is no accurate census of Hungarian Jewry, but it is thought to number 80 000, of whom about 70 000 live in Budapest, with other communities in Pecs, Szeged, Gyor, Miskolc and Debrecen. Hungarian Jews are entirely Ashkenazi.

Legal Status

All Jewish organisations were centralised in the religious community in 1948 when the Communists came to power. Membership of the community is voluntary and contributions are paid voluntarily. There are laws against racial discrimination which is prohibited under the constitution. Only civil marriages are recognised, religious marriage being additional.

The Jewish community (like all other religious denominations) receives financial support from the government.

Communal Organisation

The central representative body, the Magyar Izraeliták Országos Képviselete (National Representation of Hungarian Jews), MIOK, is headed by an executive committee whose members are elected. It is recognised by the government as are its byelaws. MIOK is affiliated to the World Jewish Congress.

As Hungary is a Communist state, there are no Zionist organisations, and no other separate organisations are permitted.

Religious Life

Although the community is centralised, a separate Orthodox section is maintained in addition to the mainstream Conservative trend. The Rabbinical Council serves the Conservative Jews and the Orthodox section has its own rabbi. After the last incumbent died in 1982, he was replaced by an Orthodox rabbi from Israel. There are both Orthodox and Conservative Batei Din.

The Hungarian community supplies its own rabbis, cantors and *mohelim* and also offers these services to other Communist countries. It also produces its own *matzot*, which are similarly distributed in the Communist bloc.

The two main synagogues in Budapest are the Dohány Street (Conservative) and the Kazinczy Street Synagogue (Orthodox). There are, in all, 26 synagogues in Hungary and 13 rabbis.

Budapest has a kosher restaurant, a central kitchen and food distribution centre. There are 12 kosher butchers throughout Hungary and a kosher sausage factory.

Education

Budapest has a Jewish kindergarten and the Anna Frank Jewish High School for boys and girls between the ages of 14 and 18. Religious education is under the supervision of the National Association of Rabbis (Országos Rabbitestület). The Rabbinical Seminary (Conservative) founded in 1877, and the only institution of its kind in the whole of Eastern Europe, trains rabbis and cantors for all Communist countries. There is also an Orthodox *yeshiva* and part-time Talmud Torah classes.

A Centre for Jewish Studies, the first such centre in the Eastern bloc, was opened in Budapest in 1987 following the agreement between the Heritage Foundation for Jewish Culture and the Law Faculty of Budapest University.

Cultural Activities

Budapest has a fine Jewish museum. A library and central archive is attached to the Rabbinical Seminary. There is a smaller Jewish museum in Sopron and other exhibits of interest can be found in the Museum of the Workers' Movement, the National Museum and the Oriental Library of the Hungarian Academy of Sciences, which houses the famous Kaufman collection.

The Goldmark Choir is run by the Budapest community and the Seminary. Budapest has also 2 children's choirs. There is a club for senior citizens and cultural activities and dances on Chanuka, Purim and similar occasions. The Friday night *kiddush* at the Seminary is well attended by younger members of the community.

Press

Új Élet is published fortnightly by the community. A *luah* is published annually and a yearbook biennially.

The Hungarian State Radio broadcasts a Jewish religious programme for 15 minutes on the first Friday of each month.

There are no Jewish publishers but state publishing houses occasionally publish Jewish books which have included high quality facsimile editions of the Kaufman Haggada and the Maimoni Codex. A number of books, mainly on the history of Hungarian Jewry, have also been published under the auspices of the MIOK and funded by the Memorial Foundation for Jewish Culture in New York.

Welfare

The Charite Hospital and Nursing Home in Budapest has 200 beds. A children's orphanage and three homes for the aged have 150 beds between them.

The Central Social Welfare Committee funded by the American Joint Distribution Committee caters for the needs of the Jewish poor. Its kosher kitchens and food distribution service provide daily kosher meals in Budapest and in the larger towns.

Relations with Israel

Diplomatic relations between Hungary and Israel, broken off in 1967, were resumed in 1987 when an agreement to exchange low-level diplomatic representatives and establish interest sections in Budapest and Tel Aviv was reached. Large numbers of Hungarian Jews have settled in Israel, notably since the 1956 uprising, and Israeli tourists often visit Hungary.

Historical Sites
The Dohány Street Conservative Synagogue in Budapest, built in 1860, is the second largest synagogue in the world and the largest in Europe. It contains plaques to Hannah Szenes and to Theodor Herzl (who was born in the adjacent building). Many victims of the Budapest ghetto are buried in the courtyard attached to the Synagogue. The Szeged Synagogue is a beautiful baroque building. A fourteenth-century gothic synagogue has recently been uncovered in Budapest at the site of the medieval Jewish community of Budavar, a walled city. The thirteenth-century synagogue and *mikveh* in Sopron have been restored and are now open to the public. Victims of the Holocaust are commemorated in the Jewish cemetery of Budapest and in most provincial communal cemeteries. A street is named after Raoul Wallenberg and a statue of him was unveiled when the World Jewish Congress Executive met in Budapest in 1987.

General Position
Hungary is more liberal than other Communist countries and has maintained relations with world Jewry. The meeting of the WJC Executive in Budapest was the first such meeting to be held in the Eastern bloc. Jews are active in public life, some work for the government service and others are employed in the private sector of the economy. Good relations are maintained with the churches.

INDIA

Population: 732 000 000   Jewish population: 5600

History
The origins of the community are obscure and shrouded in myth and legend. Tradition dates the earliest arrival of Jews in India to King Solomon's time. The first historical evidence dates back to 1000 CE or thereabouts, when Joseph Rabban, the leader of the Jews of the Malabar Coast, was granted certain privileges by the local Hindu ruler. This was inscribed in an archaic form of Tamil on copper plates which are still extant as a treasured relic in the famous Pardeshi synagogue in Cochin. Apart from the Jews on the Malabar Coast there were the Bene Israel who settled on the Konkan Coast, south of Bombay city. In the nineteenth century small numbers of Jews from Iraq, Syria and Iran settled in the coastal cities of Bombay and Calcutta, and mainly engaged in trade and commerce.

Composition of the Community

There are three main Jewish communities in India: the Cochin Jews of the Malabar Coast (Kerala State), the Bene Israel of Maharashtra and Jews from the Middle East commonly known as Baghdadis.

Cochin Jews: These were divided into two communities, the so-called Black Jews (more correctly Malabaris) and White Jews. The White Jews are mostly descendants of immigrants from Europe and the Middle East who came to India in the sixteenth and seventeenth centuries, whereas the Black Jews or Malabaris regard themselves as descendants of the original settlers. The total community is now very small – about 90 White Jews, mostly elderly – as the bulk of the Cochin Jews have emigrated to Israel. Only one synagogue is still functioning, the famous Pardeshi synagogue of the White Jews which has been declared a protected monument by the Indian government.

The Bene Israel: This community traditionally claims descent from Jews fleeing from ancient Israel in the second century BCE whose ship was wrecked on the Konkan Coast to the south of Bombay. Whether fact or myth, they forsook many Jewish practices, adopting the customs and dress of their Muslim and Hindu neighbours and speaking the local language, Marathi. They clung to certain Jewish traditions, such as circumcision, the basic dietary laws and abstention from work on the Sabbath. In the past they were the local oil pressers and were known as *Shanwar Telis* (Saturday oil pressers) as they refused to work on Saturdays. They were drawn into the mainstream of modern Judaism by teachers from Cochin who appear to have 'discovered' them in the late sixteenth or early seventeenth century. But it was Christian missionaries in the early nineteenth century who acquainted them with the Bible in Marathi translation and who promoted the study of Hebrew among them. The Bene Israel are by far the largest single element in the Jewish community of India.

Though both the Cochin Jews and the Bene Israel were, like the Muslims, outside the Hindu caste system they absorbed within themselves certain of its features.

Baghdadi Jews: Several families among the immigrants from Iraq, Syria and Iran became affluent and held important positions in commerce and manufacturing. They also were active in the civic life of Bombay and Calcutta. But, among the Jews of India, they were the least influenced by the Indian way of life, identifying mainly with the British rulers of India. In the early years they spoke Arabic but they gradually came to adopt English.

The community is largely lower-middle class, engaged mainly in the service sector. However, a small number have high social and professional status in the government or armed forces. A few have their own businesses.

According to the 1981 census there are 5618 Jews in India with 3076 living in Greater Bombay and small communities in Ikane, Poona, the Raigad district (which includes Alibag, Pen and Panvel), Manipur, Mizoram and Gujarat. A small number live in Cochin, Calcutta and Delhi.

Communal Organisation
The main body is the Council of Indian Jewry founded in 1978 in Bombay. It succeeded the Central Jewish Board established during the Second World War. The Council has representatives from synagogues and other Jewish institutions and is affiliated to the World Jewish Congress, the Asia Pacific Jewish Association and the Commonwealth Jewish Council. Other organisations include the Zionist Association and a Jewish club in Bombay. There are two women's organisations: the Jewish Women's League in Calcutta and the Bene Israel Stree Mandal in Bombay.

Religious Life
There were once 35 synagogues or prayer halls in India but at present only 18 are open. There have been Iraqi and Cochini rabbis or *hahams* in the past. The Bene Israel had the services of a Reform rabbi for some years and there was a Conservative rabbi in Calcutta for a few years. There is no rabbi at present. There are two Bene Israel *mohelim* and *shochtim*, and marriage, divorce and conversion are handled by a committee and carried out by *chazanim*.

Education
With the decrease of the population Jewish education has declined. In Bombay there are five Jewish schools, but in the Sir Elly Kadoorie School, for instance, founded by the Anglo-Jewish Association, only 5 per cent of the students are now Jewish; in the Sir Jacob Sassoon School at least half the students are Jewish. There is also the E.E. Sassoon School and two ORT schools: one for boys and one for girls. Again, only half the students in the ORT schools are Jewish. There are also two schools for the very small Jewish population of Calcutta.

Press
There is no Jewish press as such. The Israeli Consulate in Bombay publishes a monthly entitled *News from Israel* and bulletins or news-letters are issued by various organisations in Bombay, Poona, Delhi and Ahmedabad.

Welfare
There are Jewish Welfare Associations in Poona and Delhi. The Elizabeth David Gershone and David Gershone Scholarship Trust offers a non-refundable scholarship for higher education, and the Bene Israel Conference Education Fund gives students grants. Bombay has a Jewish orphanage and home for the aged.

Relations with Israel
Relations with Israel are cool although India recognises Israel. There is an Israeli Consulate in Bombay which has excellent relations with the Jewish community. The Consul is confined to consular activities and is not allowed to operate in New Delhi. Indian affairs in Israel are normally handled by the British Embassy in Tel Aviv.

Historical Sites
The most important historical sites are the Pardeshi Synagogue in Jew Town Mattancherry in Cochin in Kerala State and the ancient Bene Israel cemetery at Nevagaom near Alibag in the Raigad district where the ancestors of the Bene Israel are believed to have been shipwrecked. For centuries mounds existed under which those drowned in the shipwreck were buried. A monument is being erected on the site of the mounds.

General Position
The Indian Jewish community has gone into considerable decline with the bulk of Jews of Indian origin now living in Israel. Official Indian opinion is strongly anti-Zionist but this has yet had no apparent effect on the friendly attitude of Indians of all denominations towards Jews and Judaism.

INDONESIA

Population: 165 030 000   Jewish population: 30

During the mid-nineteenth century Jews from Holland came to Batavia (Jakarta) and Semarang on Java. A number of Baghdadi Jews also settled on the island and by the end of the First World War the community numbered 2000. Between the wars there was an influx of Jews from Eastern Europe and Germany so that the Jewish population had risen to 3000 by 1945. After Indonesia was granted independence in 1949 most Jews left the country and since then the community has gradually declined.

The few remaining Jews live on Java in the towns of Jakarta, Surabaya and Bandung. The central body, the Board of Jewish Communities of Indonesia, has its office in Jakarta and the island's only synagogue is located at Surabaya.

Indonesia has no diplomatic relations with Israel.

IRAN

Population: 45 000 000   Jewish population: 25 000

History

The Jewish community of Iran is one of the oldest of all the Diaspora communities, dating back to the sixth century BCE, when the Assyrians established Jewish colonies at Rhages near modern Tehran. In 538 BCE, Cyrus, the first Achaemenid emperor conquered Babylonia and liberated Jewish exiles, who subsequently returned to the Land of Israel. Some Jews continued to live in Persia under the Achaemenids, who also controlled much of Mesopotamia and for a short while the Land of Israel itself. The books of Esther, Ezra, Daniel and Nehemiah document the relationship of the Jews to the Achaemenid Court at Suze (Shushan in Hebrew). The official language of the Achaemenid Empire was Aramaic, a language unrelated to Persian but quite close to Hebrew, and subsequently used in Jewish religious writings and, briefly, as a vernacular language.

Under the Sassanid Dynasty (226–641 CE) Jews suffered intermittent oppression and persecution. There was a period of respite after the Arab conquest of 641 but when the Safavids established Shi'ism as the dominant form of Persian Islam, religious intolerance increased. In the mid-eighteenth century the more liberal Nadir Shah allowed Jews to settle in Meshed in the north-eastern province of Khorasan but they were eventually forced to convert and became known as *Jedid al-Islam* (New Muslims).

The poverty and oppression which characterised Persian Jewry in the nineteenth century was partially relieved by the Alliance Israélite Universelle whose activities included the establishing of schools. In the twentieth century the efforts of the Pahlavi Dynasty to modernise the country benefited the Jews along with other members of the Persian middle classes. But the period of great prosperity resulting from the oil boom in the 1960s and 1970s came to an abrupt end with the revolution in 1979. In 1978 the Jewish population had reached a peak of 80 000. Since then, more than half this figure have fled abroad.

There had been an active Zionist movement in Persia, as it then was, well before the Balfour Declaration. The first group of Persian Jewish immigrants came to Jerusalem in 1886 from Shiraz. Many of the forced converts also emigrated to Israel and, by the 1930s, there were some 2000 Jews from Meshed living in Jerusalem. The main waves of Jewish emigration to Israel from Iran were: 1919–May 1948, 3632; May 1948–52, 25 972; 1953–60, 14 000. Further emigration took place after 1979 until the ban in September 1980. Approximately 55 000 Jews have left Iran since 1979.

Present Position
Approximately 60 per cent of the present Jewish population are indigenous Iranian Jews, and 40 per cent are of Iraqi origin. The majority live in Tehran with smaller communities in Shiraz, Isfahan and Meshed.

The central body is the Central Jewish Committee of Iran in Tehran. Alliance schools still function in Tehran, Isfahan, Kermanchah and Yezd with a total, in 1987, of 1650 pupils of which 360 were Jewish. ORT also runs a school. In 1982 two schools were offered to the government as they were no longer needed. Tehran has a youth centre and three central synagogues and there are also several synagogues in Isfahan.

Since the revolution and the imposition of the strict Islamic Code, Jews have been banned from entering teachers' training colleges and from teaching other than in Jewish schools. They are also prohibited from employment in government agencies. They are, however, permitted to practise their religion provided they keep a subordinate (*dhimmi*) position. The real danger derives from the virulent anti-Zionism of the regime; 'co-operation with Zionism and the State of Israel' is a capital offence in Iran, and in 1982 Habib Elghanaian, president of the community, was accused of spying for Israel and subsequently executed. A number of other Jews have also been executed on similar grounds.

It is not always easy to distinguish the regime's anti-Zionism from antisemitism particularly when, in 1984, the Iranian Embassy in London published the *Protocols of the Elders of Zion*.

Prior to 1979, Israel and Iran had good though unofficial relations, Iran having recognised Israel *de facto* in 1950. There was an Israeli Mission in Tehran, and from 1950–51 Iran had a consulate in Tel-Aviv. Israeli technical experts were also sent to Iran. In 1979 Ayatollah Khomeini handed over the Israeli Mission in Tehran to the PLO.

Amongst Jewish historical sights in Iran are the synagogues in the Mahalleh (Jewish Quarter) of both Tehran and Isfahan, the tombs of Esther and Mordecai at Hamadan in the south west and of Daniel at Shush, north of Ahwaz.

The future for Jews in Iran is bleak. As *dhimmis*, they do still retain the right, unlike the persecuted Bahais, to practise their religion but there can be no long-term future for the community so long as the present fundamentalist regime remains in power. During the latter part of 1986 the community's position was reported to have deteriorated.

There were rumours of increased persecution and discrimination and the number of refugees arriving in Vienna and Israel from Iran was said to have risen.

IRAQ

Population: 14 654 000   Jewish population: 200

History
Abraham, the Father of the Jewish people, was born in Ur of the Chaldees, in the south of Iraq, in about 2000 BCE. The Jewish community, the oldest of all Diaspora communities, was established in 586 BCE when the Babylonian King Nebuchanezzar II conquered Judea. After the conquest of Babylonia by Cyrus in 538 BCE, Jewish exiles were allowed to return to the Land of Israel but some remained in the country. Amongst the towns having an entirely Jewish population from the late sixth century BCE were Nehardea, Nisibis and Mahoza.

In the second century CE the Jews rose in revolt against the Roman occupation and temporarily captured the town and surroundings of Mahoza. A hundred years later the brothers Anilai and Asinai established an independent Jewish kingdom at Nehardea.

Perhaps the most remarkable feature of Babylonian Jewry was the institution of the Exilarchate (in Aramaic, *Resh Galuta* – Head of the Exile) which came into existence in the second century CE. The office was hereditary and the Exilarchal family claimed descent from the Royal House of David. The Jews were given considerable internal autonomy, first by the Persian rulers and, after the Arab conquest in 634, by the Arabs themselves. For a short time (513–20) the Exilarch Mar Zutra II set up an independent Jewish principality based at the town of Mahoza. The Exilarchs were usually advised by the Gaonim, the heads of the great rabbinical academies of Sura, Pumbeditha, Mahoza and Nehardea. Here, over a period of several hundred years, great scholars gathered to discuss Jewish Law based on the Mishna. Following the persecutions of the fifth century CE these discussions were set down in writing, thus creating the great Babylonian Talmud.

From the second century to the tenth the Jewish community of Iraq or Babylonia (Bavel) produced some of Jewry's greatest scholars including Mar Samuel (177–257), Rav (early second century), Abbaye (278–338), Saadiah (882–942) and Sherira (906–1006). The eighth century also saw the rise of Messianic movements, the most important being Karaism.

After the Arab conquest many Jews moved into the larger towns. They suffered a certain amount of discrimination although in 908 the

Caliph Al-Muktadir allowed them state positions as bankers and physicians. The institution of the Exilarchate started to decline in the eleventh century and continued to do so for the next 200 years. Under Mongol rule in the thirteenth century Islamic restrictions on Jews were lifted.

From 1534 to 1917 the country was under Turkish rule. Repressive measures in the late eighteenth and early nineteenth centuries, resulted in substantial numbers of Iraqi (or 'Baghdadi') Jews emigrating to India and the Far East, where many became successful merchants.

In 1868 the Alliance Israélite Universelle established a school in Baghdad. By 1904 the Jewish population of Baghdad had risen to 40 000 out of a total Jewish population of 60 000 and by 1910 to approximately 45 000. When the country was occupied by Britain in 1917, the Jews of Baghdad were dominant in commerce and professional life and under British rule many also obtained high government office. However, after the country became independent in 1932 discrimination against Jews began, this time including the suppression of Zionist activities and the teaching of Jewish history in schools. The high point of Jewish population in Iraq was reached in 1947 when there were 150 000 Jews, 100 000 of whom inhabited Baghdad province.

During the pro-German revolt of Rashid el-Gailani in 1941, an anti-Jewish pogrom in Baghdad on 1 and 2 June left 170 Jews killed and 800 injured. Jewish self-defence organisations were formed in response to this. In July 1946, there were further anti-Jewish riots. After the establishment of Israel in 1948 the promotion of Zionism and the emigration of Jews to Israel were prohibited. However, a number of Jews successfully reached Israel via Iran and Turkey. Between 5 and 7 March 1950 the Iraqi parliament legalised Jewish emigration to Israel but all Jews who registered for emigration were deprived of Iraqi citizenship and had their assets confiscated. Between May 1950 and August 1951 the Jewish Agency and the Israeli government organised Operation Ezra and Nehemiah which arranged the transportation by air of 113 545 Jews.

Those who remained were subjected to increasing pressure culminating in the abolition of Jewish community status and government appropriation of community property in 1958. After the Six-Day War in 1967 Jews were restricted to their homes, deprived of their livelihoods and prohibited from emigrating. In 1968, many were arrested on charges of spying. This was followed by public hanging and, later, secret executions. The international outcry at such activities resulted in the government allowing most of the remainder of the community to leave the country.

Present Position
Today, the small community is mostly composed of old people. One synagogue still functions and the only communal organisation is the Synagogue Committee. Iraq, as a Rejection Front Arab state, is in a

state of war with Israel. After an incredible two and a half millenia of continuous existence, what was once a great Diaspora community has all but disappeared.

IRELAND

Population: 3 508 000   Jewish population: 2000

History
A small Jewish community existed in Ireland in the Middle Ages but it disappeared after 1290 when Jews were expelled from the British Isles. In 1660 a group of Marranos (Jews forced to convert to Christianity under the Spanish Inquisition) settled in Ireland. Over the next two hundred years Ashkenazi Jews arrived in the country from Poland, Germany, Holland, Bohemia and England. By 1881 the number of Jews in the country had grown from a mere handful to about 450, rising by 1901 to 3800, the majority living in Dublin.

Composition of the Community
The present community of approximately 2000 is almost entirely Ashkenazi and concentrated in Dublin. In the last fifteen years there has been a decline of 20 per cent in the Jewish population. The community is middle class, most of its members being either self-employed or in managerial or professional positions.

Legal Status
The Jewish religion was recognised as a minority faith under the 1937 constitution.

Communal Organisation
The Jewish Representative Council of Ireland comprises delegates elected by various organisations and institutions. The Council is recognised by the government as the representative body of Irish Jewry, even though it excludes the Dublin Progressive community. The Representative Council is affiliated to the World Jewish Congress.

The Zionist Council of Ireland acts as the central Zionist body. The Joint Israel Appeal, Jewish National Fund and Friends of the Hebrew University have branches in Dublin as do the Mizrahi Society, Hadassah, Federation of Women Zionists (WIZO) and a Regional Council of Women Zionists. The Federation of Jewish Women's Societies acts as an umbrella organisation for all women's organisations.

Religious Life
The Chief Rabbi presides over both the Chief Rabbinate Committee, and the General Board of Shechita of Ireland. A Beth Din sits when

required. The Chief Rabbi does not recognise the Progressives. There are 6 synagogues in Dublin, 5 Orthodox and 1 Progressive and also an Orthodox synagogue in Cork. Sixty to seventy per cent of the population keep *kashrut*. *Shechita* is permitted and there are two kosher butchers and one kosher grocer in Dublin.

Education
There are four Jewish day-schools in Dublin: the Dublin Talmud Torah, the Yavneh Kindergarten, with 2 teachers and 25 pupils, a primary school (9 teachers and 120 pupils) and the Stratford secondary school (10 teachers and 80 pupils). There is also a Sunday school (2 teachers and 20 pupils), and an evening school (6 teachers and 70 pupils).

Cultural Activities
Dublin provides a Jewish club, a Hebrew Speakers' Circle, a Dublin Yiddish Circle, a Jewish Medical Society and the B'nai B'rith Federation of Jewish Women. Sporting activities are catered for by the Edmondstown Golf Club and the Maccabi Association. The B'nai Akiva, Scouts and Guides, the Students' Union and Jewish Youth Voluntary Service offer youth activities. The Council for Soviet Jewry and the 35's are highly active.

Press
The *Dublin Jewish News* is published quarterly and the *Irish Jewish Yearbook* annually. The JNF Dublin office has its own annual publication.

Welfare
Dublin has a Jewish Board of Guardians and a home for the aged with 40 beds.

Relations with Israel
The two countries enjoy full diplomatic relations although the Israeli Ambassador to Dublin is resident in London. An Irish-Israel Friendship League aims at furthering relations between the two countries. The Ireland-Israel Development Association promotes trade, tourism and cultural relations.

General Position
Relations with the Catholic population of the country are good and there is an active Society of Christians and Jews. Although the community is small, it is vigorous and takes pride in its identity, situated as it is in a society that strongly respects religious affiliation. The first Chief Rabbi

of Ireland, Isaac Herzog, later became the Chief Rabbi of Israel and his son, Chaim, now Israel's President, spent much of his youth in Dublin. Both Cork and Dublin have had Jewish mayors.

ISRAEL

Population: 4 375 000   Jewish population: 3 590 000

History
The history of the Jews in the land of Israel dates back to 2000 BCE with the first Jewish state established following the conquest of the land in *c.*1250–1200 BCE. Saul became the first king of Israel in *c.*1020 BCE and was succeeded by David (1004–965) who was followed by Solomon (965–28). After Solomon's death the kingdoms of Judah and Israel divided.

The Southern kingdom of Judah (from which Jews are descended) was occupied by the Babylonians in 597 BCE. This was the beginning of a series of occupations and invasions, firstly by the Greeks, then by the Romans. Jewish independence was finally brought to an end after the unsuccessful revolt of Bar Kochba in 135–2 BCE and it was at this time that the name of Palestine was first given to the country. Although many Jews fled, a small community remained and were ruled by a succession of Patriarchs until the office was finally abolished in the fifth century CE.

Under Byzantine rule the small Jewish community continued to suffer persecution and interference in their communal affairs. For a brief period under Arab rule in the seventh century CE the Jewish situation improved but again deteriorated with increased Islamic fanaticism in the eighth century. More severe persecution was experienced with the onset of the Crusades in the eleventh century. By the late twelfth century few Jews remained in Judea but there were several settlements in Galilee and communities in Tiberias, Safed, Acre and Caesarea. The Jerusalem community was refounded by Nachmanides in 1267–70.

The fourteenth and fifteenth centuries were relatively peaceful and after the Ottoman Conquest of 1516 the Jewish community developed steadily. Safed, in particular, became a great centre of Jewish mysticism which attracted many scholars, notably Joseph Karo, author of *Shulchan Arukh*, who led the community between 1545 and 1575. Invasions and natural disasters contributed to the decline of Safed, which after the beginning of the seventeenth century ceased to be of any importance. Persecution affected the other Jewish communities but throughout the seventeenth and eighteenth centuries settlements survived and there was even a certain amount of immigration. The nineteenth century saw a gradual population increase. In 1806 there were 2000 Jews in Jerusalem, by 1856 there were 6000. Modern development really began with the building of the first suburb outside Jerusalem, Yemin Moshe, the work of Sir Moses Montefiore. In 1870 the Alliance Israélite Universelle created the Mikveh Israel Agricultural School near Jaffa and in 1878 the first modern Jewish village, Petach Tikvah, was founded in the Sharon Plain. By 1897 nineteen new agricultural settlements had been established and the total Jewish population had risen to 50 000. Tel Aviv was founded in 1909 and by 1914 the population had reached 85 000, living mostly in urban areas.

Turkish oppression during the First World War reduced the community to 56 000 but after the advent of the Balfour Declaration in 1917 and the granting of the British mandate in 1920 substantial changes took place. Immigration increased after Hitler acceded to power in Germany in 1933 but was restricted under the White Paper of 1939. After the war and the departure of the British, the Jewish community, now numbering 650 000, established its own government and identity as the independent State of Israel in 1948. Massive immigration followed eventually making Israel's Jewish population the second largest Jewish community in the world.

Composition of the Community
The main Jewish population centres are Tel Aviv/Jaffa (312 600), Jerusalem (327 700), Haifa (205 800), Bat Yam (131 200), Holon (138 000), Petach Tikvah (129 300), Ramat Gan (116 000) and Beersheba (110 000). There are marginally more Jews of Sephardi than Ashkenazi origin.

Legal Status
As the Jewish state, Israel has no separate secular community. The official language is Hebrew and Jewish festivals are public holidays. The Law of Return grants all Jews the right to settle in the country and acquire Israeli citizenship. Marriages and divorce are covered in the Law of Personal Status which is based on religious law and dealt with in religious courts. There are separate courts for each religious denomination.

Communal Organisation
The Knesset, a unicameral legislature, is Israel's parliament and has non-Jewish members. The headquarters of the World Zionist Organisation are in Jerusalem. The Israel Section of the World Jewish Congress is also based in Jerusalem.

Religious Life
The Ashkenazi and the Sephardi Chief Rabbis have equal authority and preside over a ten-member rabbinical council. The major cities of Tel Aviv, Jerusalem, Haifa and Beersheba also have two chief rabbis.

There are 24 Batei Din and the supreme religious court is the Rabbinic Court of Appeal in Jerusalem. The position of Dayan (Beth Din judge) is a permanent civil service appointment.

Religious affairs are presided over by local religious councils under the general authority of the Ministry of Religious Affairs. Other religions are also under this Ministry's jurisdiction. Synagogues are maintained by the state through subventions from the local religious councils. Neither the Reform and Liberal Movements nor the ultra-Orthodox Agudat Israel recognise the authority of the Chief Rabbis. In Israel the role of the rabbi and the synagogue is limited to the purely religious sphere.

There are several religious political parties: the National Religious Party, Agudat Israel, Poale Agudat Israel and Shas (Sephardic Guardias of the Torah). They regularly resist the secularization of the laws of personal status.

Education

There are a total of 7470 schools and approximately 60 000 teachers in Israel. Two types of education are offered – the religious and the general – both supported by the government. Outside the state system are Orthodox schools run by Aguda and two private schools, the Herzlia Gymnasium in Tel Aviv and the Reali School in Haifa. A few schools run by Hassidim offer instruction in Yiddish.

There are seven institutes of higher education: the Hebrew University of Jerusalem (founded 1925), the Israel Institute of Technology (the Technion) in Haifa (1924), the Weizmann Institute of Science in Rehovot (founded as the Daniel Sieff Research Institute in 1934), Tel Aviv University (1956), Bar Ilan University in Ramat Gan (1955), Haifa University (1963) and the Ben Gurion University of the Negev in Beersheba (1969). Instruction is in Hebrew and there are many faculties of Jewish Studies. The Reuven Shiloah Institute for African and Asian Studies in Tel Aviv is run by the Histadrut. The Hebrew University in Jerusalem also houses the National Library.

Specialist Jewish studies are taught at the 120 *yeshivot* at secondary level and 240 at higher education level. A network of *ulpanim* teaches Hebrew, specifically to new immigrants.

Cultural Activities

Museums. The Israel Museum in Jerusalem covers several acres and contains an archeological collection, an art gallery and the Dead Sea Scrolls housed in the imaginatively constructed Shrine of the Book. The Yad Vashem memorial to the Holocaust on Mount Herzl has an adjoining museum. Nearby is the Herzl Museum which houses Herzl's study exactly as it was in Vienna in 1904.

Of Tel Aviv's many museums perhaps the most unusual is the

Museum of the Diaspora (Beth Hatfutsot) which contains no historical artefacts and instead presents a continuous display illustrating the history of Diaspora Jewry. It also has a computer on which are recorded details of towns and villages, however small, in which Jews once lived. Tel Aviv has a number of specialist museums including the Haganah Museum of the pre-state defence forces, the Tel Aviv History Museum and the House of the Bible (Beth Hatanach). Also of interest is the Museum of Clandestine Immigration in Haifa and the museum of Jewish ritual objects in the building of the Chief Rabbinate.

Theatre. The oldest theatre company is the Habimah which was founded in Moscow in 1918 and brought to Palestine in 1931. It is based in Tel Aviv as are two other large companies, the Cameri and the Tzavta. There are two theatres in Jerusalem, the Jerusalem Theatre and the Khan Theatre, and municipal theatres in Haifa and Beersheba. The Haifa theatre concentrates on contemporary Hebrew plays.

Music and Dance. Among Israel's many fine orchestras the most internationally renowned is the Israel Philharmonic based in the Mann Auditorium in Tel Aviv. Both Jerusalem and Beersheba have symphony orchestras and the Israel Chamber Orchestra is based in Tel Aviv. Other orchestras include the Kibbutz Chamber Orchestra, the Israeli Police Force Orchestra and the Rinat National Choir. The Israel National Opera has its home in the Opera House in Tel Aviv. The Rubin Academy of Music is in Jerusalem and there is also an Israel Composers' Association which has approximately 700 members.

Dance companies include the Batsheva, the Bat Dor and the Inbal. Music and dance festivals take place regularly and include the annual Israel Festival of Music and Drama, the annual Ein Gev Music Festival and the International Choir Festival (Zimriya) which is held every three years. Kibbutz Daliah also holds a folk dance festival every three or four years.

Literature. Hebrew has been successfully revived as a modern literary language and a substantial body of literature has been established, recognition of which came with the awarding of the Nobel Prize to S.Y. Agnon. Contemporary writers include Amos Oz and A.B. Yehoshua who have been published extensively in translation. Much poetry is written and published. There are about 750 public libraries in Israel.

Youth and Sport
The largest youth movement, Hanoar Haoved Vehalomed (Working and Learning Youth), is connected with Histadrut and the Kibbutz movement, and has about 100 000 members. The Scouts have both Jewish and Arab members. B'nei Akiva, affiliated to the National

Religious Party, has about 30 000 members; Hashomer Hatzair, affiliated to Mapam, has 16 000 members and Hanoar Hadati Haoved Vehalomed, affiliated to Hapoel Hamizrachi, has 15 000 members.

The Maccabiah – an international sports event – is held every four years. Basketball and football are played throughout the country and in 1977 Israel won the European Basketball Championship.

Press

Israel's most influential daily is the non-party *Ha'aretz*. The daily *Davar* represents the views of the Israeli Labour Party. The most widely read are the evening papers *Ma'ariv* and the more popular *Yediot Ahronot*. The *Jerusalem Post* is published in English and has a weekly international edition distributed throughout the world. It leans slightly towards Labour. There are many other daily papers (some in the language of immigrant groups), weeklies and monthlies. A widely circulated popular weekly is the *Haolam Hazeh*.

The Israel Broadcasting Authority provides radio and television programmes in Hebrew and Arabic, and in many foreign and Diaspora languages (including Moghrabit, the Moroccan Jewish dialect). It also broadcasts its overseas service on short wave and so can be listened to by Diaspora Jewry.

Welfare

Israel has a sophisticated welfare system and the highest doctor/patient ratio in the world. Health insurance is covered by Histadrut and a number of smaller agencies. National Insurance is compulsory, as in the UK. There are many excellent hospitals including the Hadassah on the outskirts of Jerusalem, the Shaare Zedek, run on religious principles and the Rambam and Rothschild Hospitals in Haifa. Homes for the aged include those providing facilities for parents of younger immigrants. The Israeli Red Cross organisation, Magen David Adom, is well supported by Diaspora Jewry.

Relations with the outside world and the Diaspora

Israel has full diplomatic relations with: most of Western Europe (a notable exception being Greece); Rumania; Egypt; in Black Africa with Cameroon, Ivory Coast, Lesotho, Malawi, Liberia, Zaire and Swaziland; in Asia with Burma, South Korea, Japan, Thailand, Nepal, Philippines and Singapore; South Africa, Australia and New Zealand. Israel has full diplomatic relations with most of the countries on the American continent, notable exceptions being Nicaragua and Cuba.

Based in Tel Aviv are friendship associations with France, Africa and the Malagasy Republic, United States, Britain and the Commonwealth,

Ireland and Switzerland. Close relations exist between the Diaspora communities and Israel, and many Diaspora families have relatives living in Israel.

Historical Sites
The most important site is the Western Wall of the Second Temple, sometimes called the 'Wailing Wall'. For centuries it has welcomed Jews in prayer and pilgrimage. In the Jewish Quarter of the Old City of Jerusalem are many synagogues dating from the sixteenth and seventeenth centuries and others with medieval foundations which are currently being restored.

On Mount Zion stands the site of the tomb of King David and nearby the memorial Cave of the Holocaust. Beneath the city of Jerusalem is the ancient Tunnel of Hezekiah built around 700 BCE and with an inscription written in classical Hebrew. There are many archeological treasures being excavated in and around the Old City including the site of the Davidic City, just outside the Jewish Quarter.

The Valley of Kidron contains tombs dating from the first century and nearby is the ancient Jewish cemetery of the Mount of Olives. Galilee also has some first century synagogues and the town of Safed has a group of synagogues dating from the sixteenth century. A network of underground tombs can be found at Beth Sh'arim near Haifa. These date from the first and second centuries and have some Hellenistic sculptures.

ITALY

Population: 57 128 000   Jewish population: 34 500

History
Italy has the oldest Jewish community in Western Europe, dating back to the second century BCE. Its condition was satisfactory until the Edict of 313 CE which made Christianity the official religion of the Roman Empire and thus began a period of persecution. In the Middle Ages Jews settled in Rome, Southern Italy, Sicily and parts of Northern Italy, and during a relatively peaceful period transmitted Talmudic scholarship to Northern Europe, but the thirteenth century brought persecution against Jews in Naples resulting in some conversions to Christianity. Meanwhile Jewish communities in the North of Italy were established, largely through the successful activities of Jewish loan bankers.

In the fifteenth century, after the Spanish conquest of parts of Southern Italy the community was subjected to anti-Jewish diatribes and accusations culminating in the expulsion of Jews from Sicily in 1492 and from Naples in 1541. Elsewhere, however, the Jewish community flourished throughout the Renaissance period. In 1555, Pope Paul IV issued the Bull *cum nimis absurdam*, condemning Jews to live in segregated areas (ghettos) and restricting their choice of trades. It was not until after the French Revolution that ghettos were abolished and under Napoleonic rule Jews were emancipated. The unification of Italy in 1870 gave Jews equal rights.

Mussolini seized power in 1922 but despite his fascist policies did not display any antisemitism until he allied with Germany in 1938. At this time many Jews left Italy. On 16 September 1943 Northern Italy was occupied by Germany, and during the months of October and November 1943 8360 Italian Jews were deported to Auschwitz, of whom 7749 were killed.

Composition of the Community
The Italian Jewish community is largely Sephardi. The main centres of Jewish population are: Rome, 15 000; Milan, 10 000; Turin, 1630; Florence, 1400; Leghorn, 1000. There are smaller communities in Bologna, Ferrara, Mantua, Ancora and Padua. In 1956 Italy received 2500 Egyptian Jews, in 1967 3000 refugees from Libya, of which 2000 remained in the country. Fifty-six per cent of Italian Jews have a diploma or university degree; 34 per cent are engaged in trade or business; 13 per cent are professionals; 5 per cent are workers and 4 per cent are teachers.

Legal Status
From 1930 to 1984 the Jewish community was entitled to levy a tax on its members to help finance its institutions. The 1984 Concordat repealed this law and a new agreement (Intesa) between the community and the government was signed in 1987. Among other things the agreement established parity between Judaism and other religions in its relations with the state.

Communal Organisation
Italian Jewry's representative body, based in Rome, is the Unione delle Communità Israelitiche Italiane. It is one of the founder members of the World Jewish Congress. Individual communities function autonomously.

Religious Life
Each community is responsible for its own religious services. The vast majority of synagogues follow the Sephardi rite but there are a few Orthodox Ashkenazi synagogues. There is a Chief Rabbi and a Rabbinical Council. A branch of the Lubavitch movement is active in Milan.

Education

There are Jewish kindergartens and elementary schools at Florence, Genoa, Leghorn, Milan, Rome and Trieste, and a kindergarten in Vercelli and secondary schools at Milan, Rome and Turin. Institutions for advanced Hebrew studies include the Talmud Torahs in Milan and Rome, the Margulies Rabbinical School in Turin, the Italian Rabbinical College in Rome and a Higher Institute for Hebrew Studies (both run by the Unione), and the Italian Association for the Study of Judaism. Chairs of Hebrew have been established at the Universities of Rome, Milan and Naples. About 65 per cent of Jewish children in Rome attend Jewish schools.

Cultural Activities

Italy's Jewish museums include the Community Museum in Rome, the Hebrew Museum in Casale Monferrato and the Jewish Museum in Venice. Permanent exhibitions are on display in Rome and Florence. Library and archive facilities are available at the library of the Italian Rabbinical College (on the premises of the Unione), at Milan's Centre for Contemporary Jewish Documentation and at the Centre for Jewish Culture in Rome. Community archives are in Rome and Florence. The Vatican Museum has a special Jewish collection closed to the public.

Community facilities include two Jewish social centres and a club in Milan, and a cultural centre and youth club in Rome. Smaller youth clubs exist in other communities. Channel 2 on Italian television broadcasts a fortnightly half-hour programme on Jewish life and culture and radio programmes are broadcast before Jewish festivals.

Press

There is no daily or weekly Jewish press in Italy. However, 10 000 copies of *Shalom* are published monthly as is *Bollettino delle Comunità*, published by Milan's Jewish community. Bi-monthly publications include *Il Portavoce dell'ADEI-WIZO, ALEF-DAC* (published by the cultural department of the Unione), KKL's *Karnenu* and the Jewish Youth Federation's *Ha-Tikvah*. Quarterlies include publications by the Zionist Federation and the Unione and the scholarly journal *La Rassegna Mensile d'Israel*. Jewish books are published by Carucci in Rome and Giuntina in Florence.

Welfare

Rome's Jewish hospital has 300 beds. There are homes for the aged in Rome, Milan, Florence, Turin, Venice, Mantua and Trieste. Rome and Milan both have OSE centres and Rome also has a welfare and a family centre.

Relations with Israel
Full relations at ambassadorial level exist between the two countries.

Historical Sites
Five synagogues still stand at the site of the original ghetto in Venice. At Ostia, near Rome, an ancient synagogue was uncovered in 1961–2. Rome's six catacombs are the most ancient of all Jewish historical sites in Western Europe, and Venosa in Southern Italy also has many elaborate Jewish catacombs. At the Forum in Rome the Arch of Titus, erected by Emperor Domitian, commemorates Rome's victory over the Jews in 70 CE. Its bas-reliefs depict the Temple victory spoils of the seven-branched Menorah and silver trumpets.

General Position
The community is ancient and well-established. Jews have important positions in business and the professions, and in the academic world.

The Lebanon war in 1982 aroused some antisemitic feeling, notably in the universities, and more serious manifestations including the machine gun attack on the Great Synagogue in Rome, when a two-year-old boy was killed. The neo-fascist party, the Movimento Sociale Italiano, is represented in Parliament, voted in by 5 per cent of the electorate. Other neo-fascist organisations exist.

The community celebrated an important advance in its relations with the Catholic Church when Pope John Paul II visited the Rome Synagogue in 1986.

JAMAICA

Population: 2 296 000   Jewish population: 800

History
Marranos probably lived in Jamaica before the British occupation in 1655, after which more Sephardim followed. Ashkenazim from England arrived in the eighteenth century. All Jewish disabilities were abolished in 1831, earlier than in England itself. Although at its peak the community had congregations at Port Royal, Spanish Town, which had two synagogues, and Montego Bay, the community dwindled, and the Ashkenazi and Sephardi communities combined to form one community in Kingston in 1921.

A considerable number emigrated after independence in 1962 fearing that Jamaica might go the way of Cuba. These fears proved unfounded.

Composition of the Community
The community is mixed Ashkenazi-Sephardi, many of whom are descendants of the early immigrants.

Communal Organisation and Religious Life
One organisation, the United Congregation of Israelites, deals with both religious and secular affairs. Its synagogue, Shaarei Shalom, normally draws a congregation of about 100 people on High Holy Days. It is formally Conservative, but has Reform influence as well as a number of traditional Sephardi customs. The United Congregation is affiliated to the World Jewish Congress.

Cultural Activities
The Jewish Institute in Kingston is the community's cultural and social centre. There is also a B'nai B'rith Lodge and a WIZO group.

Relations with Israel
Israel has an embassy in Kingston with a resident ambassador, as well as a separate consulate in Kingston with an honorary consul general.

Historical Sites
The synagogue in Kingston has a sand floor like that in Curaçao. Some of the synagogue silver, such as the Torah crowns, date from the beginning of the eighteenth century.
   The island has some very old Jewish cemeteries, dating from at least the eighteenth century, although many of the tombs are not in good repair.

General Position
The Jamaican community has suffered no disabilities or antisemitism for the past 150 years, and is now declining through assimilation and mixed marriages. Jews have played a considerable role in Jamaican life, notably in government and the press.

JAPAN

Population: 121 047 000   Jewish population: 700

History
Jews first came to Japan from Russia and Poland in 1861, merchants from Iraq followed and the community was formally established in Nagasaki in 1894, growing to 100 members in its first decade. It increased its size after an influx of refugees from Russia, Germany and China before 1939. During World War Two, Jews experienced no persecution, but Zionist fund-raising and support for 'Jewish national movements' was banned.

Composition of the Community

All foreigners in Japan are classified as aliens regardless of length of stay. Thus none of the Jewish community hold Japanese citizenship. Most Jews live in Tokyo and are engaged in manufacturing and commerce or cultural and educational work. There is a small community of 75 at Kobe and 200–300 American Jewish personnel serving with the US forces at Okinawa. A large proportion of the community is transient, mostly from the US.

Legal Status

The community is regarded as a private voluntary organisation. Both civil and religious marriages are recognised, but there is no *shechita*.

Communal Organisation

The central body is the Executive Board of the Jewish Community of Japan. This consists of a Chairman, President and 12 members, elected at a general meeting. The Board is recognised by all sections of the community and is affiliated to the World Jewish Congress. Zionist activity is organised by the Zionist Federation of Japan and the Japan-Israel Women's Welfare Organisation.

Religious Life

The community is mostly Conservative/Reform. The synagogue in the Tokyo community centre has its own rabbi. There is also a synagogue at Kobe and a Reform rabbi with the US army holds services for Jewish military personnel at Okinawa.

Education

The rabbi in Tokyo organises a Sunday school with 70 pupils of pre-barmitzvah age. There is a large staff of full and part-time teachers.

Cultural Activities

The community centre in Tokyo has a library of Judaica.

Press

The Tokyo community publishes a monthly bulletin.

Relations with Israel

Japan and Israel have full diplomatic relations. However, Japan relies heavily on Arab oil supplies and ties with Israel are therefore limited. There is a Japan-Israel Friendship Society and good cultural links exist.

Historical Sites

Cemeteries dating back over a century are in Nagasaki and Yokahama.

The community is mostly transient, although some of its members have remained in Japan for long periods. It is affluent and independent and has a well-established communal structure.

In the mid-1980s, more than a dozen books were published alleging an international Jewish capitalist conspiracy to destroy Japan. Two books by Masami Uno on this subject sold more than half a million copies. While the Japanese are not antisemitic this surge of antisemitic publications deserves to be taken seriously.

KENYA

Population: 20 000 000   Jewish population: 330

The site of the Uganda Scheme, a project to settle Jews in East Africa which was presented to Herzl in 1903, was in fact in Kenya. The project was discussed at the Sixth Zionist Congress in August 1903, and finally turned down at the Seventh Zionist Congress in July 1905.

The first Jewish settlers came to Nairobi in 1903 and a community was founded in 1904. The Nairobi synagogue was built in 1912. In 1945 there was an influx of Jewish immigrants from Europe, many of them survivors of the Holocaust. Communal life centres around the synagogue of the Nairobi Hebrew Congregation which is affiliated to the World Jewish Congress. The WIZO Federation organises social and cultural activities.

Though Kenya does not have formal diplomatic relations with Israel, relations between the two countries are good. Some 200 temporary Israeli experts, mainly connected with the construction industry, work in the country, and this augments the small resident Jewish population. The Kenyan government helped Israel in its dramatic Entebbe rescue mission in 1976.

Jews have been active in the economic life of Kenya, particularly in the hotel industry, commerce and the professions. In 1955–7 a former president of the congregation, Colonel Issy Somen, a close friend of President Kenyatta, was mayor of Nairobi. He later served as the community's representative on the Board of Deputies in London.

LEBANON

Population: 3 500 000   Jewish population: 100

History

The territory of Lebanon has had Jewish inhabitants since ancient times. In the first century CE King Herod the Great gave a temple to his Jewish subjects living in the city of Tyre. He also gave benefactions to the Jewish community in Beirut. The Jewish population of the country steadily increased and by the sixth century there were synagogues in both Beirut and Tripoli.

In 1944 the Jewish population had reached over 6000. The number increased when Jews from Syria emigrated there in 1948. Despite restrictions imposed after 1948 Lebanon treated its Jews far more tolerantly than any other Arab country and by 1952 the Jewish population numbered 10 000. Three thousand of these were so-called 'tourists' from Syria carrying residents' permits granted by the Lebanese government. After the Six-Day War in 1967 there was steady Jewish emigration and after the civil war of 1976 most of the remaining Jewish population left the country. Before 1976 there was a Jewish Community Council, two Jewish schools, two synagogues and several prayer houses in Beirut and a Jewish school in Sidon.

Present Position
Today the community is virtually non-existent but there is a committee in Beirut representing its 100 or so Jewish residents. Relations with Israel are complicated and to a certain extent have reflected the country's internal conflicts. From 1976 to 1982 the PLO occupied territory in South Lebanon which was used as a base to attack Israel. This base was destroyed in 1982. Since the late 1970s Israel has maintained a relationship with the Christians in the far south who make up the Israeli-backed South Lebanese Army but the Shi'ite Muslims, who were initially not unfriendly to the Israeli forces in 1982, have now become actively hostile. Some of the most prominent members of the Lebanese Jewish community have been kidnapped and murdered.

LIBYA

Population: 3 800 000   Jewish population: nil

History
The first Jewish settlement was in the Benghazi area in the third century BCE. The suppression of a Jewish revolt in Cyrenaica between 115 and 117 CE resulted in the temporary disappearance of Jews from the country. A community in Benghazi was re-established in the fifteenth century and Libya received refugees from Spain after the expulsion of 1492. In the twentieth century the community prospered after the Italian occupation of 1911 but persecution began in 1936 when Mussolini introduced the anti-Jewish laws. Nevertheless by 1941 a quarter of the population of Tripoli was Jewish, though they were concentrated in the Hara Kebira (Great Ghetto) and there were 44 synagogues in the city. In 1942 under

German occupation the Jewish Quarter of Benghazi was sacked and 2000 Jews were deported across the desert, a fifth of whom died.

The post-war period saw a succession of anti-Jewish pogroms. Between 4 and 7 November 1945 more than 100 Jews were murdered in circumstances of great brutality and most of the synagogues were sacked. Three years later 280 Jewish homes were destroyed and 12 Jews were murdered. In 1967, after the Six-Day War there was further rioting, destruction and murder, and those Jews still alive fled to Israel.

Present Position
In 1970 Colonel Qaddafi confiscated all Jewish property and cancelled all debts owing to Jews. The Jewish population in 1948 before the first major exodus numbered 38 000. In 1967 before the Six-Day War it had fallen to 4500. By 1974 only about 20 remained and today it is believed there are none.

LUXEMBOURG

Population: 365 900   Jewish population: 1200

History
The small medieval Jewish community in Luxembourg was destroyed in an appalling massacre in 1349 and it was not reconstituted until 1791 after Napoleon I had incorporated Luxembourg into France. Jews started to return to the duchy, where they then automatically enjoyed the same civic rights as the French Jewish community. In 1795 all restrictions on Jewish rights of residence were abolished and Luxembourg welcomed Jews from Germany and Lorraine. The Imperial Decree of 10 December 1808 gave the community statutory rights. The Jewish population remained very small until an influx of immigrants followed the Franco-Prussian war of 1870. The synagogue erected in 1894 was destroyed by the Nazis in 1942. From 1935 a steady flow of Jewish refugees poured into Luxembourg, increasing the Jewish population from 1800 to 3500. Following the Nazi invasion in 1941, Jews were either expelled or deported. Some 750 of the original Luxembourg Jewish population perished in the Holocaust.

Composition of the Community
The community is largely upper middle-class Ashkenazi, its members mainly engaged in business.

Legal Status
The Jewish religion is officially recognised and the rabbi and secretary of the Consistoire are state functionaries. Only civil marriages are recognised by the state. *Shechita* is permitted but has not been practised for the last 15 years for economic reasons.

101

Communal Organisation
The central organisation, the Consistoire Israélite, is affiliated to the World Jewish Congress. Other institutions include the B'nai B'rith, Keren Kayemet, a Zionist organisation, Keren Hayesod, ORT, WIZO, Union des Dames Israélites de Luxembourg and, for young people, the Union des Jeunes Gens and Youth Aliya.

Religious Life
There are two synagogues, but only one rabbi, who has the title of Grand Rabbin. The services are conducted in the Orthodox tradition. There is no Beth Din so matters needing such assistance must be referred to Paris. The building of the new synagogue, which replaced that destroyed by the Nazis, was financed by the state. About 10 per cent of the Jewish population keep *kashrut* and all kosher meat has to be imported from France.

Education
There is a kindergarten and a Sunday school.

Press
No Jewish press exists as such, but there is a monthly communal bulletin.

Welfare
Luxembourg has a home for the aged with 30 beds. A welfare organisation, ESRA, dispenses funds to the few who are in need.

Relations with Israel
Relations between Israel and Luxembourg are at ambassadorial level through the Israeli embassy in Brussels.

General Position
Inter-faith relations are very good and the Jewish community belongs to the Association Interconfessionelle de Luxembourg. The small community is clearly very comfortable and unconcerned by antisemitism. About 50 per cent of the younger generation intermarry.

MALAYSIA

Population: 15 767 000   Jewish population: 10

Most of the small Jewish population of Malaysia, mainly refugees from Russia, have now left and there is no longer a formal community. There is a Jewish cemetery in Georgetown on Penang Island.

Malaysia is a staunchly Islamic state and has no diplomatic relations with Israel.

MALTA

Population: 332 000   Jewish population: 50

Jews originally settled in Roman times. They were expelled in 1492
and did not become re-established until the late eighteenth century, with
the arrival of Jews from North Africa. From 1530 Jewish prisoners were
held to ransom on the island and during their enforced stay established
a synagogue. In 1912 a synagogue was built in Valetta, but it went out of
use in 1979. A new synagogue in the same area was inaugurated in 1984.
The Jewish Community of Malta, which is affiliated to the World Jewish
Congress, consists of a largely Sephardi population. Relations with Israel
are cool although there is an Israeli embassy.

MEXICO

Population: 78 800 000   Jewish population: 35 000

History
The first Jews in Mexico were Marranos who accompanied the
Conquistadores in the sixteenth century. An Inquisitional Tribunal
was set up in 1571 and was active for some 200 years, thus discouraging
Jewish immigration. Nineteenth-century Mexico was rent by fanaticism
so even then only a small number of Jews settled in the country, many
having no connection with organised Jewry.

The first Sephardi community of Jews from Aleppo was established
in 1885 and a synagogue was built in 1887. A mixed Ashkenazi-Sephardi
community was established in 1912. The community expanded after the
First World War with the influx of Ashkenazim from Eastern Europe
and Sephardim from the Eastern Mediterranean. Immigration of German
refugees in the 1930s was curtailed in 1937 by restrictive laws.

Composition of the Community
Fifty-five per cent of Mexican Jews are descendants of Ashkenazim from
Eastern Europe, Germany and Hungary, and 45 per cent are Sephardim
from the Eastern Mediterranean. The great majority live in Mexico City
with the remaining population divided between Guadalajara, Monterrey,
Tijuana and Puebla. The largely affluent community is composed of
academics, professionals and businessmen.

A 100-strong Mexican Indian community who practise Judaism live in
the village of Venta Prieta near Pachuca about 70 miles north of Mexico
City. It is now thought that they are descendants of Marranos who married

103

Indian women and practised their Jewish religion in secret. Today they have their own synagogue, several of them have visited Israel and even served in the Israeli army. The official Mexican Jewish community does not recognise them as Jews.

Communal Organisation

The central body, based in Mexico City, is the Comité Central Israelita de Mexico (CCIM). It is affiliated to the World Jewish Congress. The umbrella Zionist organisation is the Zionist Federation of Mexico. A Sephardi Zionist organisation also exists. B'nai B'rith, WIZO and the Mexican Council of Jewish Women are active in Mexico City. Other organisations include the Mexican Magen David Adom, the Dor Hemshech Institute, the KKL, Emunah (the women's Mizrahi group) and Brit Ivrit Olamit.

Religious Life

Nidje Israel is the central Ashkenazi body (Kehilla) and the Union Sefaradi del Mexico is the Sephardi body. There are 16 synagogues and houses of worship in Mexico City, of which 14 are Orthodox and 2 Conservative. The Conservative Beth El Community Centre is English speaking. In the provinces there are synagogues at Guadalajara, Monterrey and Tijuana. The Jewish families of Puebla do not have a synagogue of their own but visit Mexico City for religious purposes.

There are two kosher restaurants in Mexico City, one in the building of the Nidje Israel synagogue. *Kashrut* is hardly observed at all by Mexican Jewry. Although there is a kosher hotel and restaurant with a synagogue on the premises at both Cuernavaca and Acapulco, these are mainly patronised by tourists.

Education

Mexico City has six Jewish day schools, a girls' school, two *yeshivot* and a seminary for teachers of Hebrew and Yiddish. There are also Jewish schools at Guadalajara and Monterrey. Courses in Jewish studies are available at the Talmud Torah of the Beth El Congregation and the Sunday school of the Beth El Community Centre. Adult education courses in Jewish culture take place at the Centro de Estudios Judios Contemporaneos (Centre for Contemporary Jewish Studies), which is run by the Mexican Jewish Community with the aid of the American Jewish Committee. Mexican universities offer biblical and Jewish studies. The Aluma Institute, founded in 1974 and situated in the Centro Deportivo, provides training in youth leadership.

Cultural Activities

The Centro Deportivo, the great Jewish sports and cultural centre in Mexico City, has some 23 000 members. The CCIM sponsors youth activities. Zionist movements include B'nai Akiva and Hanoar Hatzioni. There are social clubs at Tijuana and Monterrey and a sports centre at Guadalajara. An annual festival of Jewish music, sponsored by the Ashkenazi Kehilla, Nidje Israel, is held at the Palace of Fine Arts in Mexico City.

Press
The community publishes *Der Weg* twice a week, in Spanish and Yiddish on Friday and only in Yiddish on Tuesday, *Di Shtime*, a Yiddish language weekly, and the main Spanish language weekly *Prensa Israelita*. The bi-monthly *Tribuna Israelita*, is published in Spanish by the Anti-Defamation League, a branch of the CCIM. The other important periodical is the Yiddish language Bundist *Forois*. The community also publishes an 11-volume Jewish encyclopaedia, *Enciclopedia Judaica Castellana*, and the 10-volume *Tesoros del Judaismo*.

Welfare
The Mexican Council of Jewish Women co-operates with other welfare agencies in community work.

Relations with Israel
These are on full ambassadorial level, with an Israeli embassy in Mexico City and a Mexican embassy in Tel Aviv. Trade relations between Israel and Mexico are good but were jeopardised in 1975 when American Jews boycotted the country after Mexico had voted in favour of the 'Zionism is Racism' resolution. Cultural exchanges are furthered by the Mexican-Israeli Cultural Institute and the Shalom Club.

General Position
As in other Latin American countries, Mexican Jewry tends to have a secular or Zionist orientation, with synagogue attendance virtually limited to High Holy Days and little observance of *kashrut*. The community does, however, have an excellent school system. Although there is little antisemitism, the PLO office in Mexico City promotes anti-Zionism. The Jewish community maintains contacts with the Centre for Ecumenical Studies and with Catholic organisations.

MONACO

Population: 28 000 Jewish population: 1000

History
The few Jews living in Monte Carlo before the Second World War were mostly employed in business and banking. False identity papers given to them during the war by the authorities helped to save their lives.

After the founding of the community in 1948, the first services were held in a private house. In 1958 small premises were rented and a rabbi engaged for sabbath and High Holy Day services and in 1972 a house was purchased to act as a synagogue and community centre. Between 1960 and 1965 some North African Jews settled in Monaco.

Composition of the Community
The community is approximately half Ashkenazi and half Sephardi, with about 40 per cent of British origin, the remainder being French-speaking Jews comprising the local Ashkenazim, the recent immigrants from North Africa and a dozen Turkish families who arrived in 1979. Sixty per cent of the Jewish population are retired people.

Legal Status
When the community expanded in the early 1960s its official status was established.

Communal Organisation
The central body, the Association Cultuelle Israélite de Monaco, which is affiliated to the World Jewish Congress, has a membership of about 40 per cent of the Jewish population. There is a branch of WIZO and a very active B'nai B'rith.

Religious Life
The house purchased in 1972 has developed into one of the most beautiful synagogues on the Côte d'Azur. There is one rabbi and a kosher butcher.

Education
The community's Talmud Torah is run by the rabbi.

Cultural Activities
The Jacques Mimran Community Centre is in the same building as the synagogue and the Association Cultuelle.

Relations with Israel
Israel has a Consul General accredited to Monaco, based at the Consulate General in Marseilles. The reigning Prince and the late Princess have always attended the Weizmann Institute Gala.

General Position
Over half of this small community are retired people and it is largely an offshoot of the French and British communities.

106

MOROCCO

Population: 22 109 000   Jewish population: 13 000

History
Jews have lived in the area of Morocco since Roman times. Amongst
the ruins of the ancient northern city of Volubilis is a Jewish tombstone.
Prior to the Arab conquest a number of Berber tribes converted to Judaism
and in the seventh century the legendary berber Queen Dahia el-Kahana
fought against the Arab invaders. Arab rule in the eleventh century was
tolerant towards the Jews who during this period established communities
and seats of learning notably at Fez and Sigilmasa. Fez became the
home of the Talmudic scholar Isaac ben Jacob Alfasi, known as the
Rif (1013–1103) and of the Maimonides family who fled there from
Spain in 1160.

The Almohad rule of the mid-twelfth century suppressed Jewish
life in Morocco but from 1391 the community revived with Jewish
refugees arriving from Spain. During this period local Jews maintained
a separate community, referring to themselves in Hebrew as *toshavim*
(residents) and the refugees as *megorashim* (literally 'those who have
been driven out'). In 1438 the Jews of Fez were confined to a special
quarter for their own protection. This was known as the *Mellah* which
is the Arabic for salt and was used because the Jews in Morocco, prior
to French rule, were forced to carry out the job of salting the heads
of executed prisoners prior to their public display. Subsequently, other
mellahs were established in Moroccan cities, largely for the purposes
of segregation, much like that of European ghettos. The Muslim
rulers enforced the *dhimmi* status of the Jews, even limiting their
clothing so that they had to wear black cloaks instead of the
Muslim white. As in other Muslim countries, individual Jews could,
and did, rise to prominence at Court but the general position was
unstable.

With the establishment of the French Protectorate in 1912, the situation
improved despite a serious outbreak of violence in the Jewish quarter of
Fez when 60 Jews were killed. Many Jews began to be influenced by
French culture, partly as a result of the work of the Alliance Israélite
Universelle, established in 1862. The twentieth century has seen the rise
to pre-eminence of the Casablancan community, an increase in prosperity
and the growth of a Zionist movement. Although Morocco was under
Vichy rule in the Second World War, King Mohammed V prevented
the deportation of the Jews. After 1948, Jews started to emigrate to
Israel but also to France, the USA and Canada. When Morocco gained
independence in 1956, Jews became Moroccan citizens with equal rights.

The community enjoys a certain amount of protection from King Hassan II and government officials often attend Jewish functions. Overt Zionist activity is suppressed.

Composition of the Community

The mainly Sephardi community is concentrated in Casablanca, with smaller communities in Marrakesh, Rabat, Meknes, Tangier, Fez, Tetuan, Agadir, Safi and El-Jadida. Thirty per cent are affluent business and professional people, 30 per cent small businessmen and shopkeepers, 30 per cent labourers and artisans, whilst about 10 per cent are on welfare.

Legal Status

Under King Hassan II the community has been granted full suffrage and freedom of movement to and from Morocco. In 1956 the rabbinic courts came under the jurisdiction of the general courts and the rabbinic high court was dissolved in 1965. The rabbinic courts are now limited to jurisdiction on domestic Jewish affairs.

Communal Organisation and Religious Life

The Casablanca-based Conseil des Communautés Israélites du Maroc co-ordinates the Regional Committees and negotiates with the government. It is headed by a Secretary General and all Presidents of Regional Committees are members by right. Its several functions presided over by assistant Secretaries General include external relations, general matters, communal heritage, finance, the maintenance of holy places, youth activities and cultural and religious life. The Council is allowed to participate fully in the World Jewish Congress.

Regional Committees at Fez, Kenitra, Marrakesh, Meknes, Tangier, Tetuan, El-Jedida and Agadir are responsible for welfare and religious life. Each has its own *kashrut* commission and is responsible for rabbis and judges. There are synagogues in all the communities, several in Casablanca and kosher restaurants in Casablanca, Fez, Rabat and Tangier.

Education

Morocco has a sophisticated system of Jewish education organised by four groups: the Alliance (Ittihad), Lubavitch, ORT and Otzar Hatorah. The former Alliance schools are now under the control of Ittihad Maroc, but still have strong links with the Alliance in Paris. In 1987 the total number of pupils in the Ittihad-Maroc schools was 1186. Several schools are run by the Lubavitch movement, ORT has a school in Casablanca and Talmud Torahs are to be found in Rabat, Meknes, Fez, Marrakesh, Kenitra, Tetuan and Tangier. Specialist religious education is provided by a Lycée Yeshiva and a Kolel in Casablanca and a Lycée Seminaire in Rabat.

Cultural Activities
Cultural activities are directly controlled by the Council of the Communities. There are two major youth organisations: the Department for Education and Jewish Youth (DEJJ) with 450 members and the Eclaireurs Israélites du Maroc with 430 members. These offer free holidays for their members at camps in Immouzer and other activities for non-members.

Press
The last Jewish newspaper closed down in 1963.

Welfare
Welfare is the responsibility of the Regional Committees who provide financial aid for some 1200 people. A craft workshop has been set up in Casablanca to help with rehabilitation. OSE supplies medical aid to the needy and dental and therapeutic facilities in Jewish schools. Some 1700 meals are served daily in the schools to underprivileged children. There are homes for the aged in Casablanca, el-Jedida, Fez, Marrakesh, Meknes, Rabat and Tangier. The American Joint Distribution Committee makes a major contribution to all the welfare activities.

Relations with Israel
Morocco, as a member of the Arab League, does not have diplomatic relations with Israel but appears to have acted as intermediary at the start of the Egypt-Israel peace talks. Amongst the many foreign guests at the Congress of the Jewish Communities of Morocco, held in Rabat in May 1984, were a number of Israelis, including several members of the Knesset. The Moroccan Crown Prince and Prime Minister were guests. In 1986, the Israeli Prime Minister, Shimon Peres, paid an official visit to the country.

Between 1946 and 1964, 226 000 Moroccan Jews settled in Israel. Prior to 1961, the majority of these immigrants came from the lower socio-economic classes (much of the elite having settled in France).

Historical Sites
In Fez, the twelfth-century House of Maimonides still stands and in many towns one can still see the old walls and gates of the medieval *mellahs*, that at Meknes being particularly fine.

General Position
The 2000-year-old Jewish community of Morocco, which reached its peak population of 285 000 in the early 1950s is in decline. Many young

people who are educated abroad do not return and recently the excellent Jewish schools have had difficulties in recruiting new teachers. Although the community remains vigorous, many of its members are ageing and its future is uncertain.

THE NETHERLANDS

Population: 14 454 000   Jewish population: 25 000

History
The small medieval Jewish community was virtually destroyed through persecutions at the time of the Black Death and Dutch Jewry only really dates from the end of the sixteenth century when Marranos from Antwerp settled in Amsterdam, followed by Jews from Portugal, Italy and Turkey. Ashkenazi Jews from Germany, Poland and Lithuania followed from 1620. Freedom of worship was established by the early seventeenth century. Jews played an important part in the expanding economy of the Netherlands and during the next hundred years the community became a centre of world Jewry, with a flourishing intellectual life, but its importance decreased in the nineteenth century. Its population also began to decline in the first half of the twentieth century and at the outbreak of the Second World War it numbered 140 000.

The Nazis invaded Holland in May 1940. Amsterdam's 90 000 Jews were separated from the rest of the community and the wearing of the yellow star was made compulsory. A transit camp for deportees was established by the Nazis at Westerbork in North East Holland. By the end of the war some 100 000 Jews had perished.

Composition of the Community
Over 90 per cent of the community are Dutch-born Ashkenazim. The Orthodox congregations have about 11 000 members, the Liberal over 2000 and the Sephardi about 1500. A very large proportion of the Jewish community are not affiliated to any religious congregation. Approximately 50 per cent of Dutch Jews live in Amsterdam. There are large communities in Rotterdam and The Hague and smaller ones throughout the country. Most Jews are middle or upper-middle class, self-employed or working in the professions.

Legal Status
Jews were formally emancipated in 1796 under the French occupation. From 1815 until the end of 1983 some Jewish religious ministers were paid by the state, and since 1797 Jews have been admitted to parliament.

110

The main communal organisations, Kerkgenootschappen, are recognised by the government as representative bodies of the Jewish community. They have the right to levy taxes on their members. Only civil marriage is recognised by the state, and has to precede religious marriage. There are effective laws against discrimination.

Communal Organisation

The main governing body of Dutch Jewry is the Nederlands-Israelitisch Kerkgenootschap (Ashkenazi Jewish Community, NIK). Sephardim are organised in the Portugees-Israelitisch Kerkgenootschap (Sephardi Jewish Community) and Liberal Jews in the Verbond van Liberaal Religieuze Joden (Federation of Progressive Jewish Communities). The Dutch Zionist Organisation has 1600 members and WIZO has 2500 members. The Federation of Liberal Jewish Women is also active. Holland's six youth movements include B'nai Akiva (350 members), Ichud Habonim (250), Student Movement (200), Reform Youth (100) and Ezra (50).

Religious Life

The chief rabbinate covers both the Ashkenazi and Sephardi communities. There are 12 synagogues in Amsterdam and its suburb, Amstelveen; 8 Orthodox Ashkenazi, 2 East European Ashkenazi, 1 Sephardi and 1 Liberal. There are 4 Liberal synagogues outside Amsterdam and an Orthodox synagogue in most of the larger towns.

Education

Amsterdam has three Jewish day-schools. The largest, for 3–18-year-olds, has 450 pupils, an ultra-Orthodox school for 4–12-year-olds has 100 pupils and a Liberal school for children in the same age group has about 50 pupils. About 200 children in Amsterdam and 500 in the rest of the country receive some other form of Jewish education. Advanced religious education is covered by the Seminarium which has 100 part-time students, the Leiden Institute of Jewish Studies with about 50 students and the Kolel Chacham Zwi with 10 students. Courses of Jewish studies are also held at the University of Amsterdam and some other universities. Recently an educational resource centre was opened in Amsterdam.

Cultural Activities

A new Jewish Historical Museum was opened in Amsterdam in 1987. Its construction was financed by the Dutch government. There are two celebrated libraries: the Bibliotheca Rosenthaliana for Judaica and Hebraica, housed in the University Library, and the Sephardi Ets Chaim Library. The Dizengoff Youth Dance Centre Club has a regular attendance of about 200, the Maccabi Sports clubs have about 600 members of all ages and the Beit Simcha, a club for the elderly, has about 300 members.

Press
The 120-year-old weekly *Nieuw Israelitisch Weekblad* has an average circulation of 5500. The *Studia Rosenthaliana*, devoted to Dutch Jewish history, is published twice a year and sectarian publications with about eight issues a year include the *Levends Joode Geloof* (Reform), *Hakehilla* (Ashkanazi), *Habinjan* (Sephardi) and *de Joodse Wachter* (Zionist). The NIK publishes a regular yearbook and calendar containing full details of communal activities, and a number of educational and religious books. A private publisher, Amphora Books, publishes Dutch translations of Jewish literature.

Welfare
The welfare sector is over three-quarters financed by the government. An Amsterdam hospital has wards specially for Jews providing 60 beds. The six Dutch homes for the aged have a total of 500 beds between them. The modern Sinai Centre for Jewish mental patients has 200 beds. Professional help is given to about 3000 people a year by the Organisation for Jewish Social Work (JMW).

Relations with Israel
Relations are on full ambassadorial level, and until it succumbed to Arab pressure Holland maintained an embassy in Jerusalem. *Aliya* to Israel is steady and several thousand Israelis live in Holland. Dutch foreign policy towards Israel conforms to that of the EEC. Since diplomatic relations between the USSR and Israel were broken in 1967, the Netherlands have represented Israeli interests in the Soviet Union and in this capacity played an important role in the emigration of Soviet Jewry.

Historical Sites
The Portuguese Synagogue in Amsterdam and Anne Frank's House, now an international centre against discrimination, are both important landmarks. There are 234 Jewish cemeteries in Holland, the most famous being the old Portuguese Jewish Cemetery at Oudekerk-on-Amstel which contains the seventeenth century tomb of Rabbi Manasseh ben Israel, the founder of the Anglo-Jewish community. A monument on the Jonas Daniel Meijerplein commemorates the dock workers of Amsterdam who revolted in protest against the deportation of the Jews.

General Position
There is a general decline due to assimilation and an intermarriage rate of about 50 per cent. Antisemitism is not prevalent. Since the Six-Day War there has been a more pro-Palestinian attitude, although surveys still show that the population in general is pro-Israel and pro-Jewish.

NEW ZEALAND

Population: 3 308 000   Jewish population: 4800

History
The first Jews settled in New Zealand in 1829, and one of the first writers to describe the islands was Joel Samuel Polack, who travelled there in 1831–7. Jews came on the first immigrant ship in 1840 immediately following the British annexation. The first community was founded in Auckland in 1841, followed by Wellington in 1843. Auckland's first two mayors were Jews, and Sir Julius Vogel was Prime Minister in 1873–5 and 1876.

Jewish immigrants came from Eastern Europe after 1882 and from Germany and Central Europe after 1933. In 1974 65 Russian Jews settled in Wellington Province.

Composition of the Community
The community is mainly Ashkenazi. Most live in the two cities of Wellington (2300) and Auckland (2350). There are also small communities in Christchurch (80), Dunedin (60), and Hastings.

Communal Organisation
The central body is the New Zealand Jewish Council which is recognised by all groups and affiliated to the World Jewish Congress. New Zealand is also represented on the Board of Deputies of British Jews by two deputies. The Zionist Federation of New Zealand has offices in Wellington and Auckland. WIZO, Habonim, Youth Aliyah, JNF and the New Zealand Friends of the Hebrew University are all affiliated to it. There are also Zionist societies in Wellington, Auckland (established 1904) and Christchurch.

Religious Life
The main organisation is the United Synagogues of New Zealand in Wellington which has synagogues in Auckland, Wellington, Christchurch, Dunedin and Hastings. Auckland and Wellington also have Liberal synagogues. *Kashrut* facilities, including a butcher's shop, are available at the community centre in Wellington.

113

Education
Auckland has a Jewish day school with 120 pupils, but only 20 per cent are Jewish.

Cultural Activities
Community centres exist in Wellington and Auckland. The Union of Jewish Women is represented in Wellington, Auckland and Christchurch, with B'nai B'rith branches in Auckland and Wellington. Auckland also has a Jewish bookshop.

Press
The *New Zealand Jewish Chronicle* is published monthly from Auckland.

Welfare
Wellington has a home for the aged.

Relations with Israel
These are on full ambassadorial level.

General Position
The community is very assimilated and is declining. Its practice of Judaism is similar to that of Anglo-Jewry. A relatively high proportion of New Zealand's Jews have emigrated to Israel.

NICARAGUA

Population: 3 200 000   Jewish population: 10

Marranos may have lived in Nicaragua in the sixteenth and seventeenth centuries but modern Jewish settlement began in 1848 with the arrival of immigrants from France, Germany and Holland. After the First World War there was further immigration of Jews from Eastern Europe. The community continued to grow, with a synagogue and social centre built in 1964 and the formation of WIZO and B'nai B'rith groups and a central organisation, the Congregación Israelita which is affiliated to the World Jewish Congress. By 1972 approximately 50 families (comprising 250 people) were living in the country, concentrated in the town of Managua. In December 1972 an earthquake destroyed much of Managua. Many Jews left the country and by 1976 the population had fallen to 150.

Until 1979 relations with Israel were good. Joint ventures between the countries included the establishment of two Nicaraguan agricultural settlements ('Israel' and 'Jerusalem') built with the expertise of Israeli-trained technicians. Israel also helped with the re-planning of Managua after the earthquake. In July 1979 the extreme left-wing Sandinistas seized power. They confiscated Jewish property (including the synagogue) and imprisoned Abraham Gorn, the leader of the community. Gorn subsequently escaped and fled the country as did the remainder of the community. Since 1979 there has been virtually no Jewish community and relations with Israel have ceased.

NORWAY

Population: 4 146 000   Jewish population: 950

History

The first Jews were allowed into the country in the seventeenth century, provided they had 'Letters of Protection'. The Ministry of Justice gave immigration rights to Portuguese Jews in 1844 but Jews in general were not legally admitted in the country until 1851 after much agitation on their behalf by the poet Henrik Wergenland (1808–45). Large scale immigration started after 1881 with an influx of Jews from Eastern Europe. Emancipation came in 1891, and the oldest Norwegian communities, 'The Mosaic Congregations', were founded in Oslo in 1892 and Trondheim in 1905. The 1920 census recorded 1457 Jewish inhabitants.

By 1940 the Jewish population of Norway had risen to 1800. During the Nazi occupation persecution began in 1941 and by the autumn of 1942 was widespread. In two raids 770 Jews were captured and deported via Stettin to Auschwitz. About 930 Jews fled to Sweden and about 60 remained in hiding in Norway. Quisling's government had facilitated the persecution of the Jews by ordering their forced registration and then the confiscation of their property. A letter of protest against these measures was composed by the Bishops of the Church of Norway and signed by the other Protestant Churches. It was read out on 6 and 13 December 1942 and quoted in the 1943 new year message. Many Norwegians helped Jews to escape to Sweden. After the war Jewish survivors numbered about 800. The Norwegian government extended a special invitation to Jews who had survived the camps to settle in the country.

Composition of the Community

Norwegian Jewry is largely Ashkenazi, descended from the East European immigrants who arrived after 1882, and a number of more recent refugees from Central and Eastern Europe. Most Jews live in Oslo, with a small community in Trondheim, and a few in Bergen.

115

Legal Status

The 1891 Dissenter Law permitted the establishment of Jewish communities, and the 1969 law dealing with religious communities guaranteed financial support from the government and municipalities on the same basis as the state church. *Shechita* is prohibited under a 1929 law governing animal slaughter.

Communal Organisation

Norwegian Jewry comprises two communities, the southern centred on Oslo and including Stavanger, and the northern centred on Trondheim and including Bergen. The Oslo communities' governing board is elected twice yearly and Trondheim's annually. The boards are responsible for decisions on budgets and taxes. Between 80 and 85 per cent of Jews are community members. The Mosaiske Trossamfund (Jewish Community) of Oslo represents Norwegian Jewry in the World Jewish Congress. In Oslo are two JIA committees, a Zionist organisation, a B'nai B'rith Lodge and a WIZO. There is a WIZO branch in Trondheim. The Union of Jewish Women is also active in the community.

Religious LIfe

Oslo's rabbi is under the authority of the Communal Board. His functions include the supervision of a kosher food centre. Both Oslo and Trondheim have synagogues.

Education

A kindergarten was opened in Oslo in February 1981. Since the appointment of a rabbi in 1980, study groups have been operating in Oslo. Hebrew classes in the city offer up to two hours' weekly tuition preparing children for bar or bat mitzvah. There is a summer camp for Norwegian Jewish children.

Cultural Activities

Oslo has a Jewish youth organisation, a B'nai Akiva group and a community centre. There is a community centre in Trondheim.

Press

Since 1976 the Oslo and Trondheim communities have jointly published a 60-page review which appears three times a year.

Welfare

The orphanage and homes for the aged both closed down as they were no longer required, but there are plans to build apartments for old people in Oslo. Oslo's social committee organises visits to the old and the sick.

Relations with Israel

There are full relations at ambassadorial level. From 1977 to 1981 approximately two-thirds of all members of parliament were members of a pro-Israel group.

General Position

There is little antisemitism although anti-Zionist manifestations sometimes have antisemitic overtones. The neo-fascist organisations do not have any influence. Racial and religious discrimination are punishable by law. On average 17 per cent of the population intermarry. The average is, however, higher for both men and women in the 20–29 age group.

PAKISTAN

Population: 94 700 000   Jewish population: 5

Organised settlement began in what is today Pakistan in the nineteenth century. There is a synagogue, the Magain Shalome, in Karachi to which is attached a Bene Israel Relief Fund Society. It is believed that only one Jewish family remains in Pakistan.

There were antisemitic incidents during the 1948 and 1956 Arab-Israeli wars. Anti-Zionist and antisemitic material has been published in English in Pakistan for international distribution.

Pakistan has no relations with Israel.

PANAMA

Population 2 040 000   Jewish population 3800

History

Although there were Jews in the Spanish expedition to Panama in the early sixteenth century, serious settlement did not begin until the mid-nineteenth century. The first Jewish settlers were in fact on their way to California during the Gold Rush of 1849 but stayed in Panama. Several years later there was a severe earthquake on the Danish Caribbean island of St. Thomas and the Sephardi Jews who settled there fled to Panama. In 1876 the first Jewish community was established after a further influx of Jews from Curaçao and other Caribbean islands. The community in Colon was called Kol Kodesh Yaacov. In 1880 a second community, Kol Shearit Israel, was established in Panama City. The Jews of these communities played an important part in trade and industry. Before the First World War the Jewish population increased with the arrival of Sephardi Jews from the Middle East and Ashkenazi Jews from Poland, Russia and Rumania. Refugees from Germany and Austria arrived in the thirties.

Composition of the Community
The community is approximately 60 per cent Sephardi and 40 per cent Ashkenazi. The majority live in Panama City and there are smaller communities in Colon, David, Chitre and Bocas del Toro.

Legal Status
Although Catholicism is the official religion of the country, there is freedom of religious worship.

Communal Organisation
The Consejo Central Comunitario Hebreo de Panama, founded in 1964, co-ordinates Panama's three separate communities and the Human Rights Committee of B'nai B'rith. It is affiliated to the World Jewish Congress. Zionist movements include the Zionist Organisation of Panama, the Jewish National Fund and WIZO.

Religious Life
Panama City has three synagogues and is the home of the Chief Rabbi. The largest synagogue is the Orthodox Sephardi Sociedad Israelita Shevet Ahim. The other synagogues are the Conservative Ashkenazi Beneficencia Israelita Beth El and the Reform Kol Shearit. Kosher food can be bought in Panama City. The United States National Jewish Welfare Board maintains a Jewish community centre and a synagogue for the armed forces at Balboa.

Education
The Central Council maintains the Albert Einstein Institute in Panama City, a school which was founded in 1954 and is attended by nearly 1000 pupils (about a third of whom are not Jewish and often the children of government officials) from kindergarten to high school level. A second school, the Academia Hebrea de Panama, is also in Panama City.

Cultural Activities
B'nai B'rith is active and there are also several youth groups.

Relations with Israel
Relations are on full ambassadorial level. The Panama-Israel Cultural Institute promotes friendship between the two countries.

General Position
Panama is the largest and most vigorous of all the FEDECO communities and many of its members have held important government positions.

PARAGUAY

Population: 3 500 000   Jewish population: 900

History
A few Jews from France, Switzerland and Italy settled in Paraguay at
the end of the nineteenth century but were ultimately absorbed into the
general population. At the beginning of the twentieth century a Chevra
Kadisha was formed from small groups of Ashkenazi Jews from Poland
and Russia and Sephardi Jews from Palestine. The first Sephardi synagogue
was built in 1917, following the arrival of immigrants from Greece and
Turkey. In the 1920s Ashkenazi Jews arrived from Russia and Poland and
established the Unión Hebraica de Paraguay. The migration from Central
Europe between 1933 and 1947 saw more than 10 000 Jews pass through
Paraguay on their way to Argentina, but only few remained. Ironically, in
recent years Paraguay has welcomed Jews escaping the repressive regime
of Argentina's former military junta.

Composition of the Community
The majority of the community are Ashkenazi and live in the capital
city, Asunción. Most are engaged in commerce, the remainder are in
the professions.

Communal Organisation
Consejo Representativo Israelita del Paraguay, known as CRIP, is the
central body. It is run by a permanent president and a public relations
committee and maintains relations with the government. It is affiliated to
the World Jewish Congress. Zionist movements include the Organización
Sionista del Paraguay, WIZO, Magbit, the JNF and Friends of the Hebrew
University.

Religious Life
The main religious and social organisation is the Unión Hebraica
founded by the Ashkenazim. Other organisations include the Templo
Israelita Latino, the German Unión Israelita de Socorros Mutuos and
the Polish Poilisher Farband. These are in the process of merging into
one united Kehilla with two synagogues.

Education
The Alianza Israelita maintains the Jewish cemetery and acts as a burial
society. It also runs Paraguay's Jewish school, the Colegio Integral Estado
de Israel, which caters for pupils from kindergarten up to secondary level.
Ninety-five per cent of the total Jewish school-age children attend the
school which also has a small number of non-Jewish pupils. It has

four Israeli teachers and in addition to the normal Paraguayan school syllabus offers specialist Jewish subjects.

Cultural Activities
There is a Jewish community centre in the CRIP premises. Zionist organisations include the youth movement Hanoar Hatzioni and a branch of WIZO.

Press
The Union Hebraica del Paraguay publishes the monthly *UHP*.

Relations with Israel
There is an Israeli embassy and a consulate general in Asunción. An Israeli ambassador resides permanently in the city. Trade and cultural relations are good. Recently a team of Israeli technicians arrived in the country to help maintain Paraguay's state airline. Approximately 100 Paraguayan Jews have settled in Israel.

General Position
Assimilation is the main concern of the community, with the current intermarriage rate running at about 10 per cent of the population. So far, however, the majority of couples in mixed marriages send their children to the Jewish school. The community is prosperous, with some families among the wealthiest in the country. General Stroessner acted in October 1986 to stamp out incipient antisemitic activity.

PERU

Population: 19 700 000   Jewish population: 5000

History
The first Jews in Peru are thought to have been among the leaders of the Spanish invasion in 1532. But these would have been 'crypto-Jews' (those who practised their religion in secret). In the late sixteenth century crypto-Jews from Portugal were very prominent in trade and commerce in Peru. However, the Inquisition began in 1570 and continued until the beginning of the nineteenth century. Many Jews died in particularly gruesome circumstances, burnings at the stake being common. The last execution was in 1736.

The modern history of Peruvian Jewry began in 1870 when a group of European immigrants, mostly from Alsace, formed the Sociedad de Beneficencia Israelita and five years later acquired a cemetery. But this community did not survive. Its members either intermarried with the local population or converted. A group of Sephardi Jews from North Africa arrived in Peru in 1880, drawn by the rubber industry. They settled in the north-east region of the Amazon at a town called Iquitos. The next wave of immigration was after the First World War with refugees from the Ottoman Empire. They were followed by Jews escaping from Nazi Germany. By the end of the Second World War the Jewish population had reached its peak figure of 6000.

Composition of the Community
Ninety-eight per cent of the Jewish population live in Peru's capital, Lima. The community is 75 per cent Ashkenazi, 10 per cent German Ashkenazi and 15 per cent Sephardi. Jews are particularly prominent in the textile trade, in business and industry, and in the professions.

Legal Status
In 1897 a law was passed permitting civil marriage. In 1915 non-Catholics were permitted to have their own cemeteries, and this, in a sense, amounted to a recognition of religions other than Catholicism.

Communal Organisation
The Asociación Judia del Perú, which is affiliated to the World Jewish Congress, co-ordinates the three main congregations or Kehillot. These are the Ashkenazi Unión Israelita, the Sephardi Sociedad de Beneficencia Israelita Sefaradi and the German Ashkenazi Sociedad de Beneficencia Israelita de 1870. The Presidency of the Association is rotated between the three organisations. The main Zionist organisation is the Federación Sionista del Perú which shares the Jewish National Fund premises in Lima. Other groups include WIZO, Pioneer Women, Friends of Magen David Adom and Friends of the Hebrew University.

Religious Life
There are four synagogues in Lima. Three are Orthodox and one is Conservative. There are two resident rabbis. Services are held daily in the Ashkenazi Great Synagogue and in the Sephardi synagogue. Occasionally Sabbath services are conducted by young people. There are no kosher restaurants.

Education
Approximately 98 per cent of Lima's Jewish children attend the Colegio León Pinelo. Founded in 1946 it has maintained high educational standards ever since and has a reputation for academic excellence. In 1982 it began a scheme under which pupils are sent for a few months to study at a college in Israel.

Cultural Activities
The Hebraica Club is the main social centre and it provides a varied range of activities including sports and things of cultural interest. There is a B'nai B'rith lodge in Lima and a Jewish Scientific Society attached to YIVO.

Press
There are two papers: the Hebraica Club's weekly bulletin and the Community's monthly *La Unión*.

Relations with Israel
There are full diplomatic relations with Israel. The Israeli embassy is in Lima and the Peruvian embassy in Tel Aviv. Relations between the countries have been good dating back to Peru's support of Israel in the UN Partition Resolution of 1947. In 1975 Peruvian intellectuals vigorously attacked the 'Zionism is racism' resolution. A number of Peruvian Jews have settled in Israel.

Historical Sites
The cemetery at Iquitos built by the nineteenth-century Sephardi settlers is still extant.

General Position
The community is, on the whole, flourishing though assimilation and intermarriage are on the increase. Antisemitism is barely a problem but there have been attacks on Jewish property which are thought to have been the work of the Maoist organisation Sendero Luminoso.

PHILIPPINES

Population: 55 000 000   Jewish population: 150

History
A few Marranos came to the Philippines after the Spanish Conquest in the sixteenth and seventeenth centuries. They were followed by a number of Jewish traders, mainly from Alsace Lorraine, in the late nineteenth century. Immigration continued after the American occupation in 1898, with Jews coming from the USA and Europe, followed by Russian Jews after the First World War. The first official congregation was established in Manila in 1922, and a synagogue was built in 1924. After 1933 Jewish refugees fleeing both the Nazis in Europe and the Japanese in Shanghai

arrived in the country, with some 2000 settling there between 1939 and 1940. During the Japanese occupation of 1943 the entire Jewish population was interned. The community was re-established in 1945.

Composition of the Community
One hundred and fifty Jews are residents and about the same number are temporary residents, mostly Israeli. There are also some Jews among the American servicemen at the Clark and Subic Bay bases. In addition there are a number of Filipino converts. Only about 20 per cent are Philippine nationals. It is a fairly affluent community, almost entirely based in the capital Manila.

Legal Status
The Jewish Association of the Philippines is officially registered as a non-profit making religious organisation. Only civil marriage is recognised by the state. *Shechita* is permitted.

Communal Organisation
The central body is the Jewish Association of the Philippines which is affiliated to the World Jewish Congress. Its board of five trustees is elected annually, and is recognised by the whole community. There are no Zionist organisations but there is a women's organisation.

Religious Life
There is no rabbi, *mohel* or *shochet*; a professional *mohel* is brought in from abroad as the occasion demands. Services are held in the community centre and conducted by various lay members of the community. A small number observe *kashrut*. There is a Jewish cemetery. Religious services are also held by the US army at the Clarke Air Base near Angeles City, which civilians may attend.

Education
Three professionally trained teachers hold twice weekly Hebrew classes. There are 28 pupils divided by age into three classes.

Cultural Activities
The community centre was built in 1982–3, and contains a 220-seat synagogue, social hall, and classrooms, as well as a number of ancillary rooms.

Relations with Israel
The two countries have full diplomatic relations. Israel's embassy is in Manila, and the Philippines' embassy in Tel Aviv. Relations are good, and Filipinos have been trained in Israel under a technical co-operation programme. There is a certain sympathy for Israel because the largely

Christian Philippines has to contend with staunchly Islamic neighbours and its own radical Muslim minority. However the Philippines is also dependent on Arab oil.

General Position
Philippine Jewry is a very small but active community of immensely diverse origin. It includes a large transient population but its new centre and synagogue should help give it greater stability. Filipinos are friendly towards the community and there does not appear to be any antisemitism.

POLAND

Population: 36 745 000   Jewish population: 6000

History
Poland has played an important and tragic role in the history of the Jewish people for 700 years. From the thirteenth century to the 1940s it was the centre of Jewish activity and culture; in the Second World War it became the graveyard of European Jewry.

Jewish settlement began in the ninth century, though the recorded history of the community starts with Boleslaw the Pious' 1264 Charter of Protection, known as the Statute of Kalisz, inviting Jews to Poland to help redevelop the country after the Tartar invasions. The Statute of Kalisz was ratified and broadened by King Kazimierz the Great (1333–70) who favoured Jews as skilled middlemen making an important contribution to the economic development of Poland. However, under the rule of the Lithuanian Wladyslaw II Jagiello (1386–1434), these rights were not reconfirmed and Jewish privileges were virtually abolished in 1454, with Jews being expelled from Warsaw in 1483 and Cracow in 1491.

During the sixteenth century many Jews became fiscal officials. Rabbinic schools were established and Jews were granted autonomy when the Council of the Four Lands was formed. The constituents of the Council (which functioned from the mid-sixteenth century until 1764) were the Jewish communities of Great Poland (Poznań region), Little Poland (Cracow region), Galicia (Lvov region) and the province of Volhynia. The Council of the Land of Lithuania was a similar self-governing body in the Grand Duchy of Lithuania.

The Cossack and peasant revolt of 1648, led by Bogdan Chmielnicki, resulted in a succession of massacres of Jewish communities in the Ukraine and Eastern Poland. By 1658, having been caught between warring Russians, Poles and Swedes, 700 Jewish communities had been destroyed.

During the sixteenth and seventeenth centuries Jewish culture and scholarship flourished with major developments in Talmudic learning, rabbinic studies and Yiddish language and literature. Cabbalistic studies also began at this time, later developing into hassidic mysticism. A strange offshoot of these two movements was Messianism and the appearance of false Messiahs, including Shabtai Zvi, who managed to attract a considerable following.

At the end of the eighteenth century Poland was divided between Russian, Prussian and Austrian rule. The largest Jewish concentrations fell within the Russian occupied area, which became part of the Pale of Settlement in 1835. While the nineteenth century saw steady economic progress among Polish Jewry, growing antisemitism threatened their security. A pogrom in Warsaw in 1881 was followed by the discriminatory May Laws (see under USSR), and eventually by mass emigration to the West.

The 1919 Minorities Treaty granted special status to the minorities, which constituted one third of the population. The concessions given to Jews as the second largest group (the largest being the Ruthenians) included the recognition of the Yiddish language and sabbath observance, and special protection in education. Out of the 437 seats in Poland's 1922 parliament, 83 were held by the National Minorities' bloc and 36 of those were held by Jews.

On 1 September 1939 the German army crossed the Polish border. On 28 October 1939 all Jews in Poland were confined to ghetto areas. Extermination camps were established at Treblinka, Chelmno, Sobibór, Majdanek, Belzec and Oświęcim (Auschwitz). Jews from all over Europe were brought to these camps to be murdered. Many Polish Jews formed partisan units or joined Polish partisans, and others revolted. In the Warsaw Ghetto Uprising of 1943 Jews tried to resist deportation and succeeded in driving out a German military unit in April 1943. However the Germans retaliated by systematically destroying the ghetto and on 8 May the resistance leader, Mordechai Anielewicz, was killed. Approximately 56 000 Jews died in the fighting.

By the liberation, approximately three million Polish Jews had died. Those who survived mostly did so by taking refuge in the USSR. The majority of them were repatriated to Poland between 1945–7 and in 1956–8. After the war, a number of antisemitic incidents took place including the 1946 pogrom in Kielce where 41 were killed. Many Jews took fright and emigrated, mostly to Israel. Between 1948 and 1958 about 140 000 Jews left for Israel, including most of those who were repatriated from the Soviet Union. After the Six-Day War in 1967 there was a further outbreak of antisemitism in the form of an 'anti-Zionist' campaign and many Jews were dismissed from their jobs, resulting in a new wave of emigration to Israel and elsewhere. This reduced the community to its present figure of 6000.

125

Composition of the Community
The community is entirely Ashkenazi. The post-war Polish Jewish community emigrated in the years 1946–50, 1956–8 and 1967–9. The main centres of Jewish population are Warsaw (2000), Wrocław (1000), Cracow (600) and Łódź (600). Today the community is mainly composed of elderly people.

Legal Status
Jews have equal rights and the Jewish religion is treated like all other religions. The Jewish secular organisation (see below) is connected with the Administrative and Social Department of the Ministry of the Interior and with the Ministry of Culture and Arts through its Department of Libraries, Houses of Culture and Socio-Cultural Activities. The religious organisation is under the supervision of the Office of Religious Affairs.

Communal Organisation
After the war, Polish Jewry formed two central bodies. The secular Zarząd Główny Towarzystwa Społeczno-Kulturalnego Żydów w Polsce (Central Board of the Cultural and Social Association of the Jews in Poland, known as TSKŻ) runs 14 clubs in Warsaw and in the various provincial communities. The community sends observers to the meetings of the World Jewish Congress. Zionist activity, which temporarily revived after the war, ceased with the Communist takeover.

Religious Life
The religious organisation is the Związek Religijny Wyznania Mojżeszowego (Mosaic Religious Association). There are four functioning synagogues but no rabbis. A rabbi from abroad (usually Hungary) conducts services on High Holy Days. The Nożyk Synagogue in Warsaw was reconstructed in 1982 and re-consecrated during the 40th anniversary commemorations of the Warsaw Ghetto Uprising in April 1983. The Religious Association provides a dozen canteens, serving about 50 000 kosher meals a year.

Education
In 1925 there were 113 schools teaching in Yiddish and 71 in Hebrew. Today there are no Jewish schools.

Cultural Activities
The Jewish Historical Institute in Warsaw has a library, archives and a museum. The Memorial Foundation for Jewish Culture in New York supports some of its research projects. The Yiddish State Theatre stages regular performances mostly for non-Jewish audiences. The TSKŻ's 14 centres, situated throughout the country, arrange a variety of cultural activities including lectures, dramatic performances and song recitals.

Press
The TSKŹ in Warsaw publishes the weekly *Folks-sztyme*, with 9 pages in Yiddish and 3 in Polish. The Jewish Historical Institute publishes a scholarly journal, *Biuletyn*, and the annual Yiddish-language *Bleter far Geszichte*.

Welfare
The TSKŹ provides aid for the needy, but there are no Jewish homes for the aged or hospitals.

Relations with Israel
Poland broke off diplomatic relations with Israel after the Six-Day War as did other Communist countries excluding Rumania but in October 1985 an agreement was reached to exchange low-level diplomatic representatives and set-up interest sections in Warsaw and Tel Aviv. A number of Israeli scholars have visited Poland over the past few years to research at the Jewish Historical Institute and other archives.

There is a large Polish Jewish immigrant population in Israel. In 1956 it numbered 331 300. Of the approximately 300 associations of Polish Jews in various towns, about half are linked with the Association of Immigrants from Poland. Many of the immigrants have served in the Cabinet, and two have been prime ministers.

Historical Sites
Remains of the ancient Jewish community can be found all over the country: ruined synagogues, wall plaques, cemeteries and surviving buildings of the *shtetlach*.

In Cracow the Old Synagogue (Alte Schul), dating from the fourteenth century, has been restored and is now a museum. The fifteenth-century Remuh (or New) Synagogue is still in use, as is the Temple, dating from 1844. The Kupa (1595), the Wysoka (High) Synagogue (1663), the Popper (1620), and the renaissance-style synagogue of Eisig Reb Yekels are all no longer in use. A number of famous rabbis including the Rema (Moses ben Israel Isserles) are buried in the cemetery attached to the Remuh Synagogue.

At Góra Kalwarja, south of Warsaw, the home and synagogue of the Gerer Rebbe has been converted into a store-room. Synagogue buildings are still standing in Działoszyce (early nineteenth century) and at Krzepice, near Przytyk. Important cemeteries are in Warsaw (the Gęsia), Lublin and Przytyk. Of the 400 cemeteries scattered all over the country only 22 are in a reasonable condition in spite of efforts by the Polish Public Committee for the Preservation of Jewish Cemeteries and Cultural Monuments.

There is an unusual memorial at Lukow in Eastern Poland: a pyramid of Jewish gravestones built in 1946 by survivors of the Holocaust before they emigrated. Other Holocaust memorials include the large memorial to the Ghetto Uprising in Warsaw and a museum with a Jewish Pavilion at Auschwitz. Memorials can be found on the sites of many other camps, most of which are open to the public. Resistance to the Nazis is recorded by plaques around the country.

General Position
With no rabbi and a declining population, the future of Polish Jewry looks bleak. Antisemitism still exists, usually manifested in attacks on 'Zionists' as in the 1981 disturbances. Some antisemitic material was published during the early 1980s. Among the positive developments are the increased contacts between the community and world Jewry due to numerous visits by Jewish leaders and scholars from the West. A revival of interest in Jewish history and culture manifested itself in a number of conferences, seminars and other cultural events on Jewish themes held since 1983.

PORTUGAL

Population: 10 129 000   Jewish population: 300

History
Although some Jews may have settled in Portugal during the medieval period of Arab rule there is no detailed information on the community before the thirteenth century. An already growing community was significantly expanded in 1492 with the influx of refugees from the Spanish inquisition. However, following the repeal of an expulsion order in 1496 Jews were forcibly converted to Christianity. These converts were known as New Christians or Marranos. The next 400 years saw Jews gradually drifting back into Portugal but the community was not radically altered until the Second World War when about 70 000 refugees from Central Europe passed through the country, some of them remaining. In 1945 the Portuguese community numbered about 1000.

Composition of the Community
The community is largely upper middle class with many businessmen, engineers and professional people such as doctors, economists and professors. Most Jews live in Lisbon, with a handful in Oporto and Algarve.

Communal Organisation
The central organisation is the Comunidade Israelita de Lisboa which is affiliated to the World Jewish Congress. A WIZO group is active in the community.

Religious Life
There are two synagogues, one Sephardi and one Ashkenazi, and one rabbi. Lisbon has a kosher kitchen.

Cultural Life
Lisbon has a Jewish centre, the Centro Israelita de Portugal. A Jewish youth association, Hehaber, is attached to it.

Welfare
The Jewish Hospital has now been converted into a home for the aged. There are also special arrangements for geriatric medical care.

The Marrano Community
Descendants of the original Marranos still live in and around the town of Belmonte in the Northern province of Beira Alta. They are uncircumcised and baptised but otherwise practise Judaism in secret, lighting their sabbath lamps in the cellar. They do not eat pork, they marry amongst themselves and are known by their neighbours as Judeos – Jews. They are not officially recognised by world Jewry. Discovered in 1917, attention was not drawn to them until the neighbouring town of Guarda was 'twinned' with the Israeli town of Safed in 1982.

Relations with Israel
Israel and Portugal have full ambassadorial relations. Israel has an embassy in Lisbon but Portugal does not have an embassy in Israel. Many Portuguese Jews have emigrated to Israel.

General Position
The community has declined to a population of only 300 (this figure does not include the Marranos). There is considerable anxiety about the long term future.

PUERTO RICO

Population: 3 350 000   Jewish population: 2000

History
A very small number of Jews came to the island after 1898. At the outbreak of the Second World War the community still numbered only 35 families. It began to develop when US troops, among them many Jews, flooded into the island in the early part of the war. A community centre was established in 1942. Subsequently a number of American Jews settled in Puerto Rico either on a permanent or temporary basis.

After the Cuban revolution of 1959 many Cuban Jewish refugees fled to the island.

Composition of the Community
Most Jews are now of Cuban origin but there is also a large number of Americans. Most are engaged in business and nearly all live in San Juan-Santurce.

Religious Life
Of the two synagogues, the main one, Shaarei Zedek, is attached to the Jewish Community Centre in San Juan. It can seat 500 people and has 250 affiliated families. The other is the Temple Beth-Shalom (Reform). All affiliated families are American. However, there is no rabbi for either synagogue.

Communal Organisation
The focus of Jewish life is the Jewish Community Centre which is housed in a building originally built by a pupil of Frank Lloyd Wright, which has been designated a national monument. It has been extensively renovated and was reopened in 1984. The Hebrew school classes are also held in the building. The United Jewish Appeal and Hadassah are the largest communal organisations and are attached to the Centre. Most cultural activities are Israel oriented.

Relations with Israel
There are no separate relations with Israel as foreign affairs are conducted through the USA.

General Position
Although Jews have not been prominent in public life, the first Chief Justice of the Puerto Rico Supreme Court was a Jew.

ROMANIA

Population: 22 600 000   Jewish population: 23 000

History
Jews settled in what is today Romania as early as the fourth century and there is archeological evidence for their existence in the Northern Carpathian region two centuries earlier. In 1367 Jewish refugees arrived from Hungary and by the end of the sixteenth century communities existed in Jassy, Botosani, Suceava and Siret. In the seventeenth century Jews fleeing from the Chmielnicki massacres in Poland and the Ukraine settled

in Moldavia and from the beginning of the eighteenth century Moldavian rulers granted special charters to attract Jews.

The first Haham Bashi (see under Turkey) of Jassy was appointed by the Sultan in 1719. Jews tended to be concentrated in Moldavia, in the North East, where the Boyars invited Polish Jews to set up markets destroyed in fighting between Russians and Turks. In the late eighteenth and early nineteenth century there was a steady Jewish immigration. In this period Jews suffered from the continuous warring between the Turkish and Russian Empires. After 1861 Bucharest replaced Jassy as the main Jewish centre. Between 1826 and 1916 there were at least 200 regulations restricting Jewish freedom and the 1878 Treaty of Berlin's demands for equal rights for Jews were ignored. From 1900 to 1906, about 70 000 Jews left the country and while equality was formally granted in 1918–19, the discriminatory atmosphere remained. After the First World War, the Jewish community was augmented by the large Hungarian Jewish community of Transylvania when this territory was attached to Romania in the Treaty of Trianon.

In 1937 the largely hassidic Romanian community was subjected to discriminatory legislation – Hebrew and Yiddish papers were banned, Jews lost their citizenship rights and the right to practise in the professions. At the outbreak of the war Romania was allied with Germany and in 1940 introduced legislation based on the Nuremberg Laws. Many Jews were then deported to camps in Transdniestria and later to Auschwitz. Several massacres took place, the worst being in June 1941 near Jassy when 14 000 Jews were shot by German and Romanian troops. Approximately 385 000 Romanian Jews died in the Holocaust, out of a pre-war population of around 800 000.

After the war and the return of surviving deportees the Jewish population numbered 400 000. When Communist rule was established in 1946, a Democratic Jewish Committee, modelled on the old Soviet *Eevsektsiya*, was set up under government control. In 1948 the Jewish Communists expelled the Zionists and in 1950 the Zionist leaders were arrested and not released until the Committee was finally abolished in 1955.

Between 1948 and 1952, 125 000 Jews left for Israel. Emigration was banned until the end of the 1950s but recommenced when the ban was lifted and has continued ever since.

Composition of the Community
The community has a majority of Ashkenazi Jews. Just under half the population live in Bucharest (10 478) with 500 Jews living at Jassy and 450 at Dorohoi in Moldavia and a further 65 communities and 20 congregations scattered throughout the country. Ninety-one other localities have groups of less than 10 Jews. Forty-eight per cent of the population is over the age of sixty.

Legal Status

As a religious-ethnic group the Jewish community is recognised and financially supported by the state. The Jews do not have national minority status, although Yiddish is accepted as the Jewish 'national language'. The Chief Rabbi, as head of a religious community, is automatically granted a seat in the national parliament.

Communal Organisation

The central body, the Federatia Comunităţilor Evreiesti Din Republica Socialistă România (Federation of Jewish Communities in the Socialist Republic of Romania), is headed by the Chief Rabbi and was the first organisation of its kind in a Communist country to receive permission to join the World Jewish Congress. Zionist groups are not permitted.

Religious Life

The central body headed by the Chief Rabbi represents both Ashkenazi and Sephardi groups. There are 84 synagogues whose prayer leaders are provided by the Federation. There are 11 kosher restaurants throughout the country and 5 *shochtim* supervised by the 10 Hahams of the Federation.

Education

Talmud Torah classes are provided for approximately 500 students in 25 towns and cities.

Cultural Activities

Bucharest has a museum of Romanian Jewish history (in the same building as the Synagogue of the Tailors), a Romanian Jewish History Research Centre and the Federation's Jewish Library and historical archives. There are Talmud Torah student choirs in 17 towns and youth orchestras in Bucharest, Brasov, Jassy and Dorohoi. A Yiddish State Theatre holds performances in Bucharest.

Press

The community's paper, the *Revista Cultului Mozaic* (literally Mosaic Religious Review), is published fortnightly in an edition of 10 000. Founded in 1956, it is written in four languages: Romanian, Yiddish, Hebrew and English. The Federation publishes a calendar.

Welfare

Homes for the aged cater for over 400 people and are situated in Bucharest (2), Timisoara, Arad and Dorohoi (2). The American Joint Distribution Committee provides 80 per cent of the finance for a range of welfare schemes including a meals on wheels service (feeding 300 in

Bucharest, 400 in the provinces), financial assistance and food and clothing for the old and infirm. Approximately 5000 receive such benefits. The Federation administers convalescent homes situated in mountain areas and near the Black Sea.

Relations with Israel
Romania is the only Communist state which maintained full diplomatic relations with Israel after the Six-Day War.

In the pre-war years, about 13 000 Romanian Jews settled in Israel followed by a further 350 000 post-war. Since 1980 the average annual figure has been 1000, with 1348 in 1986.

Romanian immigrants have actively contributed to the development of Israel, particularly in the founding of many kibbutzim. The Hungarian-language paper, *Uj Kelet*, published in Tel Aviv, was founded in Transylvania. The Romanian-speaking community in Israel publishes its own paper, *Viata Noastra*.

Historical Sites
The 450-strong Jewish community of Dorohoi near the Soviet border constitutes the last remaining *shtetl* in the world. The town of Jassy has a fifteenth-century synagogue and a statue of Avram Goldfaden, who founded the Yiddish theatre in 1876.

General Position
The Jewish community of Romania is highly centralised under the strong leadership of its Chief Rabbi, Dr Moses Rosen, who was appointed in 1948. Although there is considerable Jewish activity, there is a high rate of emigration and the community's numbers are steadily declining.

SINGAPORE

Population: 2 529 000   Jewish population: 300

History
The community was founded in 1841 by Baghdadi Jewish traders from Bombay, Calcutta, Baghdad and Rangoon, who were mainly drawn to Singapore because it was developing into an important trading centre. By 1858 there were 20 Jewish families, in 1870 the community numbered 172, and immigration continued until the early 1930s. The first synagogue, the Maghain Aboth, was built in 1878, and the second, the Chesed El, in 1904, by the magnate Sir Manasseh Meyer, who was also active in the running of the Colony itself.

During the Japanese occupation most of the community was imprisoned, and their property seized. After the war the Jewish Welfare Board was founded, and David Marshall became its first president in 1946. He was subsequently to become Singapore's first Chief Minister, following independence in 1965.

Composition of the Community
The community is about 75 per cent Sephardi, and 25 per cent Ashkenazi. Just under 25 per cent are not Singapore citizens, being mainly US, Israeli, British or Australian. About 70 per cent are affluent businessmen and there are also a number of professional people and civil servants. About 10 per cent, mainly the aged and sick, rely on the welfare services.

Legal Status
The community is organised as a private voluntary association. There are laws against incitement and racial hatred, and *shechita* is permitted.

Communal Organisation
The central body is the Jewish Welfare Board, which since 1978 has been referred to in its Constitution as the Jewish Community of Singapore. Elections to the Board are held annually. There is a small WIZO group.

Religious Life
There is one rabbi and two synagogues, both Sephardi, but there is no Beth Din. Most of the community adhere to *kashrut*, and meat products are mainly imported from Denver, Colorado, although the rabbi is a qualified *shochet*. A local Jewish surgeon acts as a *mohel*.

Education
A Sunday school (Talmud Torah), Sir Manasseh Meyer's Hebrew School, under the aegis of the Jewish Welfare Board, is available for some 30 children from kindergarten age up to 13. Some of the teachers are from Israel and some from Singapore itself. There is also a separate school for the children of Israelis working in Singapore. About 40 children attend the classes which meet once a week in the evenings.

Cultural Activities
These are based on the Sir Manasseh Meyer Communal Centre which is opposite the Chesed El Synagogue and includes the Hebrew School. It possesses an auditorium and is used for drama, sport and dancing. The school has a library of historical and religious significance. Young people belong to a youth group, which holds picnics and summer camps, as well as discussions on Jewish affairs and Jewish history.

Press
There is no Jewish press as such. However, annual reports and circulars are produced.

Welfare
The community has one old-age home, as well as a communal lodging-house.

Relations with Israel
Diplomatic relations, established in 1969, are on ambassadorial level. Relations are good, with Israelis working in Singapore in commerce and industry, particularly in building. However, Singapore prefers a low profile on some matters affecting Israel in view of its closeness to Malaysia and Indonesia.

Historical Sites
The Chesed El Synagogue is listed as a historical monument under the Singapore Monuments Act, and the older Maghain Aboth Synagogue is also of architectural significance.

In 1984 the Thomson Road cemetery, which contained the marble mausoleum of Sir Manasseh Meyer, was removed due to the building of an underground railway. The Singapore authorities agreed to defray the costs of removal of the graves, and an Israeli rabbinical authority supervised the transfer. Unfortunately the Meyer Mausoleum could not be rebuilt and had to be demolished.

General Position
Although there are no Jews in parliament, some are prominent in public life, such as the former Chief Minister, now ambassador to France. The community is generally professionally based and prosperous and there is no antisemitism. However the community is in decline and there has been a steady emigration, mainly to Australia and the West Coast of the USA.

SOUTH AFRICA

Population: 31 010 000   Jewish population: 120 000

History
It is likely that there were some settlers of Jewish extraction in the seventeenth century but it was not until the nineteenth century that Jews were officially allowed into the country and to practise their religion openly. The first Jewish congregation was established in Cape

Town in 1841 and others followed in the Cape Province in subsequent years. These included Port Elizabeth (1857), Kimberley (1875) and East London (1901).

Jewish settlement in the Transvaal dates from 1886 when gold was discovered in the Johannesburg area. The Jewish community was established soon after the establishment of Johannesburg itself and from very early on Jews played an important part in the development of trade and industry.

The nature of the community began to change in the 1880s with the beginning of large-scale immigration of Jewish refugees from Eastern Europe. By 1910 South Africa had received approximately 40 000 Jewish immigrants, the majority coming from Lithuania.

The Quota Act of 1930 restricted immigration and was followed in 1937 by the Aliens Act which specifically banned immigration of Jews from Germany. Nevertheless the population continued to increase and from a figure of 38 101 in 1904 reached 118 120 in 1970 and some 120 000 in 1986.

Composition of the Community
The South African Jewish community is mainly of Ashkenazi origin although there is a small Sephardi community in Cape Town. The largest concentration of Jews is in the Transvaal (65 per cent) in the Johannesburg region. The South African Board of Deputies figures for major areas of Jewish population are: Johannesburg, 63 620; East Rand (Germiston), 4440; West Rand, 940; Cape Town and Peninsula, 28 000; Durban, 6420; and Port Elizabeth, 2740. Throughout South Africa are scattered about 200 Jewish communities, some of them quite small.

The Jewish community is affluent, well-educated and middle class with double the proportion of employers compared to the rest of the white population.

Legal Status
Jews, as an integral part of the white population, have full equality. Synagogues are private voluntary organisations and membership of the community is not compulsory. The community does not have the right to levy taxes. *Shechita* is permitted.

Communal Organisation
The central body of the community is the South African Jewish Board of Deputies whose headquarters are in Johannesburg with the provincial committees in Cape Town, Durban, Bloemfontein, Port Elizabeth and Pretoria. The Board, which represents all the important Jewish organisations and congregations, is recognised by the government as the official spokesman of South African Jewry. It is governed by an

executive council elected by a biennial national congress and is affiliated to the World Jewish Congress.

An organisation of equal importance in the community is the South African Zionist Federation with headquarters in the Zionist Centre in Johannesburg. Most Zionist groups are affiliated to it and also have their offices in the Centre. Amongst them are the United Zionist Association, the Zionist Revisionist Organisation of South Africa, the Democratic Zionist Association and the South African Labour Movement.

Of the many women's movements the most influential is the Union of Jewish Women which works extensively in the field of social services and fundraising. The Women's Zionist Council of South Africa is an equally important organisation in the community. Other groups include the Women's Mizrahi (Emunah), the United Temple Sisterhoods of South Africa (who contribute to welfare and educational programmes for underprivileged black Africans) and various women's benevolent societies.

Fund-raising is centralised through two bodies, the United Communal Appeal which provides funds for domestic needs, and the Israel United Appeal which raises money for Israel.

Religious Life

The largest religious body is the mainstream Orthodox Federation of Synagogues of South Africa to which 65 synagogues are affiliated and which operates in all areas apart from the Western Province of the Cape. The Cape's parallel organisation (based in Cape Town) is the South African Jewish Ecclesiastical Association (JEA). The Chief Rabbi of the Federation is the country's leading religious authority with an Av Beth Din under the auspices of the JEA in Cape Town.

The two extreme Orthodox groups in Johannesburg are the Adath Yeshurun Congregation – mostly of German origin – and the Kollel Yad Shaul, devoted to religious studies. The Lubavitch have centres in both Johannesburg and Cape Town.

There are approximately 14 Progressive congregations incorporating some 18 000 members and having a total of 12 rabbis. The congregations are affiliated to the South African Union for Progressive Judaism whose religious body is the Central Ecclesiastical Board.

Education

Jewish education is organised by the South African Board of Jewish Education in Johannesburg, the Cape Board of Jewish Education in Cape Town and the South African Council for Progressive Jewish Education (also in Johannesburg). Between them these organisations provide a total of 69 nursery schools, 10 primary schools and 8 high schools. Of these the most distinguished are the King David schools and the Yeshiva College in Johannesburg, Hillel schools in Benoni, Carmel schools in Pretoria, Herzlia schools in Cape Town, the Theodor Herzl school in Port Elizabeth and Carmel College in Durban. Independent schools in Johannesburg include the Lubavitch Torah Academy, the ultra-Orthodox Shaareh Torah and the Yiddish Folkschool.

Specifically Jewish education is provided by the 25 schools in Johannesburg affiliated to the United Hebrew Schools of Johannesburg and the 29 Hebrew schools in the rest of the country. Between them the schools cater for approximately 1700 pupils. Hebrew teachers are trained at the Rabbi Zlotnick Hebrew Teachers' Training College in Johannesburg. The Board's Pedagogic Centre in Johannesburg is an educational resource centre.

Institutes which provide rabbinical training include the Yeshiva Gedolah attached to Yeshiva College in Johannesburg and the South African Jewish Ministers' Training College. The Isaac and Jessie Kaplan Centre at the University of Cape Town offers courses in Jewish Studies at undergraduate and postgraduate research level and there are Hebrew courses available at several other English speaking universities.

Cultural Activities
South Africa has three Jewish museums: the Harry and Friedel Abt Jewish Museum in Johannesburg, the Jewish Museum in Cape Town and a Jewish collection at the C. P. Nel Museum at Oudtshoorn in Cape Province.

Libraries in Johannesburg can be found at the Zionist Federation, the Pedagogic Centre and the Board of Deputies (which also has an archive collection). Other libraries include the Landau at the University of Witwatersrand, the Kollel Library of religious works and the Kaplan Centre's library.

Umbrella youth organisations are the South African Maccabi Council and the South African Zionist Youth Council. Of the four main youth movements the largest is Habonim with approximately 2600 members, followed by B'nei Akiva (1800 members), Betar (1700 members) and the Progressive organisation, Maginim (800 members).

Press
English language weeklies include the *Zionist Record and South African Jewish Chronicle* (organ of the Zionist Federation), the *South African Jewish Times* and the *Jewish Herald* (Revisionist). The independent *Afrikaner Yiddische Zeitung* is a Yiddish-language weekly. The South African Board of Deputies publishes two monthlies: *Jewish Affairs* (English-language) and *Buurman* (Afrikaans-language). Other publications include the *Federation Chronicle* (Federation of Synagogues), the *Pretoria Jewish Chronicle*, *Hashalom* (Durban) and two Yiddish periodicals, the

monthly *Yomtov Bletter* – which also has an English-language section – and *Dorem Afrika*, a literary quarterly. Swazi Radio broadcasts a regular Sunday evening Jewish programme run by the Lubavitch Movement.

Welfare
Jewish homes for the aged include the Witwatersrand Home and Our Parents' Home (founded by the German community) in Johannesburg and Highlands House in Cape Town. Leading charitable organisations are the Jewish Helping Hand and Burial Society, and the Cape Jewish Board of Guardians. Both were founded at the end of the nineteenth century. Institutions for the handicapped include the Selwyn Segal Institute in Johannesburg, the Glendale Institution in Cape Town and the Kadimah Industries which gives employment to those unable to fend for themselves. Hatikvah House in Johannesburg provides a home for psychiatric patients and the mentally handicapped.

Relations with Israel
Israel has an embassy in both Pretoria and Cape Town. Relations are cordial though the future is uncertain. There is some *aliya* to Israel and there are approximately 20 000 Israelis living in South Africa. Israel recently imposed a ban on new military contacts with South Africa.

Historical Sights
At West Park cemetery in Johannesburg is the Holocaust Memorial, a striking sculpture by the South African Jew, Herman Wald. The Yad Vashem memorial at the Etz Chaim Synagogue ws sculpted by the artist Ernest Ullman. The Mooi Street Synagogue, which was founded by Lithuanian immigrants from the shtetl of Poswohl, has been declared a national monument.

General Position
A wealthy and ardently pro-Zionist community, the Jews of South Africa find themselves in an uncertain position as the country's internal problems remain unsolved. The community is committed to a peaceful dismantling of apartheid but has little political influence. In 1985 the South African Board of Deputies passed a resolution explicitly rejecting apartheid and has since urged Jews to co-operate in achieving non-violent reform.

Although not a major problem, antisemitism in South Africa seems to be gaining ground. It is manifested within the white community largely among extreme right-wing Afrikaaner organisations, including the neo-Nazi Afrikaaner Werstandsbeweging. Black left-wing groups include anti-Zionism as part of their programmes, regarding South African Jews as part of the capitalist white community and connected to the alleged 'special relationship' between Israel and South Africa. The large Muslim community is strongly pro-Arab and its more extreme element has produced antisemitic propaganda, notably during Israel's involvement in Lebanon.

The community is active in public life, in the legal profession and in the academic and cultural life of the country. However, the worsening political situation has caused an increase in emigration mainly to Israel, the USA and Australia. The continued existence of the community will obviously depend upon how the country's internal difficulties are resolved.

SOUTH KOREA

Population: 42 000 000   Jewish population: 50

A small number of Jews, mainly refugees from Russia, lived in Korea during the Japanese occupation. The bulk of the community arrived as part of the United States occupation force after the Second World War.

The majority of the community are US military personnel but there are also a few Jewish businessmen working in the country. Both groups live mainly in the capital, Seoul, and do not have Korean citizenship. There is a Jewish Community Council, which is recognised by the government.

The one rabbi provided by the US army for its Jewish personnel serves a two-year tour of duty and is then replaced. There is a Beth Din and religious services are held at the US Religious Retreat Centre on Friday evenings. Only civil marriages are recognised by the army authorities. Kosher food can be obtained. A Sunday school is available for children.

South Korea and Israel have full diplomatic relations but the Israeli ambassador is resident in Tokyo.

SPAIN

Population: 38 818 000   Jewish population: 12 000

History
Reference to the existence of Jews in Spain at the time of the Roman Empire can be found in passages of the Talmud, Flavius Josephus and the Book of the Maccabees. Many of the early Jewish settlers were farmers and landowners, and lived in comparative freedom until the anti-Jewish

measures executed at the Third Council of Toledo in 589. A hundred years later one of the Visigothic Kings, Egica (687–701), reduced all Jews to the status of slaves. When the Arab Muslims conquered Spain in 711 Jews were granted freedom to practise their religion even though they did not have equal rights.

Under Arab rule Jewish culture blossomed and individual Jews rose to prominence, such as Hasdai ibn Shaprut (c.915–70), Chief Diplomatic Adviser to successive Caliphs. Jews were not free from persecution, however, and massacres occurred, notably in 1066 when 3000 Jews were killed in Granada. The next two hundred years saw the rise of important figures in Jewish scholarship and literature including Abraham ibn Ezra (1089–1164), Moses de Leon (died 1305), Rabbi Moshe ben Nachman, known as Nachmanides or Ramban (1194–1270), Bahya ibn Pakuda, Yehuda Halevi (1086–c.1142), author of 'the Kuzari', and Solomon ibn Gabirol (c.1021–56).

After the Almohad invasion of 1136, the practice of Judaism was forbidden, but life in the expanding Christian north became easier. At this time the most important of all Jewish philosophers, Moshe ben Maimon, known as Maimonides or Rambam (1135–1204), was born in Cordova. He was forced to flee the country at the age of thirteen to escape the Almohad persecution. The situation in the Christian north continued to improve until by the mid-thirteenth century the Court of Castile saw considerable Jewish intellectual activity. But from 1391 the Jewish community began to decline and suffered massacres and persecutions. The once flourishing communities of Andalusia, Levante and Cataluna were destroyed, leaving the only Jewish settlements in Castile. Jews were forced to convert but many kept their faith in secret. These 'New Christians' (or Marranos) were often attacked and in 1478 the Inquisition was established as an instrument of persecution. In 1492 Jews were expelled from Spain and about 50 000 actually fled. The Inquisition continued to seek out Marranos until the end of the eighteenth century.

The Inquisition did not formally end until 1834. In 1869 non-Catholics were granted rights of residence and freedom to practise their religion. After this date Jews began to drift back into the country. The law prohibiting the building of synagogues was abolished in 1909.

Spain received about 3000 Central European refugees after 1933 and during the Second World War large numbers of refugees passed through the country. Until 1943 Jews with partial or full Spanish citizenship were given protection by Spanish Consulates abroad. At a later stage of the war, Spain participated in the rescue operation of Hungarian Jews by giving protection certificates to 2750 Jews who were not Spanish citizens.

A large number of Sephardi Jews settled in Spain in the 1950s. On 29 June 1967 non-Catholic communities were given the right to own property and legal recognition and the repeal of the edict of expulsion was made explicit for the first time in 1968 on the occasion of the official recognition of the Madrid Jewish community.

Composition of the Community

The community consists largely of recent or fairly recent immigrants: Central and Eastern Europeans from before and after the Second World War, Moroccans in the late 1950s and Latin Americans who came in the late 1970s and early 1980s. Barcelona has a number of Middle Eastern immigrants, mainly from Turkey and Greece. The community is overwhelmingly Sephardi with a minority of Ashkenazim. The main centres of Jewish population are Madrid, 3000; Barcelona, 3000; Malaga, 1200. On the Moroccan coast, the two Spanish enclaves of Ceuta and Melilla have a total population of about 1500 Jews. Majorca is the last home of the Spanish Marranos, known as the Chuetas. The majority of Spanish Jews are relatively affluent members of the middle class.

Legal Status

In 1968 the Expulsion Order of 1492 was finally abolished. All other restrictions had been abolished earlier. A declaration of religious liberty for non-Catholics was passed by referendum on 14 December 1966, for incorporation into the Basic Law.

The Law on Religious Liberty of 29 June 1967, was the first legislation granting status to non-Catholic communities. The Constitution of 1978 proclaimed universally recognised principles of religious liberty, including the basic one that the Spanish state has no official religion, thus separating church and state for the first time in Spanish history. The Law on Religious Liberty of 6 July 1980 and its subsequent Constitutional mandate made negotiations possible between the Spanish state and those religions which are strongly established in the country. Three such agreements are contemplated: with the Catholic Church, the Federation of Jewish Communities and the Federation of Protestant Communities.

Communal Organisation

The Federación de Comunidades Israelitas de España (Federation of Jewish Communities of Spain), is based in Madrid. It comprises 11 different communities, the 5 with permanent offices being Madrid, Barcelona, Malaga and the Spanish Moroccan towns of Ceuta and Melilla. The remaining 6 are Seville, Valencia, Alicante, Majorca and the two Canary Island communities of Gran Canary and Tenerife. The Federation is affiliated to the World Jewish Congress.

Various Jewish organisations including WIZO, Consejo Español de Mujeres Israelitas (Spanish Council of Jewish Women) and the Committee for the Support of Oppressed Jews, operate within the framework of the community structure. In addition there is a B'nai B'rith lodge.

Religious Life

The two synagogues – one Sephardi, one Ashkenazi – in Barcelona's community centre, were the first synagogues to be opened after the Expulsion. Modern synagogues exist in Madrid (founded 1968), Malaga, Marbella, Seville, Torremolinos, Valencia and Gran Canary. Barcelona, Madrid and Malaga have resident rabbis. Kosher meat is obtainable in Barcelona, Madrid, Malaga and Torremolinos.

Education

Spain has two Jewish day-schools: the Liceo Sephardi in Barcelona, founded in 1971 and which now has 120 pupils, and the Colegio Estrella Toledano in Madrid with 180 pupils of which 30 per cent are not Jewish. In Melilla there is a Talmud Torah supported by the municipality.

The Barcelona community runs a youth summer camp outside the city under the direction of an Israeli *madrich*. The Madrid community runs a similar camp, Massade, at Hoya de Manzanares.

The Church-supported Centre for Judeo-Christian Studies, founded in 1972, organises courses for the Catholic clergy and, in conjunction with the Jewish community, annual seminars for Spanish and Israeli university professors, held alternately in Spain and Israel.

Cultural Activities

The Barcelona community centre, with its two synagogues, was the first Jewish building to be erected in Spain after the Expulsion. Today, it is a cultural centre with a Ladies' Guild (whose activities are similar to those of WIZO) and a youth group (Maccabi). Madrid's community centre provides similar facilities. There is also a community centre in Malaga. The library of the Arias-Montana Institution (a non-Jewish body) contains a magnificent 16 000-volume collection on Sephardi Jewish history.

Press

The Federation of Jewish Communities of Spain publishes a monthly Spanish-language bulletin, *Hakesher*.

Relations with Israel

Spain and Israel established full diplomatic relations in 1986. Trade and cultural relations between the two countries are good and the Spanish state airline, Iberia, flies directly between Barcelona and Tel Aviv.

Historical Sites

Some of the world's finest examples of medieval architecture can be found in Spain, notably the old Juderias (similar to ghettos). In many Spanish towns churches are converted synagogues. In Lucena, an almost entirely Jewish town in the Middle Ages, the St. James's Church (Iglesia de Santiago) is referred to locally as 'La Sinagoga'. In Catalonia a dramatic conservation project is underway to restore the Call (Jewish community) of Gerona, famous for its thirteenth century Cabbalistic School, headed by Nachmanides. The recently established Isaac the Blind Centre, named after the thirteenth century cabbalist, acts both as a study centre and a museum for objects discovered as part of the project.

Toledo, the main centre of Spanish Jewry in the Middle Ages, contains some striking antiquities including the Transito Synagogue built by Samuel Halevi Abulafia (c.1320–61) with fine decoration and Hebrew inscriptions. Attached to the synagogue is the Sephardi Museum, containing medieval Jewish artefacts. Nearby, Abulafia's palace still stands. The palace subsequently became the house of the painter El Greco, and is today a museum of his work. The Toledo Juderia is well marked, with an interesting entrance arch. There is also a cemetery and several other synagogues, and many original houses of the Juderia are still standing. The fourteenth-century synagogue in Cordova was recently restored to coincide with the 850th anniversary of Maimonides.

In Granada, archaeologists now think that the Alhambra may have been the original eleventh-century palace of Joseph ibn Nagrela, where he lived prior to the massacre of 1066, although, in this case, very little remains of the Juderia itself.

Apart from the old Juderias and synagogues converted into churches, there are several modern statues of important Jewish figures of the past, including that of Shlomo ibn Gabirol in Malaga, and Maimonides in Cordova.

General Position
The largely immigrant community has grown significantly since the end of the war, with Ashkenazim and Sephardim successfully fusing into one community. In recent years there has been an immigration of Latin American Jews, in particular from Argentina, some of whom tend to remain aloof from the rest of the community.

The community has steadily increased over the past two decades, but is now relatively stable. Over a short period a vigorous community has successfully established effective institutions including two Jewish day-schools.

There are for the most part good Jewish-Christian relations and very little antisemitism. Some right-wing antisemites are assembled in small groups such as the ultra-conservative Warriors of Christ the King and the neo-Nazi CEDADE (Circulo Espanõl De Amigos De Europa).

Non-Jewish Spaniards are remarkably interested in preserving the heritage of Sephardi Jewry to the extent that the Spanish government intervened in several instances on behalf of Sephardi Jews abroad, for example, at the time of the Six-Day War of 1967.

SURINAM

Population: 370 000   Jewish population: 350

History
Marranos fleeing from Portuguese persecution in Brazil came to Surinam in 1639, making it the oldest permanent Jewish settlement in the Americas. A semi-autonomous Jewish agricultural colony, Jodensavanne, was also established in the seventeenth century. It was known to English writers of the period as 'The Jew Savannah', 100 miles up the Surinam river, and a synagogue was built there in 1685. By the eighteenth century the Sephardi settlers had been joined by Ashkenazim in Paramaribo. In recent years, more than 300 Jews have emigrated, mainly to Holland, but also to the United States and Israel.

Composition of the Community
The Sephardi and Ashkenazi parts of the community have been intermarrying for some time and virtually all of them now live in the capital, Paramaribo.

Legal Status
The two Jewish congregations are regarded as private voluntary organisations. The Boards of the congregation are recognised by the government and have the right to levy taxes on their members. Only civil marriages are recognised by the state.

Regulations against discrimination or incitement to racial or religious hatred were inserted in the Surinam Penal Code in 1971, but antisemitism was not specifically mentioned. *Shechita* is permitted, but is not performed as there is no *shochet*.

Communal Organisation
The Sephardi congregation, the Nederlands Portugees Israelietische Gemeente (Dutch Portuguese Jewish Community), and the Ashkenazi congregation, the Nederlands Israelietische Gemeente, both have boards of five elected members and they co-operate closely. The Sephardi congregation is affiliated to the World Jewish Congress. The Zionist Association was active from 1941 to 1956. Now there are no Zionist groups. A representative of the Keren Hayesod collects annual contributions.

Religious Life
The two synagogues in Paramaribo hold alternative services, and both follow the Sephardi rite. There is no rabbi, but a part-time cantor conducts services and is assisted by laymen on the High Holy Days. A Jewish doctor acts as a *mohel*. There is no Beth Din.

145

Education
An evening class is held once a week with 2 teachers and 20 pupils.

Press
Surinam has no Jewish press. A Dutch language monthly, *Teroenga* (from the Hebrew, *Teru'a*), was published from 1959 to 1968.

Relations with Israel
The Israeli ambassador to Venezuela acts as ambassador to Surinam. The embassy and consular services are in Caracas. A few Israeli families are resident in Surinam.

Historical Sites
There are plans for the restoration of the two old Paramaribo synagogues, described by an English soldier-adventurer who visited them in the 1770s as 'two elegant Jewish synagogues, one German, the other Portuguese'. The seventeenth-century synagogue at Jodensavanne was restored in 1973.

General Position
This community, which was protected from the Inquisition by the Dutch, is experiencing an amicable fusing of Ashkenazim and Sephardim into one community, but it is clearly undergoing a slow decline.

SWEDEN

Population: 8 343 000   Jewish population: 16 000

History
The Jewish community of Sweden dates back to 1774 when Aaron Isaac from Mecklenburg received permission from King Gustav III to establish a Jewish community in Stockholm and conduct public worship. Before this, Jews resident in the country were forced to convert to Christianity. There was opposition to the King's decree and the Judereglemente (Jew Law) of 1782 designated the Jewish settlement as a foreign colony, with its members restricted in movement and denied the right to vote. The first Swedish Jewish community was established at Marstrand near Gothenburg. However, it was of brief duration and Jews remained thereafter restricted to Stockholm, Gothenburg and Norrkoping.

In 1815 immigration of Jews ceased though the total Jewish population was only 785. In 1838 Jews were officially designated 'believers in the

Mosaic faith', a description lasting until 1980. In 1849 they were allowed to be witnesses in court, in 1860 they were given the right to own property and in 1866 they won the right to vote (but not to stand for election). Finally, in 1870, full emancipation was granted, with the reservation that no Jew could be prime minister.

After 1882 many Jewish refugees from Russia and Poland arrived in the country; by the 1920s the community had become prosperous and integrated into Swedish society. Only a limited number of refugees from Germany and Austria arrived in the 1930s owing to the restrictive Swedish immigration policy. After the outbreak of the Second World War public opinion changed in favour of the refugees and Sweden offered asylum to the Norwegian and Danish Jews. More than 200 000 refugees of various nationalities found a haven in the country during and immediately after the war. The rescue missions of Raoul Wallenberg and Count Folke Bernadotte saved many Jewish lives.

Post-war Jewish immigration included 2500 Hungarians after the 1956 rising and Polish refugees forced out by the antisemitic policies of 1968.

Composition of the Community
Less than half of Sweden's Jewish population are descendants of the pre-war Jewish population. The rest are either refuges from Nazi-occupied Europe who settled in the late 1940s or more recent refugees from Poland and Hungary. The community is Ashkenazi with about 8000 living in Stockholm, 2500 in Gothenburg and 2–3000 in Malmö. There are small communities in Boras, Norrkoping, Vaxjo, Uppsala and Lund, and isolated individuals living in other parts of the country. Most Jews are relatively prosperous, either self-employed or in the professions.

Legal Status
Until 1952 the Jewish community was classified as an institution of public law and membership was compulsory. Its status changed to that of a private voluntary organisation where an earnings-related membership fee is voluntary. Only civil marriages are recognised by the state. *Shechita* is not permitted in Sweden.

Communal Organisation
The Judiske Forsamlingarnas Sverige Centralråd (Central Council of the Jewish Communities) in Sweden has *de facto* government recognition and is affiliated to the World Jewish Congress.

Stockholm, Malmö and Gothenburg have their own Jewish community organisations (Judiska Församlingen). The largest, in Stockholm, elects a

25-member assembly every three years, which in turn elects a nine-member executive board. The community members vote for party lists and not for individuals. Three parties have participated in recent elections: Liberal Judaism, Jewish Union (Zionist and traditionalist) and Jewish Unity (conservative).

There are 27 Jewish organisations and a number of B'nai B'rith Lodges are in operation. Judaica House is the premises of Maccabi, WIZO, the Zionist Federation, the Keren Kayemet and Keren Hayesod.

The three women's organisations include WIZO, with 2500 members (1300 in Stockholm); the socially-concerned Women's League, with 430 members; and Emunah, a group of Orthodox Jewish women. Amongst the activities organised by Stockholm's seven youth groups are a community-run summer camp for 220 children, camps in Israel and Scandinavia organised by Habonim and B'nai Akiva, and sporting functions for all ages arranged by Maccabi.

Other community centres and youth clubs exist in Gothenburg, Lund and Malmö. Lund's Jewish centre also houses the Scandinavian Resource Centre for Jewish Culture and Malmö's has B'nai B'rith rooms. The university town of Uppsala has a Jewish students' organisation.

Religious Life
Of Stockholm's three synagogues, two are Orthodox, and one, the Great Synagogue, Conservative. There are two rabbis, two cantors and several doctors who act as *mohelim*.

There are two synagogues in Gothenburg (one Orthodox and one Conservative), and an Orthodox synagogue in Malmö. The university town of Lund also has a synagogue, which only holds services on Festivals. Kosher meat imported from Copenhagen is available in Gothenburg and Malmö and a range of kosher products can be bought in Stockholm. There are no kosher restaurants. Approximately 15 per cent of the community keep *kashrut*.

Education
Stockholm has two Jewish schools: a kindergarten with 5 teachers and approximately 55 children aged between 4 and 6, and the Hillel Day-School, with 21 teachers and 225 pupils aged from 7 to 13. There is no Jewish secondary school but schools provide Hebrew education in classes with a Jewish majority with the help of either teachers from the Hillel School or a rabbi. The Stockholm community holds weekly afternoon schools where about 100 pupils aged between 7 and 16 are taught by 7 teachers. The community also organises study groups for adults. Slightly over 50 per cent of all Jewish youth attend universities.

Cultural Activities

The Stockholm community possesses a Judaica and Hebraica Library, and a 200-year-old community archive. The Stockholm community centre, Judaica House, organises a number of activities, including an Israeli folk-dance group, sports clubs and a small Jewish bookshop. The Great Synagogue has its own choir and there is also a Hebrew circle and various activities in Yiddish.

Press

The *Judisk Kronika* (Jewish Chronicle) is published bi-monthly from Stockholm in an edition of 7000 and distributed all over Sweden. *Menorah* is published four times a year by Keren Hayesod to support the fund-raising campaign and gives information from Sweden and Israel. Stockholm also has a small Jewish publishing house founded in 1969, which primarily concentrates on translating school books and non-fiction from English and Hebrew. A weekly Jewish local radio programme is broadcast in central Stockholm. The Jewish Students' Association is responsible for its contents.

Welfare

Stockholm has a small Jewish nursing home with 30 beds and 12 full-time staff, and a home for the aged with 30 beds and 11 full-time staff. Malmö also has a home for the aged attached to the community centre.

Relations with Israel

Relations are on ambassadorial level. Sweden has an embassy in Tel Aviv and a consulate in Jerusalem. There are some 1000 Israelis living in Sweden.

Historical Sites

The Conservative Great Synagogue in Stockholm was built in 1870 and is considered one of the masterpieces of the non-Jewish architect, Frederick Scholander. Classified as a Swedish national monument, parts of its interior date back to the eighteenth century. The old City Police Station in Stockholm is on the site of the second synagogue of 1785 and the women's gallery is still extant. Other interesting synagogues are at Nybrogatan (whose entire interior came from Germany), Gothenburg and Malmö.

General Position

The position of Jews and their relations with the non-Jewish population are very satisfactory. A few very small neo-Nazi groups and antisemitic propagandists exist but there are laws against racial discrimination and against incitement to racial and religious hatred. The Chief Rabbi of

Stockholm was chairman of a 'brotherhood' organisation of Jews and Christians, which holds lectures and runs cultural and social programmes. The chairmanship rotates between Catholic, Protestant and Jewish leaders.

SWITZERLAND

Population: 6 456 000   Jewish population: 18 300

History

The first Jewish communities appeared in Switzerland during the thirteenth century but in 1348 the whole of Swiss Jewry was threatened with extermination when Jews were blamed for the rapidly spreading plague. Although communities were re-established several years later, successive expulsions ultimately limited Jewish residence to the county of Baden. Until the French revolution the only Jewish communities were in Aargau, Lengnau and Oberedingen. After the establishment of the Helvetian Republic in 1798 Jews were granted freedom of movement, residence and trade and by 1866 they were guaranteed civic and legal equality. In 1897 the first of many World Zionist Congresses was held in Basle.

During the Holocaust Switzerland sheltered about 23 000 Jewish refugees, though 10 000 further applicants were refused admission. At the end of the war most of these refugees left the country. The first plenary assembly of the World Jewish Congress, established to represent Jewish interests worldwide, was held in Geneva in 1936.

Composition of the Community

The majority of Swiss Jews are Ashkenazi. However, since the war there has been a small Sephardi immigration from the Arab world, North Africa and Turkey. The community is largely middle-class, its members increasingly employed in the specialised professions, large corporations and the civil service. There are about 25 Jewish communities, of which the largest are Zurich (6713), Geneva (4321) and Basle (2577). 58.4 per cent of Jews live in the German-speaking area, 37.6 per cent in the French, and 3.9 per cent in the Italian.

Legal Status

The communities have the status of voluntary organisations. *Shechita* is prohibited, although kosher meat may be imported. While the law passed in 1973 making it illegal to slaughter animals without anaesthetic removed

150

certain objections against *shechita* it did not remove the prohibition. The central communal organisation is exclusively entitled to import kosher meat and deals with its distribution.

Communal Organisation

The Schweizerischer Israelitischer Gemeindebund (SIG – Union of Swiss Jewish Communities), based in Zurich was founded in 1904 to deal with the problem of *shechita* prohibition. Twenty-two communities are affiliated to it and they send delegates to the annual assembly, which elects its 25-member central committee. The SIG acts as Swiss Jewry's spokesman on political and social problems, not necessarily exclusively Jewish, and has special committees for Press and Information, Religion, Culture and Youth. The individual Swiss communities, however, remain autonomous. The SIG is one of the founder members of the World Jewish Congress.

The Zionist movement is represented by the Schweizerische Zionistenverband (Zionist Federation) and a large WIZO organisation with offices in Basle, Fribourg and Zurich. The Jewish Agency and the WIZO European Head Office is in Geneva, with its Swiss Office in Zurich. The Union of Jewish Women's Societies acts as an umbrella organisation for all women's organisations. Both the Jewish National Fund and Keren Hayesod are very active. Swiss Jewry is one of the highest per capita donors for Israel, largely through the Israel Appeal.

Religious Life

There is no overall Chief Rabbinate: the communities of Basle, Geneva and Zurich have their own Chief Rabbis. The Religious Committee of the SIG supervises the distribution of kosher food and negotiates with military and educational authorities in matters of kosher food and religious holidays. It also helps in recruiting religious teachers and cantors for the smaller communities. Twenty-two communities are affiliated to SIG but 3 Liberal and 3 Orthodox remain independent.

Zurich has 1 Liberal and 3 Orthodox synagogues and a prayer room at the airport. Geneva has 1 Orthodox Ashkenazi, 1 Sephardi, and 1 Liberal synagogue. Basle has 2 Orthodox synagogues, and Lugano 1 Orthodox and 1 Conservative. There are synagogues in Baden, Berne, Biel-Bienne, Fribourg, La Chaux-de-Fonds, Lausanne, Lucerne, Vevey-Montreux, St. Gallen, Vevey and Winterthur. Despite restrictions on *shechita*, kosher food is generally available at all main centres partly because Switzerland is a major centre of tourism. Some resorts have at least one kosher hotel.

Education

There are two Jewish day schools in Zurich. Otherwise Jewish tuition is given in the religious classes of the communities, ranging from 2 to 15 hours per week. There is a Chair of Judaism at Lausanne University. Orthodox education is provided by the Beth Jacob Seminary in Lucerne and a *yeshiva* just outside Lucerne at Kriens.

Cultural Activities

The library of the Jewish community of Zurich houses a fine collection of German language Jewish books and a catalogue of Switzerland's Judaica. The only Jewish museum is in Basle.

The Youth Committee of the SIG organises summer and winter camps, and annual meetings of the smaller communities. Jewish students meet in Basle, Geneva and Zurich where there is also a ski club and discotheque. There are Jewish bookshops in Basle and Lucerne and two in Zurich.

Press

The SIG's press and information committee, which operated the 'Juna' service throughout the war, has valuable documentation on the history of that period. Today it provides information on the problems of the Middle East, the Diaspora and antisemitism. There are two weekly newspapers, the *Jüdische Rundschau*, published in Basle, and the *Israelitisches Wochenblatt* in Zurich and a monthly published in Zurich, *Das Neue Israel*.

Welfare

The principal welfare organisation, the Verband Schweizerische Jüdische Fürsorgen (VSJF – Union of Swiss Jewish Welfare Organisations), is a committee of the SIG, but operates more or less independently. The VSJF's centre at Les Berges du Leman in Vevey, offers shelter for refugees and a permanent home for the aged. Other homes for the aged are at Basle, Geneva and Lengnau.

Relations with Israel

Switzerland has full diplomatic relations at ambassadorial level. The Israeli Embassy is in Berne, and there is a Consulate General in Zurich. Switzerland is one of the few countries to have a friendship association in Israel.

Historical Sites

The most important historic site is the Stadt-Casino in Basle, where the First Zionist Congress was held in 1897. In the little villages of Lengnau and Endlingen, where the Jews resettled in the seventeenth century, there are ancient synagogues.

The international Jewish organisations, AJDC, HIAS, OSE and the World
Jewish Congress, maintain offices in Geneva. The International Council of
Jewish Women has its headquarters in Geneva. The community is affluent
and has strong links with Israel. Antisemitism is virtually non-existent but
there is a high intermarriage rate and increasing assimilation.

SYRIA

Population: 9 840 000   Jewish population: 4000

History
Before the Assyrian conquest of the eighth century BCE there was
conflict between the Aramean Kingdoms in what is now Syria and
the Kingdoms of Israel and Judah. After the Greek conquest of the
fourth century BCE Jewish communities in the region were subjected to
hostility, as they were later under the Byzantines, when many synagogues
were turned into churches. Following the Arab conquest of the seventh
century CE, Jews came under the usual Muslim restrictions.

According to Benjamin of Tudela who visited the country in 1173 there
were 3000 Jews in Damascus itself, 1500 in Aleppo, and 2000 in Palmyra.
In the late fifteenth and early sixteenth centuries, Jewish refugees from
Spain settled in the country and from the sixteenth century to the end
of the First World War Syria was part of the Ottoman Empire.

In 1840, Damascus was the scene of a notorious blood libel,
involving the arrest and forced confession of a number of leading Jews
in connection with the disappearance of a superior of the Franciscan
monastery. An international outcry ensued.

After the French occupation of 1918 Jews were given equal rights, but
growing anti-Zionist feeling led to outbreaks of violence. In 1945 the Great
Synagogue in Aleppo was looted, prayer books were burnt in the street and
in December 1947 fierce anti-Jewish rioting caused the deaths of many Jews
and the destruction of much Jewish property. In August 1949, a bomb was
thrown into a synagogue on the sabbath, killing 12 Jews and injuring 26.

Eventually the Jewish Community Council in Damascus was dissolved
and a special Government Committee on Jewish Affairs was set up. Many
Jews emigrated, mainly to Israel until a ban was imposed on emigration.
After the Six-Day War the situation deteriorated still further, with a
pogrom in Kamishli in which 57 Jews were killed, and the imposition
of more anti-Jewish restrictions.

As a dictatorship, Syria has a poor human rights record, but
the status of Jews is considerably worse than that of the rest of the
population. A particularly onerous code of restrictions came into force

in 1967, including a total ban on emigration; prohibition of movement of more than 3 kilometres from place of residence without special permit; a 10 p.m. curfew; education restricted to six years' elementary schooling without special permission; prohibition on working for the government and on the ownership of a radio or a telephone. The property of deceased Jews is confiscated, descendants having to pay for its use and Jewish identity cards carry the word 'Jew' (*Moussawi*). Some of these restrictions (particularly those relating to the transfer of property) were relaxed in 1976 but were re-imposed in 1979.

Present Position
The Jews of Syria are Sephardim, with some 3000 or more living in Damascus, about 700 in Aleppo and 200 in Kamishli in the extreme north-east. In all three cities, they are segregated in ghettoes. In 1943, there were some 29 770 Jews in Syria. Damascus now has a Jewish Community Council and a rabbinical court with a rabbi. The El Ferenje Synagogue has about 50 to 60 worshippers daily. There are two schools in Damascus, the Maimonides School and the Alliance School, both with non-Jewish pupils and a part-Muslim staff.

TAIWAN

Population: 19 135 000   Jewish population: 150

History
The Taiwan Jewish community was founded in 1975 by a group of businessmen and employees of Israeli and American companies working in the country.

Composition of the Community
The community is almost entirely concentrated in the capital Taipei. It is made up of the transient workers and their families, mainly from the USA and Israel.

Legal Status
The community is registered with the state but not considered a religious entity. Only civil marriages are recognised, *shechita* is permitted but not practised.

Communal Organisation
The community is headed by a president and an executive board of nine members elected annually by a general meeting. Each member of the board is a chairman of a special sub-committee dealing with the separate areas of the community's activities.

Religious Life

The community has no rabbi, *shochet* or *mohel*. When one is required he is brought from Hong Kong or Japan. The only synagogue is in the community centre in Taipei. Services are conducted by members in turn and are essentially Conservative in style. There is no Jewish cemetery.

Education

About 18 pupils attend a Hebrew school which has two classes. The school employs two professional teachers and one voluntary assistant, and meets for two hours every Sunday morning.

Cultural Activities

Most cultural activities are held in the Taipei community centre which houses the small synagogue, library, classrooms and various recreation facilities. Organised events include communal brunches every alternate Sunday and cultural meetings every Tuesday evening.

Press

A community bulletin is published monthly.

Relations with Israel

No official relations exist between Israel and Taiwan. However, unofficially there is an exchange of representatives as well as trade and defence links. Taiwan has close ties with Saudi Arabia and other Islamic states.

General Position

Jews in Taiwan maintain fairly good relations with the native Chinese. The community is not wealthy and struggles to survive financially, dependng on membership fees and fund-raising activities. The centre in Taipei is leased on a short-term basis.

THAILAND

Population: 50 800 000   Jewish population: 200

History

The community was established only recently, the first communal buildings being opened in 1966.

Composition of the Community

Very few of the resident Jewish population are Thai nationals. They are mainly Sephardim of Syrian and Lebanese origin and Ashkenazim from Eastern Europe and Shanghai. Apart from Israeli embassy staff, there are some Jewish temporary residents, a number of Americans, and a group of Orthodox Iranians and Afghans. The majority of the community live in the capital Bangkok.

Communal Organisation
The Jewish Association of Thailand (JAT) organises all aspects of communal life. Its status is that of a secular and private body as Judaism in Thailand is registered as an association rather than as a religion. The JAT is affiliated to the World Jewish Congress.

Religious Life
Although there is no rabbi, the community has a modern synagogue where the JAT holds a sabbath service once a month. A separate group of Orthodox Sephardim conduct their own daily and sabbath services in a converted house which serves as a synagogue. While there is no permanent *shochet*, kosher meat is imported via the Jewish community in Singapore.

Education
There are very few young children in the community and no organised Jewish education. The children of Israeli embassy staff receive private tuition in Hebrew.

Relations with Israel
Israel has a resident ambassador in Bangkok and Thailand has an embassy in Tel Aviv. Relations are good and a number of Israelis have come to work in the country.

General Position
This is a small community of mixed origin organised around its own synagogue and community centre. Relations with the Thai government are good and there is no antisemitism.

TRINIDAD AND TOBAGO

Population: 1 216 000   Jewish population: 10

History
Organised Jewish life in Trinidad began in 1930. In 1938 refugees from Central Europe arrived and more came during the war years. By the end of the war there was a vigorous community of some 800 people. However, the goal of many of the refugee immigrants had originally been the United States, Canada or Venezuela, and when the opportunity came, they went to those countries. Many also followed their children who had

been sent abroad for education, with the result that the community has steadily declined.

Composition of the Community
The community is Ashkenazi of mainly Central European origin. No births or marriages have been recorded for a long time and most of the population are in their seventies or eighties. All live in the capital, Port of Spain.

Communal Organisation
The few remaining Jews are still informally grouped around what was the central body, the Jewish Religious Society. Contributions are still collected on behalf of Israel, but the WIZO closed down for lack of members.

Religious Life
There is no *minyan* and therefore no synagogue or services.

Relations with Israel
The Israeli ambassador to Venezuela in Caracas is Israel's non-resident ambassador.

TUNISIA

Population: 7 205 000   Jewish population: 3500

History
Jews are known to have lived in Latin Carthage c.200 CE but they settled in the country long before then. The community declined after the Byzantine conquest in 535. Under Muslim rule in the seventh century, Jews established what was later to become a flourishing community in Kairouan, the new capital of the province of Ifriqiya. It became the centre of Jewish learning in the West during the Gaonic period and its leader was given the title Nagid (Princely Leader). However, from the mid-eleventh century Muslim repression increased and Jews were finally banned from living in what was considered to be a Muslim holy city. This ban remained in force until the late nineteenth century. Elsewhere in Tunisia life became increasingly difficult during the Almohad rule in the twelfth century with many Jews forced to convert to Islam. During the short period of Spanish conquest (1535–74) persecution increased.

The Jews in Muslim Tunisia lived as *dhimmis* until the 1837 accession of the more liberal Ahmed Bey. His cousin, Mohammed, succeeded him in 1855, and continued many of his liberal practices. However, he also established a special religious court which had the right to sentence a Jew to death for blaspheming against Islam solely on the evidence given by a Muslim. When a Jew was executed on such grounds there was an outcry against the injustice. The French intervened and promulgated the Fundamental Pact of 1857 which modernised the laws and provided for a Jewish assessor in any such trial. In 1881, Tunisia came under French protection and, in 1910, Jews were allowed to acquire French citizenship. However, in 1917 the Jewish quarter was looted by Tunisian troops.

From November 1940 Tunisia came under Vichy rule and antisemitic and discriminatory laws were imposed on Jews. Nazi Germany occupied Tunisia from November 1942 until May 1943. During this time Jews were subject to confiscation of property, deportation and execution. Some 4000 were sent to labour camps and others to European concentration camps.

After Tunisia achieved independence in 1956, the position of the Jews deteriorated again. The Rabbinical Tribunal was abolished on 27 September 1957 and on 11 July 1958 the Community Councils of Tunis and Sfax were dissolved, although individual Jews continued to hold prominent positions. With the outbreak of the Six-Day War on 5 June 1967, anti-Jewish rioting broke out and the Great Synagogue of Tunis was burnt down. Subsequently, however, Tunisia's President arranged compensation to the community, the re-building of the synagogue and punishment of the rioters.

There has been a steady decline in the Jewish population of Tunisia: from 105 000 in 1949, it fell to 67 000 in 1959 and to a mere 8000 in 1973. Today the population numbers approximately 3500. Recent emigration has been to Israel and to France.

Composition of the Community
More than half the Jewish population is concentrated in the city of Tunis, with two other important communities on the island of Djerba (Hara Kebira and Hara Sghira). About 200 Jews live in the Sousse-Monastir region on the Gulf of Hammamet, and there are other small communities scattered in various towns. About 2 per cent are affluent, 30 per cent are middle class and 68 per cent working class.

Legal Status
The individual community committees are appointed and accepted by the government. Jews are not compelled by law to belong to the community which is entitled to levy taxes on kosher meat and wine. *Shechita* is permitted.

Communal Organisation
Each community has a committee appointed by the government. Tunis had an active Zionist movement which closed down with independence in 1956.

Religious Life
The chief rabbinate is in Tunis. There is a second rabbi in Djerba and four other rabbis in the country. Most Jews observe *kashrut*.

Education
Djerba has one full-time kindergarten with 25 children. There are six primary schools: three in Tunis, two on Djerba and one at Zarzis on the coast just south of Djerba. There are two full-time Jewish secondary schools in Tunis and two on Djerba. Approximately 350 children receive part-time Jewish education. Religious education is organised by *yeshivot* in Tunis and Djerba (the *yeshiva* in Tunis being run by the Lubavitch movement). A very small percentage of Jewish youth receive their higher education in Paris.

Cultural Activities
The community does not have specific organisations for cultural activities but meetings are regularly held in the home of the Lubavitch rabbi. Some 200 children go to camp every summer.

Press
Le Réveil Juif was once an important Zionist paper published in Sfax and distributed in Tunisia, Algeria, Morocco and France. Today, however, there is no Jewish press.

Welfare
There are two homes for the aged with a total of 80 beds, and an outpatients clinic in Tunis. Much of the help given to the needy in Tunisia is organised by the American Joint Distribution Committee which has a branch in Tunis.

Relations with Israel
Although Tunisia is the home of the Arab League, and in 1982 became the headquarters of the pro-Arafat faction of the PLO, it has always been one of the most moderate of the Arab states. The former President, Habib Bourgiba, called for Arab recognition of Israel and allowed emigration to Israel. Since 1967, however, Tunisia has moved steadily closer to the rest of the Arab world and this process was hastened when Israeli planes attacked PLO headquarters in Tunis in 1985. Between 1948 and 1972, some 56 000 Tunisian Jews emigrated to Israel.

159

Historical Sites

The ancient El Ghriba synagogue still stands in the village of Hara Sghira on Djerba. There are other interesting synagogues on Djerba and in the southern town of Medenine. The beautiful Zarzis synagogue in the south was burnt down in October 1983, probably by Palestinians. Colourful rituals include the celebration of Jewish Holy Days and the annual Lag B'Omer pilgrimage on Djerba. The Bardo Museum in Tunis has a section devoted to Jewish ritual objects.

General Position

What was once a great Jewish community has sadly declined. Most educated Tunisian Jews have emigrated to France. The community's confidence in their safety was shaken when in 1985 Jews leaving the Djerba synagogue were shot and killed by a security guard.

TURKEY

Population: 51 429 000   Jewish population: 23 000

History

There were settlements of Jews in the area of Asia Minor from ancient times. However, the first important community with a synagogue under Turkish rule was established at Bursa in 1326. In the fifteenth century the Turks advanced to capture Salonica (1430) and Constantinople (1453), both of which had Jewish communities, and the Jews were much better treated under the Turks than under the Byzantines.

Following the expulsion from Spain in 1492, Sultan Bayazit II (1481–1512) invited the Jews to settle in the Ottoman Empire. Bayazit later appointed one of the refugees, Joseph Hamon, as his personal physician. The influx of Sephardim altered the nature of the community and the original 'Romaniot' Jews were swamped by the newcomers and totally absorbed, so that the language of Turkish Jews became Ladino. The few Ashkenazi immigrants who came later were similarly absorbed. This led to the communities of Constantinople (Istanbul), Adrianople (Edirne) and Smyrna (Izmir) developing and flourishing. However, restrictions on the Jews became more severe during the seventeenth century, until the issuing of the Imperial Firman of 1856 which made all non-Muslims equal to Muslims.

The break-up of the Ottoman Empire after the First World War and the secular reforms of Atatürk caused some problems for the Jewish community but they also ensured that Muslims and non-Muslims were on equal footing in their dealings with the authorities. In

1938, after Atatürk's death, many of the religious restrictions were eased. During the Second World War, when Turkey was pro-Axis, Jews were unfairly taxed causing bankruptcy and arrests. With the approaching defeat of the Axis, a law was passed in 1944 releasing all defaulters and cancelling all unpaid tax. Between 1948 and 1950, large numbers (around 37 000) of the community emigrated to Israel. With the general economic recovery of the country, the position of the Jewish community improved but the violence of the late 1970s caused further emigration.

Composition of the Community
The community is approximately 95 per cent Sephardi and 5 per cent Ashkenazi. Figures for the Jewish community are only estimates as any form of community census is illegal.

About 20 000 Jews live in Istanbul, 1500 in Izmir and smaller communities in Bursa (200), Ankara (100) and Edirne (80). The few hundred Jews who lived in the towns of Adana, Mersin and Gaziantep in South East Anatolia left because of the threat of assimilation through demographic decline.

Turkish Jews are engaged in commerce and live in urban areas. The majority are self-employed or in managerial or clerical posts with a small number of lawyers, doctors, dentists, engineers and architects. The community is mostly upper-middle or middle class, with some 8 per cent needing welfare assistance.

Legal Status
Synagogues are classified as religious foundations and as such come under the General Directorate of Vakifs which exercises some financial control. Although children are registered at birth as Jews, it is not compulsory to belong to the community. The community cannot levy taxes but may request donations.

Communal Organisation
The structure of the Turkish Jewish community differs very considerably from that of most other Diaspora communities and in its present form is based on an Ottoman imperial writ of 1864, establishing the method of election of the Chief Rabbi and of the rabbinical and lay councils who assist him. There are central bodies that look after synagogal problems and fund-raising for communal needs. However, as a result of the millet system it is the Chief Rabbi who is the head of the community. Izmir though has a Jewish community council of its own.

There are no Zionist organisations because Turkish citizens are not allowed to belong to international organisations.

Religious Life

The head of the community is the Haham Bashi or Chief Rabbi. The title of Haham Bashi dates from 1453. He is accepted by the entire rabbinate community. The Karaite minority in Turkey number about 100 and do not accept the authority of the Chief Rabbi but consult him occasionally. There is a Beth Din.

Because of the recent decline of the population, a number of synagogues are not functioning. However, some 15 Sephardi synagogues are in use in Istanbul, as well as one Ashkenazi Orthodox and one Karaite. There are two synagogues in Izmir and one in Ankara.

Education

Istanbul has a primary school with about 150 pupils and a secondary school with over 300 pupils. In Izmir there is a primary school with some 50 pupils.

Cultural Activities

Although Turkish law does not permit ethnically or religiously-based organisations, there are several sporting and recreational associations with a predominantly Jewish membership. However, non-Jews are entitled to be members. In effect, this means that there are four Jewish clubs in Istanbul as well as a community centre and four Jewish youth clubs.

Press

Shalom is the only Jewish paper in Turkey. Primarily in Ladino, it does have articles in Turkish. (Under the Ottomans, Jews did not normally speak Turkish, only Ladino, which remains the language of the older generation, although young people now speak Turkish as their first language.)

A community calendar exists and is distributed free to all those who have made charitable donations to the welfare bodies.

Welfare

Jewish hospitals exist in Istanbul (110 beds) and Izmir (50 beds). The two cities each have a home for the aged. There are also a number of welfare societies, providing clothes for needy school children and for the sick and poor.

Relations with Israel

Turkey keeps a legation in Tel Aviv and a consulate in Jerusalem. Israel has a legation in Ankara and a consulate-general in Istanbul. Nearly 40 000 Turkish Jews have settled in Israel since 1948.

Historical Sites
Old synagogues, notably the Ahrida, are to be found in the Balat area. Other old synagogues are at Yanbol and Cana. At Cana is the prison of the old Beth Din while at Ahrida the headquarters of the medieval Jewish police can be seen.

General Position
The Turkish community has declined, largely through emigration and continues to do so as marriage rates fall. In the past, the community has been deprived of active involvement in world Jewry through the banning of the affiliation of Turkish groups to foreign organisations. However, since 1983 this has changed as the community can now send observers to World Jewish Congress meetings.

The community suffered a serious blow in 1986 when a terrorist attack on the Neve Shalom synagogue in Istanbul resulted in the death of 21 worshippers. The rise of militant Islam has brought problems for the community although there are laws against racial and religious discrimination.

UNION OF SOVIET SOCIALIST REPUBLICS

Population: 276 290 000   Jewish population: 1 810 876

History
The earliest Jewish settlements in the Roman period were in the southern Ukraine and the Crimea and the existence of groups further north was reported in the Middle Ages. In general however, Jews were not allowed into Russia and were expelled from Russian-occupied territory. But in 1795, after large areas of Poland and Lithuania were annexed, Russia acquired a large Jewish population.

Lithuania had a Jewish population in the fourteenth and fifteenth centuries, centred on the cities of Vilna, Grodno and Kovno. A sixteenth-century charter granted them a monopoly on trade and tax farming. A self-governing Jewish body, the Council of the Land of Lithuania, was formed in 1623. From the seventeenth century Lithuania became a great centre of Jewish scholarship with the city of Vilna known as 'the Lithuanian Jerusalem'.

In 1835 Jews were officially restricted to the western provinces of the Russian Empire. This restriction remained in force until 1915 and was legally abolished in the Revolution of 1917. The area, known as the Pale of Settlement, included the whole of Russian Poland, Latvia, Lithuania, Byelorussia, the Ukraine and the Crimea, except for the cities of Kiev, Nikolaev, Sebastopol and Yalta, which were barred to Jews without a special permit. Some Jews did live outside the Pale, but mostly without permission.

In 1827 notorious regulations were issued forcing the Jewish community to supply conscripts who had to serve 25 years in the Russian army where they were subjected to attempts to convert them to Christianity. Conditions slightly improved under Alexander II (1855–81), during whose rule Jews were admitted into Moscow, but after his assassination in 1881 and Alexander III's accession (1881–94), anti-Jewish pogroms began, culminating in 1891 with the expulsion of Jews from Moscow.

The antisemitic May Laws of 1882 combined with the rapid expansion of the Jewish population and economic depression produced one of the greatest migrations in Jewish history, as Russian and Polish Jews in their thousands travelled across the world to Britain and the USA. Meanwhile a flowering of Hebrew literature occurred among remaining Russian Jewry.

At the outbreak of the First World War, the Jewish population of Russia, including Poland, numbered 5 600 000. The 1917 Revolution brought civil war, resulting in the abolition, on 2 April, of anti-Jewish legislation. Two years later at the establishment of the Soviet regime non-Communist Jewish institutions were abolished and antisemitism was made a criminal offence. But the Civil War was accompanied by pogroms in the Ukraine in which over 100 000 Jews were murdered. After the restoration of order, economic conditions improved but religious practices were restricted and Zionism was gradually suppressed.

In 1941 the Nazis invaded the USSR, occupying Ukraine, Byelorussia and the Crimea, the site of the old Pale. Although about 300 000 Jews escaped to safety beyond the Volga, others were trapped and fell into the hands of 'killing squads' known as Einsatzgruppen. The total number of Jews murdered in the German conquered areas of the Soviet Union (post-1939 borders) was 2 350 000. Jews played an important part in the fight against the Nazi invasion; about half a million served in the Red Army during the war and it is estimated that up to 20 000 were active in the partisan movement.

After the war the Soviet government attempted to suppress Yiddish culture and many leading intellectuals 'disappeared'. The antisemitic campaign of Stalin's last years culminated in the 1952 'Doctors' Plot'. A group of Jewish doctors were charged with treason but were released after Stalin's death. Later, pressure eased slightly, but in general Jewish cultural life continued to be heavily suppressed.

Composition of the Community
About 87 per cent of Soviet Jews are Ashkenazi and the remainder may be described as 'Oriental' rather than Sephardi. The Ashkenazim are further divided into *zapadniki* (Westerners) and 'Core Jews'; the *zapadniki* living in the provinces of the USSR annexed during the Second

World War and the 'Core Jews' being the pre-war inhabitants of Russia. The former are more intensely Jewish, with many speaking Yiddish, and the latter are more integrated into Russian society.

The 'Orientals' comprise three groups: the Georgian-speaking Jews who are culturally cohesive and live separately from other Georgians; the so-called 'Mountain Jews' of Daghestan on the Caspian coast who speak Tat, a form of Azeri Turkish; the largest group, the Bukharans, who live principally in the cities of Tashkent, Samarkand and Bukhara in the Uzbek SSR and speak Tadzhik, a language closely related to Persian.

Soviet Jews live mainly in urban areas. According to the 1970 census (equivalent data of the 1979 census are not available), the largest settlements are in Moscow (251 000), Leningrad (162 000), Kiev (152 000), Odessa (120 000), Karkhov (80 000), Tashkent (56 000), Kishinev (50 000), Minsk (47 000), Sverdlovsk (40 000), Riga and Lvov (25 000 each), and Kazan and Zhitomir (20 000 each).

The highest percentage of Jews in any Soviet republic is to be found in the Moldavian SSR, formerly Bessarabia, on the Rumanian border, where the 80 127 Jews constitute 2 per cent of the population. In the Ukraine, the 634 154 Jews constitute 1.3 per cent and in Byelorussia, with 135 000, 1.4 per cent. Jews constituted 0.7 per cent of the population of the USSR as a whole according to the 1979 census which gave them a total population of 1 810 876. There are indications that there has been a further numerical decline. According to the 1959 census, Jews had constituted 1.1 per cent of the population, with a total of 2 267 814. The so-called Jewish Autonomous *Oblast* of Birobidzhan in Eastern Siberia has a Jewish population of only 10 166.

Soviet Jewry is highly concentrated in the upper socio-economic levels of Soviet society, even being described as a scientific and technical elite, strongly represented among scientific workers, lawyers, doctors, artists, writers and journalists. Although the Jewish minority comprises only 0.7 per cent of the population, some 15 per cent of all Soviet physicians are Jews; 4.1 per cent of all employees with higher education are Jews, as are 1.4 per cent of employees with special secondary education. Jews are no longer to be found in any numbers in the party and state apparatus, the army and the diplomatic corps.

Legal Status

The USSR, like some other East European countries, has a dual concept of nationality: *grazhdanstvo* (literally 'citizenship') and *natsionalnost* (literally 'nationality'). Jews are legally classified as a nationality in this second sense, which refers to ethnic origin, but unlike other Soviet nationalities, they lack a territorial base, as Birobidzhan has failed as a Jewish autonomous region. Compulsory internal passports state the nationality (*natsionalnost*) of their

165

owner. Children of Jewish parents are registered as Jews on their passports but a child of mixed parents may choose to which nationality he or she wishes to belong.

Religious practice is permitted in the USSR, although frowned upon, and 'believers' of groups of 20 are permitted to form religious societies (*dvatsatka*). Each Jewish *dvatsatka* is under joint control of the local Soviet and Council for the Affairs of Religious Cults, which appoints and dismisses members of the synagogue's governing board. The synagogue is administered by the *dvatsatka* under a lease agreement with the local Soviet. An argument often used by the authorities for closing synagogues is that the number of members has fallen below 20. There are also *minyanim*, groups functioning without registration, though under Soviet law, unofficial prayer groups are permitted providing the authorities receive notice of each service.

Communal Organisation
There is no central Jewish body and no organised community. The post-revolutionary party controlled Jewish sections of the local administration (*Eevsektsiya*) were disbanded by Stalin in 1930. Today the only officially recognised groups are the local *dvatsatka*s whose members represent a very small proportion of Soviet Jewry and have no official links with each other. There are no other Jewish organisations.

Religious Life
There is no overall religious body but there are an estimated 61 synagogues and about 300 *minyanim*. A 1979 semi-official Soviet estimate of 60 000 observant Jews is probably too low. There is no Chief Rabbi. The principal rabbi of the more important of Moscow's two synagogues is sometimes referred to by the Soviet authorities as the 'Chief Rabbi' of Moscow, but this is an unofficial title with no practical meaning. Jewish religious books are very rarely printed in the USSR and are difficult to obtain from overseas. Ritual objects are not manufactured in the country and are unobtainable. At Passover, *matzot* are baked, but supplies are often insufficient and their import has from time to time been prohibited.

Education
There are no Jewish schools or separate Jewish educational institutions of any kind in the USSR. A very small number of Soviet rabbinical students were trained in Budapest during the 1970s and 1980s. An attempt is being made by the authorities to ban the teaching of Hebrew, although this ban is unconstitutional. The 'unofficial' classes in existence run the risk of police harassment as do private courses on Jewish history and similar subjects.

Although the Jews are one of the best educated of the national minorities,

166

the number of Jewish students has been declining proportionately faster than the decline in Jewish population. The 1970 figure of 512 students per 10 000 of the Jewish population was reduced to 300 per 10 000 in 1979. This may be caused by discrimination in university admission.

Cultural Activities

Most Jewish theatre companies have amateur status, apart from the Moscow Jewish Dramatic Ensemble (formed in 1961) and the Jewish Musical Chamber Theatre (formed in 1978 and officially based in Birobidzhan). Both of these professional companies are without permanent premises and the number of performances they are permitted to give is severely limited, especially in areas of Jewish concentration. Other theatres include the Vilnius Jewish People's Theatre, the Birobidzhan Yiddish People's Theatre, the Kishinev Jewish People's Theatre, and a Jewish Music Hall company in Moldavia. Regulations affecting these companies vary according to region – for instance, they are barred from Latvia and do not perform in Leningrad. A small number of Yiddish books and translations from Yiddish into Russian are published. Very occasionally an original Russian novel with a Jewish theme also appears. There are known to be a number of sculptors and painters who use Jewish themes. The Sholem Aleichem Museum is in Pereyaslav-Khmelnitsky.

In recent years numerous unofficial attempts by Jewish activists have been made to hold seminars on Jewish cultural subjects and Jewish refusenik scientists have held scientific seminars and conferences in private homes. There are no official (government-sanctioned) Jewish cultural activities, libraries, lecture courses or clubs.

Press

Two Yiddish-language Jewish periodicals are published, *Sovetish Heymland* (a monthly) and *Birobidzhaner Shtern* (five times a week). Both promote the official Communist line. The Jewish *Samizdat*, the unofficial 'underground' press, is published irregularly in Russian and in a limited number of issues.

Welfare

No separate Jewish welfare organisations exist in the USSR.

Relations with Israel

In 1948 the USSR followed the USA as the second country to recognise Israel. However, Moscow severed diplomatic relations at the time of the Six-Day War in 1967. The arrival in Israel of a Soviet Consular delegation in 1987 is an example of the recent improvement in Soviet-Israeli relations.

Many of the leaders of the State of Israel, including the first three presidents and several prime ministers have been of Russian Jewish origin as were some of the earliest pioneers including the original fourteen members of the *Bilu*. Russian Jewish settlement goes back to 1777 when 300 *Hassidim* settled in Tiberias and Safed. Between 1882 and 1948 (from the beginning of the First to the end of the Fifth *Aliya*), approximately 100 000 Jews emigrated to Palestine. After the establishment of the State of Israel to 1965 approximately 24 000 Soviet Jews settled in Israel.

For many years permission for Jews to leave Russia has been granted very sporadically. This changed in 1968 when Jews were regularly allowed to leave, only for Israel, for the purpose of reunification of families and the figures have varied considerably from year to year. In the peak year of 1979, 51 333 left, not all going to Israel, whereas in 1986 only 914 were allowed to leave. In the period between 1968 to 1986, 266 587 Jews left the Soviet Union with Israeli visas; 163 763 of these went to Israel.

New liberalisation policies introduced under Gorbachev have led to a limited increase in emigration. Thus in 1987, 8155 Jews were allowed to leave the Soviet Union. Among those granted exit visas were several of the most prominent refuseniks and activists.

General Position
Antisemitic activity was legislated against in 1917. Since then Jews have theoretically had equal rights. There are a number of reasons why this has not worked out in practice. First, antisemitism remained part of the Russian outlook. Second, atheist propaganda affected the Jewish minority differently from other national minorities because their religion is at the core of their national identity. Finally, anti-Zionist propaganda is sometimes antisemitic and based on the tsarist forgery, *The Protocols of the Elders of Zion*. It is also hard for the Jews to maintain their identity and culture when they have no geographical base and are a minority wherever they have settled.

The 1979 census indicated that the use of Yiddish or other Jewish languages as mother tongues had fallen to 14.2 per cent of the Jewish population. The difficulty in obtaining books on Jewish culture and the restrictions on the teaching of Hebrew, have both contributed to the decreasing Jewish knowledge of the average Russian Jew. Russian Jewry is the only Jewish community in the world prohibited from having organisational contacts with Jews in the rest of the world.

The marked decline in the Jewish population from 2 267 814 in the 1959 census to 1 810 876 in the 1979 census has been caused by a combination of ageing, emigration, assimilation and mixed marriage.

World Jewry's support for Soviet Jewry has undoubtedly contributed to the successful emigration of about a quarter of a million

Jews but its success has been limited in modifying internal Soviet policy.

Soviet Jewry lacks any central organisation and with its declining population, assimilation and difficulty in obtaining access to Jewish culture is likely to continue to decline.

UNITED KINGDOM

Population: 56 376 800   Jewish population: 330 000

History

By the middle of the twelfth century there were Jewish communities in most large cities in England. The first recorded blood libel occurred in Norwich in 1144 and anti-Jewish riots began in 1189. In York, the entire Jewish community met voluntary death in order to escape massacre. In 1290 the English medieval Jewish community was expelled by Edward I. The present community dates back to the 1656 negotiations between Rabbi Manasseh ben Israel of Amsterdam and Oliver Cromwell which resulted in Dutch Sephardim being admitted into Britain. A small number of Ashkenazim followed in 1692. Immigrants from Central Europe arrived in the eighteenth century, many of them settling in London or in the South and West of England and eventually becoming merchants in the South Coast ports. From 1760, representatives of the Ashkenazi congregations began to act with the *deputados* of the Sephardim as a watch committee which eventually became the London Committee of Deputies of British Jews. This later included representatives of the provincial and colonial congregations.

Immigration continued throughout the nineteenth century. Full emancipation was achieved in 1858 when Lionel de Rothschild took his seat in Parliament. Following the May laws of 1882 in Russia, large numbers of Jews arrived in the United Kingdom, some only intending to use it as a transit point for the United Statess. However, many remained. Immigration was only curtailed by the Aliens Act of 1905. After 1933 German and Central European refugees arrived in England, with more following after the war. More recently Jews have come from Aden and other Middle East countries, South Africa and Rhodesia.

The Anglo-Jewish community was instrumental in negotiations over the development of the Jewish National Home in Palestine, the Balfour Declaration having been issued in 1917. The community remained involved in the fate of Palestine throughout the period of the British Mandate.

Composition of the Community

Some 97 per cent are Ashkenazi of whom about 75 per cent are descended from the Russian Jews who immigrated between 1882 and 1905, the remainder being descendants of eighteenth- and early nineteenth-century immigrants and refugees of the inter-war and post-war years. The few descendants of seventeenth-century Sephardi immigrants remain active in communal leadership. The majority of Sephardim are post-war immigrants from the Middle East.

About two-thirds of British Jewry live in Greater London (240 000), with large communities in Manchester (35 000), Leeds (12 000), Glasgow (11 000), Brighton and Hove (12 000), Birmingham (5500), Liverpool (5000) and Southend (5000) and small ones throughout the United Kingdom.

Legal Status

The communities have the status of private associations, but the Board of Deputies has *de facto* government recognition as the representative of British Jewry and is consulted on relevant legislation. Together with the Anglo-Jewish Association, it has the right to present addresses and petitions to the Crown. It also appoints Marriage Secretaries to solemnise synagogue marriages which are recognised in civil law. The Chief Rabbi holds a position in the state similar to that of the Roman Catholic Archbishop. *Shechita* is permitted.

Communal Organisation

The Board of Deputies (full title, the London Committee of Deputies of British Jews) has over 600 deputies, elected mainly by synagogues, and a number of organisations which are entitled to appoint deputies. The deputies elect the various committees, honorary officers and the president. The Board maintains various departments: Defence; Israel; Foreign Affairs; Education; Law and Parliamentary; Public Relations; Central Lecture Committee; Shechita; and a Community Research Unit concentrating on statistical and demographic studies. The Board also works closely with the National Council for Soviet Jewry. The Board of Deputies became the British constituent of the World Jewish Congress in 1975, a function previously filled by the WJC British Section.

Zionist groups are represented by the Zionist Federation (founded 1898). In 1983 Herut and the General Zionists withdrew and combined with the Mizrachi Federation to form the National Zionist Council. The World Zionist Organisation maintains an office which administers an *aliya* department.

The leading fund-raising organisation is the Joint Israel Appeal which is run by a team of professionals divided into profession-based committees. The Jewish National Fund (Keren Kayemet le Yisrael) has existed longer and works for more specific projects. Zionist women's groups include the Federation of Women Zionists (WIZO) (with 20 000 members, one of the largest Jewish organisations in Britain), British Na'amat (formerly Pioneer Women) and Emunah (Mizrachi Women). The League of Jewish Women is also active in the community. B'nai B'rith maintains a network of lodges organised in the District of Great Britain and Ireland and is separate from the European Continental District.

Religious Life
The major body is the United Synagogue (founded 1870) which appoints the Chief Rabbi and maintains his office and the Beth Din. The United Synagogue is Orthodox as are the large majority of synagogues in the London area. The provincial Orthodox communities are independent but recognise the authority of the Chief Rabbi. The US is generally regarded as the 'established' synagogue.

More orthodox is the Federation of Synagogues (founded 1887 by East European immigrants). The principal rabbi of the Federation is known as the Rav Rashi and the Federation has its own Beth Din. Even more orthodox is the Union of Orthodox Hebrew Congregations (founded 1926). These two right-wing Orthodox groups together cover 3.5 per cent of the population. On the other wing are the Reform Synagogues of Great Britain (13.1 per cent) and the Union of Liberal and Progressive Synagogues (7.1 per cent) who share a joint Council of Reform and Liberal Rabbis.

The Sephardim have a Beth Din and *kashrut* organisations and their main body is the Spanish and Portuguese Jews' Congregation, founded in 1657 and the oldest such organisation in the United Kingdom. Other Sephardi congregations are the Aden Jews' Congregation, and the Eastern Jewry Community. The Anglo-Jewish community has the highest level of synagogue affiliation in the Diaspora (85 per cent) and of Orthodox synagogue membership (about 80 per cent). About 50 per cent of the population keep *kashrut*.

Education
Anglo-Jewry has a very highly developed school system, run in the main by the Zionist Federation Educational Trust and the Jewish Educational Development Trust, the latter founded in 1972. England's Jewish schools include 36 nursery schools, 29 primary schools, 13 secondary day schools and 3 middle schools. Carmel College (founded 1948) in Oxfordshire, and Polack's House (founded 1878) at Clifton College in Bristol both provide a public school education for boarders. The ultra-Orthodox Gateshead Jewish School is also for boarders.

The most important rabbinical institute is Jews' College, which educates rabbis for the United Synagogue and awards degrees from London University. Parallel institutions are the Leo Baeck College, for

Reform and Liberal training, and the Montefiore College for Sephardim. There are six *yeshivot* or similar rabbinical colleges, of which the most famous is the *yeshiva* at Gateshead in the North East of England.

The Oxford Centre for Postgraduate Hebrew Studies is attached to Oxford University and some other universities run courses in Jewish Studies. Most synagogues organise children's Hebrew classes under the general authority of the London Board of Jewish Education or the Chief Rabbi and United Synagogue. There are some 10 000, mostly part-time, students and a mainly part-time teaching staff of nearly 400. A network of Hillel houses in conjunction with the Union of Jewish Students provide social and cultural facilities for Jewish university students. Adult education is provided by Yakar, an institution teaching traditional Judaism to those previously estranged from their culture, and the Spiro Institute for the Study of Jewish History and Culture.

Cultural Activities

The Jewish communal headquarters at London's Woburn House contains a museum. In the West End the Ben Uri Gallery exhibits works by Jewish artists. Libraries specialising in fields of Jewish interest include the Mocatta Library, at University College, London; the Wiener Library, with research facilities on the study of Nazism and the Holocaust; the library at Jews' College; the library at the Institute of Jewish Affairs specialising in contemporary affairs. The Hebrew department of the British Library has one of the finest collections of Hebrew books in the world. At Southampton University the Parkes Library, founded by the late Revd. James Parkes, is entirely devoted to the subject of antisemitism.

The Jewish Book Council organises an annual Jewish Book Week and more recently Jewish Music Weeks have been organised by B'nai B'rith. There are approximately 24 Jewish booksellers in London and 11 in the rest of the country.

Youth Movements

The principal youth organisation is the Association of Jewish Youth (AJY) and there is a wide range of Zionist youth movements. The Union of Jewish Students is also active. Almost all Jewish organisations and some synagogues run youth groups, and Maccabi provides sports clubs all over the country. There are several Jewish choirs and a Jewish youth orchestra. The major grant-making body in this area is the Jewish Youth Fund.

Research

The leading Jewish research organisation in the Diaspora is the Institute of Jewish Affairs in London. Associated with the World Jewish Congress, it concentrates on contemporary affairs. The Institute publishes books and periodicals, runs a lecture series and holds symposia and conferences. The

172

Wiener Library, formerly a research centre on the Nazi period, now offers only library facilities. The Jewish Historical Society and the society of Jewish Studies sponsor lectures and conferences.

Press

The weekly *Jewish Chronicle*, founded in 1841, is the organ of the whole Jewish community. It covers both international and local affairs and reaches about 80 per cent of the Jewish population. The *Leeds Jewish Gazette* and the *Manchester Jewish Gazette* are its subsidiaries in the North of England. Other local publications include the *Jewish Echo* in Glasgow and the *Jewish Telegraph* published in Liverpool, Leeds and Manchester. A Jewish cultural journal, the *Jewish Quarterly*, has been published since 1953. An independent bi-annual publication, formerly published by the World Jewish Congress, is the scholarly *Jewish Journal of Sociology*. The Institute of Jewish Affairs publishes three scholarly journals: *Patterns of Prejudice* (devoted to the problems of antisemitism and racism); *Soviet Jewish Affairs* and *Christian Jewish Relations*. The IJA also publishes periodic *Research Reports* on topical subjects of Jewish concern in the international field.

The *Jewish Yearbook* and the *Jewish Travel Guide*, are both published by Jewish Chronicle Publications. The Zionist Federation publishes a monthly bulletin, the *Zionist Review*, and the internationally-based *Zionist Yearbook*. The Jewish Educational Development Trust issues a yearbook on Jewish education. Most organisations and many synagogues produce their own small publications.

You Don't Have to be Jewish, a regular half-hour radio programme sponsored by the Board of Deputies, is broadcast every Sunday morning and Thursday evening on BBC Radio London. There are also Jewish radio programmes in Brighton and other provincial towns.

Welfare

The Jewish Welfare Board (founded as the Board of Guardians in 1859), with a staff of approximately 400, runs a number of homes for the aged and is the major Jewish welfare body. World Jewish Relief (formerly the Central British Fund for Jewish Relief and Rehabilitation), supports Jewish needs abroad and also maintains its own homes. The Jewish Blind Society (founded 1819) has day centres and a residential home in London. The Norwood Foundation cares for deprived children and B'nai B'rith maintains homes and flatlets for the aged.

There are about 18 homes for the aged in London, including the independent Nightingale House in South London, and 8 outside London in Birmingham, Bournemouth, Hull, Leeds, Liverpool, Manchester,

Glasgow and Cardiff. There is a home for the physically handicapped and for the blind in Bournemouth; Manchester has a centre for the mentally handicapped.

Relations with Israel

Relations are on full ambassadorial level. Margaret Thatcher was the first British Prime Minister to come to Israel when she visited the country in 1986. The British-Israel Chamber of Commerce is concerned with trade relations. Local Anglo-Israel Friendship Leagues affiliated to the Zionist Federation have many non-Jewish members as does the Anglo-Israel Association. The main political parties and Israeli institutions also have groups of 'Friends'.

Amongst the organisations advocating Israel's cause are the Zionist Federation and the Board of Deputies. The Britain-Israel Public Affairs Committee (BIPAC) concentrates exclusively on publicity for Israel.

Historical Sites

'Old Jewries' on the site of medieval ghettos can be found in London and many towns in the provinces. The twelfth-century house of Aaron the Jew still stands in Lincoln and the Music House, from the same period, in Norwich. Clifford's Tower in York has a plaque commemorating the massacre of the Jews in 1190.

The Bevis Marks Sephardi Synagogue in London, one of the most beautiful in Europe, was built in 1701. The ancient Ashkenazi synagogues at Plymouth (built in 1752) and at Exeter (built in 1763) are still in use, the latter having a cemetery dating back to the seventeenth century. The Cheetham Hill Sephardi Synagogue in Manchester is now a Jewish museum and London's first cemetery established at the resettlement in 1657 is still in existence, although no longer in use.

General Position

Jews occupy many important positions in public life: in government, the House of Commons and the House of Lords, in the universities and cultural institutions and in commercial life. Jewish-Christian relations are on the whole very good. The Chief Rabbi, the Archbishop of Canterbury and the Cardinal Archbishop of Westminster are ex officio joint presidents of the Council of Christians and Jews which has branches throughout the country. Organised antisemitism is limited to small fringe groups on the extreme right, but more serious is the anti-Zionism of the extreme left, which on occasion has created problems for Jewish university students.

The Anglo-Jewish community is vigorous and has many functioning organisations. Assimilation and emigration are increasing, particularly outside the centres of London and Manchester. There is an estimated intermarriage rate of 25 per cent.

174

UNITED STATES OF AMERICA

Population: 236 031 000   Jewish population: 5 835 000

History
Five of Columbus's crew on the 1492 expedition were Jewish, but
the first Jewish settlement in North America was established in 1654
by 23 Dutch refugees from Brazilian Inquisition in New Amsterdam. In
1677 Jews from Surinam and Curaçao set up a community at Newport,
Rhode Island. The first synagogue was consecrated in New York on 6
April 1730. A community was established in Savannah, Georgia in 1733
and another in Philadelphia in 1745, and a smaller number of Jews settled
in Charleston in the 1740s.

In colonial America, liberty of conscience was established from the
beginning. The exception was New York where Jews were not allowed
naturalisation until 1727, and were debarred by decrees of the New York
Assembly from voting for its members in 1737. When the country became
independent in 1776, complete freedom of religion was granted, except
for Maryland (finally granted in 1816) and North Carolina (1868).

There was a steady increase in the Jewish population from 1500 at
independence to 100 000 by 1854. Twenty-five years later, after the first
major immigration wave of 150 000 German and Polish Jews in 1860–70,
the Jewish population had tripled. The great exodus from Eastern Europe
between 1882 and 1914 brought more Jews to the United States than
anywhere else, amounting to a total of 2 million immigrants. The rise
of Hitler in the 1930s led to a further influx of 250 000 German and
Austrian Jews. By 1945 the centre of world Jewry had been transferred
to the United States.

It was not until the end of the nineteenth and the beginning of the
twentieth centuries that, with the exception of B'nai B'rith established
in 1843, the great United States Jewish organisations were founded:
the Zionist Committee (1906), the Anti-Defamation League (1913), the
American Joint Distribution Committee (1914) and the American Jewish
Congress (1918).

Composition of the Community
The occupational structure of the Jewish community is as follows:
professional, 32 per cent; managerial and administrative, 39 per cent;
sales, 15 per cent; craft and skilled workers, 4 per cent. These figures
show a large number in the most elite occupations – 71 per cent – as
opposed to the figures for the US in general of 27 per cent.

The largest single concentration of Jews in the world is in the greater
New York area with 1 742 500 Jewish inhabitants. The next in size are
Los Angeles (500 000), Philadelphia (240 000), Chicago (248 000), Miami

(253 000), Boston (170 000), Washington DC (157 000), Fort Lauderdale (110 000), Newark (95 000), Baltimore (92 000), San Francisco (80 000), Cleveland (70 000), Detroit (70 000), Hollywood, Florida (60 000), St. Louis (53 000), and Pittsburgh (45 000). There are many smaller but still substantial communities. These figures show a very heavy concentration of Jewish population in the centre of the Eastern Seaboard (New York, Philadelphia, Boston, Washington DC and Baltimore), and again in the West in California.

Legal Status
Jewish communal organisations, including synagogues, are private organisations with voluntary membership. Such organisations benefit from exceptionally liberal tax laws, which exempt charity donations, and so enable the community to give great financial backing to its institutions and to Israel.

Communal Organisation
There is no single overall central body governing or representing the United States Jewish community though there are several in particular fields. American Jewry is represented in the World Jewish Congress through its American Section which compromises 32 national organisations representing the broad cross-section of American Jewish organised life. The American Section, as well as the international headquarters of the World Jewish Congress, are located in New York.

Problems concerning Israel, and to some extent other overseas issues, are dealt with by the Conference of Presidents of Major American Jewish Organisations, abbreviated to the Presidents' Conference, to which 34 national organisations are affiliated. Founded in 1955, it articulates American Jewry's views on Israel to the United States government.

The National Jewish Community Relations Advisory Council (NJCRAC), founded in 1944, is the consultative, advisory and co-ordinating council of eleven national organisations, and 108 local community relations councils. It helps to co-ordinate attitudes on domestic political problems, inter-communal and interfaith relations, defence, Israel and overseas affairs. NJCRAC is itself a member of the Presidents' Conference.

The third central body is the Council of Jewish Federations and Welfare Funds (CJFWF) which provides national and regional services to over 190 affiliated federations and covers 800 communities in the United States and Canada. Its work in welfare, fund-raising and communal organisation covers about 95 per cent of the Jewish population of the USA.

Other large national Jewish organisations with general functions include the American Jewish Congress, the B'nai B'rith and the American Jewish Committee.

The American Jewish Congress aims to foster the creative, religious and cultural survival of the Jewish people. It actively supports Israel and presses for legal action against racial discrimination and antisemitism and more generally campaigns on issues of church-state separation and civil rights.

The American Jewish Committee concerns itself with human rights in general as well as Jewish rights throughout the world. It involves itself in many aspects of Jewish affairs through its various departments, has a wide programme of publications and maintains a library of oral history. It has traditionally a slightly patrician stance.

The B'nai B'rith, a worldwide organisation, has just under 400 000 members – the largest membership of all US Jewish organisations. Its national and international headquarters are in Washington DC. An off-shoot of the B'nai B'rith, the Anti-Defamation League was created to combat antisemitism. It carries out a thorough monitoring programme and publishes detailed reports.

The tremendous and highly effective support given to Israel by United States Jewry has backing from a number of Zionist movements loosely organised in the American Zionist Federation. Included are the Zionist Organisation of America (ZOA), Hadassah and a number of party groups. The most effective political support for Israel comes through the American-Israel Public Affairs Committee (AIPAC), based in Washington DC and founded in 1954. A lobbying organisation, it works to gain the support of community leaders to apply pressure to Congress.

The National Conference on Soviet Jewry, based in New York, is a co-ordinating agency for national Jewish organisations and local community groups acting on behalf of Soviet Jewry.

The fund-raising of the American Jewish Community is effected primarily through the United Jewish Appeal (UJA). The funds are divided between Israel (80 per cent) – through the United Israel Appeal (UIA) – domestic and other overseas projects, the latter mainly through the Joint Distribution Committee (JDC) (20 per cent). These joint fund-raising activities, which help to maintain the unity of the community, are greatly facilitated by the US tax laws.

Religious Life

Only 47 per cent of the Jewish population are affiliated to synagogues. Twenty-three per cent of Jewish households belong to a Conservative congregation. The Conservative movement has a total membership of 1 500 000 and has 830 congregations affiliated to its umbrella organisation, the United Synagogue, plus another 100 not affiliated. Thirteen per cent of households belong to the Reform movement, whose approximately 750 congregations (linked to the Union of American Hebrew Congregations, UAHC) include 1 100 000 members. Nine per cent belong to one of the 2500 Orthodox congregations, most of which are affiliated to the Union of

Orthodox Jewish Congregations of America (UJOCA). Other Orthodox groupings, including hassidic groups and the Lubavitch movement, are not affiliated to the UOJCA.

A unique feature of American Judaism is Reconstructionism. Though similar to Conservative Judaism, it regards Judaism as the evolving religious civilisation of the Jewish people.

Unlike other large Diaspora communities, such as France and Britain, there is no overall religious leader and no Chief Rabbi. There are synagogues in practically every city in the United States, including several thousand in New York City alone.

Each of the main streams of American Judaism has its own rabbinical association. The Reform movement has the Central Conference of American Rabbis; Conservatives: the Rabbinical Assembly; Orthodox: the Rabbinical Council of America and the rival Rabbinical Alliance of America. The Synagogue Council of America acts as spokesman and co-ordinates the policies of national rabbinical and lay synagogal organisations of all these branches of American Judaism.

Only 28 per cent of United States Jews observe *kashrut*, but among Jews with parents or grandparents born in the United States the level has dropped to 8 per cent. There are innumerable kosher restaurants and hotels throughout the country with varying levels of supervision, and more recently Chinese kosher food has evolved. In New York State the designation kosher is under state regulation and it is an offence to sell non-kosher food as kosher.

Education
Approximately 320 full-time Jewish day-schools are run by Orthodox congregations. The Conservative United Synagogue run 65 Solomon Schechter schools, and the Reform congregations have three day-schools, most of them being supplementary. Of the total number of 372 417 children attending Jewish schools (day and supplementary), 36 per cent are in Reform schools, 20 per cent in Conservative schools and 8 per cent in inter-denominational schools.

The foremost institution of higher education is the Yeshiva University in New York, granted university status in 1945, and originally an association of colleges, the first dating back to 1886. In addition to Jewish studies, the Yeshiva University offers general studies and particularly medical studies. Another university which *de facto*, if not *de jure*, is to be regarded as Jewish is Brandeis University near Boston. It was founded in 1948, and as well as Jewish and Middle-East Studies teaches a wide range of academic subjects. Non-Jews are admitted. The University runs an institute for Near-East Studies in Israel.

The various sectors of American Judaism train rabbis at their own institutions: Orthodox rabbis are educated either at the Rabbi Isaac Elchanan Theological Seminary (part of Yeshiva University) or one of the many other *yeshivot* granting ordination. Reform rabbis are trained at the Hebrew Union College Institute of Religion in Cincinnati, Ohio, which in 1950 amalgamated with the original Hebrew Union College (founded in 1875) and the New York Jewish Institute of Religion (founded in 1922). The New York premises house the Hebrew Union School of Sacred Music. There are other branches of the college in Los Angeles and Jerusalem. Conservative rabbis are trained at the Jewish Theological Seminary of America in New York, founded in 1886. It has branches in Los Angeles and a Student Centre in Jerusalem. Its Cantors' Institute has a joint programme with Columbia University. The Reconstructionist Rabbinical College is in Philadelphia.

There are many other institutes providing Jewish education for young adults. These include the Brandeis-Bardin Institute in California, which gives short courses of Jewish cultural and spiritual training; the Cleveland College of Jewish Studies which also trains religious teachers; Dropsie University, which specialises in Hebrew and Middle Eastern Studies in a non-sectarian format; the Spertus College of Judaism in Chicago; the Rabbi Chaim Berlin Rabbinical College in Baltimore which concentrates on traditional talmudic studies. Some 350 universities throughout the country have Hebrew or Jewish Studies departments.

The American Association for Jewish Education co-ordinates its 18 affiliated national organisations and 51 affiliated bureaux of Jewish education.

Youth Movements
Most of the synagogal and Zionist organisations have youth branches, the main umbrella groups being the North American Jewish Youth Council and the American Zionist Youth Foundation. The North American Jewish Students' Network is the American affiliate of the World Union of Jewish Students. The Reform movement sponsors the National Council of Synagogue Youth. The Conservative youth movement, Atid (Future), provides the novel 'bookmobile' which travels around university campuses selling Jewish books at a discount. The B'nai B'rith supports Jewish students through the Hillel Foundation, which covers 20–30 per cent of campus youth, and the B'nai B'rith Youth Organisation helps in providing social activities and vocational guidance. The JWB-supported Jewish community centres, the amalgamation of Young Men's and Women's Hebrew Associations (YM-YWHA), concentrate on sports and athletics, and also provide cultural activities. The largest is in New York City.

Cultural Activities

The National Foundation for Jewish Culture, through the Jewish Cultural Appeal, grants scholarships and awards for cultural efforts in the arts. It encourages Jewish studies in small and medium-sized communities.

The Jewish Welfare Board sponsors the Jewish Book Council and the Jewish Music Council. It also runs the Jewish Centre and Lecture Bureau, and acts as a service agency for Jewish community centres throughout the USA and Canada. Many scholarly societies exist including the American Jewish Historical Society, the American Academy for Jewish Research and the Leo Baeck Institute.

The United States Jewish community plays a dominant role in the cultural and academic life of the United States, particularly in literature. American Jewish writers have created their own genre in the literature of the English-speaking world, through authors such as Saul Bellow, Bernard Malamud, Chaim Potok, Philip Roth and many others.

Museums

The United States has many Jewish museums. The largest and most important, is the Jewish Museum on Fifth Avenue in New York City, which includes one of the finest collections of Jewish ritual objects in the world. In Los Angeles, the Skirball Museum of Hebrew Union College has a collection of ceremonial art and archaeological objects. Washington DC houses the Leila and Albert Small Jewish Museum and, in the B'nai B'rith building, the Philip Klutznick Museum. There are two small Jewish museums in Miami and the Temple Museum in Cleveland, Ohio contains Jewish ceremonial art objects, prayerbooks and manuscripts, and the Ratner Collection of Judean Antiquities. The largest institution of the Western States is the Judah L. Magnes Memorial Museum in Berkeley, California. The National Jewish Museum is attached to the Mikveh Israel Synagogue in Philadelphia.

Libraries

Of the many Jewish libraries in the United States, the most important are the Yivo Institute of Jewish Research Library, with 300 000 volumes, and the library of the Jewish Theological Seminary of America, with 220 000 volumes and 6000 manuscripts, both in New York. The Hebrew Union College Institute of Religion in Cincinnati has 200 000 volumes and its Music Section in New York has 50 000 volumes. The New York Public Library itself has 125 000 volumes of Judaica and Hebraica. Other New York Jewish libraries are at New York University and Columbia University (the Butler Library). In Los Angeles are at least four important Jewish libraries in addition to the Jewish Studies Collection of some 100 000 volumes at UCLA. There is also a Jewish collection at Harvard University.

Many Jewish bookshops are to be found in the major Jewish centres, particularly New York City and Los Angeles.

Press
The US Jewish community has a very large press, but there is no single leading national newspaper corresponding, for instance, to the London *Jewish Chronicle*. The Jewish Telegraphic Agency based in New York publishes the *Daily News Bulletin* which is distributed worldwide. The weekly Yiddish language *Jewish Forward* is published in New York. The other New York Yiddish paper is the Communist *Morning Freiheit*, published three times weekly. There are more than 75 weekly newspapers, including the *Jewish Exponent* (Philadelphia), *Jewish News* (Newark), the *B'nai B'rith Messenger* in Los Angeles (an independent paper not published by the B'nai B'rith), the *Jewish Week* and the *Jewish Press* in New York and the *Jewish Floridian* in Miami. Mid-West papers include the Detroit *Jewish News* and the Chicago *Sentinel*.

Of the many important monthlies the most influential is probably *Commentary* published by the American Jewish Committee, which since its foundation in 1945 has established itself as one of the leading journals of the English-speaking world, read well beyond the Jewish community. The American Jewish Committee also publishes a quarterly, *Present Tense*, and in co-operation with the Jewish Publications Society of America (JPSA) publishes the *Amerian Jewish Year Book*. *Moment* is a Jewish intellectual monthly. The American Jewish Congress issues the *Congress Monthly* and the scholarly quarterly *Judaism*. The Zionist movement produces the leading monthly, *Midstream*. All religious persuasions have their own monthly publications.

The most important Jewish publishing houses in America are the Herzl Press in New York, and the prestigious Jewish Publication Society in Philadelphia. New York City also houses the large Bloch Publishing Company, founded in 1854, and Schocken Books.

Welfare
The Council of Jewish Federations and Welfare Funds acts as an umbrella organisation for many welfare groups and community councils in individual states. These support many hospitals including the celebrated Mount Sinai and Montefiore in New York City. These hospitals receive government and state funds for their maintenance and admit non-Jews. There are many homes for the aged, child care facilities, and family service groups.

181

Relations with Israel

Although there have been occasional fluctuations in relations between the United States and Israel, the US has supported Israel since its inception when President Truman recognised the provisional government as the *de facto* authority of the new State of Israel on the very day it was established.

The United States has staunchly supported Israel and aided it with massive loans and grants. While it may be true that the Jewish lobby influences United States policy on the Middle East, this should not be regarded as the only or even the main reason for US support for Israel; Israel is important to the US strategically and is also the only democracy in the Middle East with similar ideals to that of American society. Thus the US regards Israel as the only strong and reliable ally in the region. One aspect of this support was the US legislation against the Arab boycott, which became possible without damaging the United States trade with the Arab world.

There are full ambassadorial relations between the USA and Israel. Apart from the embassy in Washington DC, Israel maintains consulates general in New York, Atlanta, Boston, Chicago, Houston, Los Angeles, Miami, Philadelphia and San Francisco. The USA has an embassy in Tel Aviv and a consulate in Jerusalem.

Large numbers of Jews from the United States have settled in Israel and some 200 000 Israelis are living in the USA.

Historical Sites

That despite its great size the United States Jewish community does not have many Jewish historical monuments emphasises the newness of the community. There are however a number of sites worthy of note.

A plaque in Battery Park, New York City, recalls the spot where the 23 Jewish immigrants landed in 1654. Also in New York City, on the roof of the Wall Street Synagogue, is a replica of the first synagogue in America of circa 1730. Other ancient synagogues in New York City include the Sephardi Shearith Yisrael, representing the oldest congregation in America and the Central Synagogue on Lexington Avenue, the oldest synagogue on its original site, and designated as a 'landmark of New York'. The Reform Temple Emmanu-El on Fifth Avenue is one of the largest synagogues in the world, and the Milton Steinberg Building which belongs to the Park Avenue Synagogue has the largest continuous stained glass facade in the world. At Chatham Square in Lower Manhattan is the site of the first Jewish cemetery.

The oldest extant synagogue is the Touro Synagogue in Newport, Rhode Island. Built in 1763, it is a fine example of colonial architecture, and has been declared a national shrine by the US government. It was immortalised in a poem by Longfellow.

Another designated historical landmark is the Beth Elohim Synagogue in Charleston, South Carolina, which was built in 1749, and the cemetery nearby is the oldest in the South, containing graves of soldiers who fell in the revolutionary war. Another Southern cemetery of interest is the one at Richmond, Virginia, containing the graves of Jewish soldiers who fell in the Civil War.

The third oldest synagogue in the USA is in Baltimore, and is being restored as a Jewish National Shrine. The old Mikveh Israel Synagogue in Philadelphia contains memorabilia of early American Jewish pioneers.

Memorials of the Holocaust include the huge sculpture by Jacques Lipschitz in Philadelphia, a bronze sculpture by Gizel Berman in Seattle. In Los Angeles the Skirball Museum of HUC has a photographic collection of destroyed Jewish landmarks in Europe. Ground has been broken for two new Holocaust Memorial Museums – near Battery Park in New York and in Washington DC.

General Position

The United States Jewish community is the largest in the world, comprising almost half the world total – the figure for 1984 was 44 per cent. Consequently, the community plays a dominant role in world Jewish affairs and has assumed the cultural leadership of Diaspora Jewry.

Antisemitism is generally minimal. There has been some concern about the activities of some neo-fascist and Christian fundamentalist groups, but the community is well able to contain them. Relations with the wider community are in fact good and the Conference of Christians and Jews is active. A more serious problem is the recent development in relations with the black community, where tension has occurred in New York City for economic reasons, and certain black leaders have been influenced by Third World anti-Zionism.

The community plays a major role in the general life of the country. Apart from its importance in academic and cultural worlds, it makes a significant contribution to political life, with Jews in both Houses of Congress and occasionally serving also in the Cabinet. There has been a Jewish secretary of state, but no Jewish president so far. However, there have been Jewish state governors ever since the first took office in Georgia as far back as 1801. It is in the legal world that Jews have particularly established themselves. A number of presidents of the Supreme Court have been Jewish, and frequently one or more of its members have been Jewish.

The characteristic of present day US Jewry is its self-confidence. It is outspokenly and unashamedly Jewish, and prepared to use its influence on behalf of Israel and world Jewry, which it does effectively. Although the community constitutes only 3 per cent of the total US population, it is the most highly educated and the most affluent of all United States minorities.

URUGUAY

Population: 2 988 000   Jewish population: 44 000

History
The first Jewish settlers in Uruguay were mostly impoverished Sephardi immigrants who came from the Middle East in the early 1900s. After the first Balkan War (1912–13) they were joined by a second more prosperous and educated wave of Sephardi Jews from the same area. The first Zionist Organisation was founded in 1911 and by 1917 several colonies had been established by the Jewish Colonisation Association.

A small number of East European immigrants arrived in the 1920s and after 1933 immigration of Jews from Central Europe steadily increased until heavy restrictions were imposed at the outbreak of the Second World War. After the war Uruguay received refugees from Europe and, several years later, from Hungary and the Middle East.

Composition of the Community
Seventy-three per cent of the present population is of East and Central European origin, 15 per cent West European. About 12 per cent are Sephardim. The majority live in the capital, Montevideo, with a small community of about 1000 in Paysandu in the west on the Uruguay River and another in Rocha in the south-east near the coast. Since the later 1950s there has been little immigration and as a result nearly 70 per cent of the population are native born. Jews are well represented in the middle class and professions, but a small part of the community is poor.

Communal Organisation
The Comité Central Israelita del Uruguay unites the four separate Kehillot: Comunidad Israelita del Uruguay (Ashkenazi), Comunidad Israelita Sefaradi, Nueva Congregación Israelita (German speaking) and Comunidad Israelita Húngara. Paysandu has an independent organisation, the Sociedad Israelita de Paysandu. The Comité Central is affiliated to the World Jewish Congress.

There are many Zionist organisations including the World Zionist Organisation (Latin American Department), the Jewish Agency, KKL and the umbrella body, Organización Sionista Territorial del Uruguay. Zionist political parties are represented by Asociación Jerut, the Federación Sionista Liberal del Uruguay, Mizrahi-Hapoel Hamizrachi and Poale Zion Histadrut.

In 1975 the government reacted to acts of terrorism by the left-wing Tupamaros by clamping down on all left-wing organisations. Jewish organisations and newspapers were affected and left-wing candidates were banned from standing in Jewish communal elections.

Religious Life
Each of the four main communities has its own synagogue and rabbi. There is also a small hassidic community. Approximately eleven synagogues or prayer rooms can be found in Montevideo. Synagogue services are poorly attended.

Education
There are four Jewish schools in Montevideo. The two largest, with 2400 students between them, are the Escuela Integral Hebrea Uruguaya and the Instituto Ariel Hebrao Uruguayo. The more traditional Yavne Institute has a few hundred pupils and there is an ORT school with about 500 students, not all of them Jewish. The local Hebrew classes are attended by about 20 pupils. There is a small Jewish school in Paysandu which has about 40 pupils. The Pnimiah for Jewish students from Paysandu and Rocha studying in Montevideo was established by the Jewish Agency in 1975.

Cultural Activities
The main organisation is the B'nai B'rith (which recently celebrated 50 years in Uruguay). There are several women's organisations, including WIZO and Pioneer Women, which are united in the Consejo de Entidades Femeninas Israelitas del Uruguay (CEFIDU – Uruguayan Council of Jewish Women's Organisations). The two largest youth organisations are the Hebraica-Maccabi Club and the young people's section of the Nueva Congregación Israelita. Both groups are strongly pro-Israel. Ideological demands are satisfied by the three Zionist youth movements, B'nai Akiva, Betar and Hashomer Hatzair. The Dor Hemshech Institute also organises cultural activities. Jews are active in the arts, particularly in the theatre; amongst them is Uruguay's most distinguished playwright, Jacobo Langsner.

Press
The main Jewish newspaper, the Spanish-language weekly *Semanario Hebrao*, is strongly pro-Israel. Other journals include the literary review *Do!*; *La Voz Semanal* published in Spanish and German and the Comité Central's information bulletin. The daily Jewish radio programme, *Voz*

de Sion en el Uruguay is broadcast in both Spanish and Yiddish and is run by the Managing Director of *Semanario Hebrao*. There is a specialist Jewish bookshop in Montevideo.

Relations with Israel
The two countries have full diplomatic relations. Between 1948 and 1970, 2400 Uruguayan Jews settled in Israel. There is much fund-raising for Israel in Uruguay. One project was the planting of the Artigas Forest in Israel which was named after the Uruguayan national hero, José Artigas. Two other forests in Israel were also sponsored by Uruguay's Jewish community.

General Position
The Jewish community is shrinking as a result of assimilation. The strongest community feeling focuses on Zionism, particularly amongst the young. There is little religious commitment or practice.

VENEZUELA

Population: 18 552 000   Jewish population: 20 000

History
Sephardi Jews migrated from the Dutch Caribbean island of Curaçao to Venezuela in the early nineteenth century. The earliest settlement, at Coro (equidistant from Caracas and Maracaibo and almost opposite Curaçao itself), was the site of the first cemetery built in 1832. The state and the Catholic Church were so closely interlinked that the great wave of European emigration between 1880 and 1914 by-passed Venezuela. Instead the modern community was founded by Middle East and North African Sephardim, including a large number from Morocco, who arrived at the turn of the century. In the 1960s many Jews from other Latin American countries started to come to Venezuela whose economy had been boosted by the development of the oil industry.

Composition of the Community
The community is equally divided between Jews of Sephardi and Ashkenazi origin. The majority live in the capital, Caracas, with smaller communities in Maracaibo and some other towns. Recent immigrants from other Latin American countries make up a significant proportion of the community, and most of them, as well as the indigenous population, are involved in commerce or industry.

186

Communal Organisation

The central body, the Confederación de Asociaciones Israelitas de Venezuela (CAIV) consists of four institutions: the Asociación Israelita de Venezuela (the Sephardi Kehilla), the Unión Israelita de Caracas (the Ashkenazi Kehilla), the Zionist Federation and the B'nai B'rith. The Union of Jewish Women, youth movements and representatives from the small towns are affiliated to the CAIV which represents the community in the World Jewish Congress. In order to join the Zionist Federation, the B'nai B'rith or even to use the community's education facilities, sports or social centres, membership of one of the two Kehillot is compulsory. Approximately 16 different groups are affiliated to the Zionist Federation. These include Keren Hayesod, an *aliya* organisation, WIZO, and various student groups. Other social institutions include six B'nai B'rith lodges, the Hillel Foundation and a Family Institute. The Weizmann Institute, the Hebrew University and Tel Aviv University are supported in Venezuela by organisations of friends.

Religious Life

The two central organisations, the Sephardi and Ashkenazi Kehillot, have synagogues and affiliated burial societies. There are nine synagogues in Caracas and one each at Maracaibo, Puerto La Cruz, Valencia and Maracay. The synagogues are all Orthodox apart from the B'nai B'rith, which is Conservative. The seat of the Ashkenazi Beth Din is at the Great Synagogue in Caracas.

Education

Approximately 90 per cent of all Jewish youth receive their primary and secondary education in Jewish schools. These are recognised by the Ministry of Education and have a national reputation for high academic standards. The most important schools are the Colegio Moral y Luces Herzl/Bialik, founded in 1947 by the Ashkenazi Kehilla and amalgamated with the Colegio Hebraica, built in 1971 by the Sephardi Kehilla, comprising kindergarten, primary and secondary schools with a total intake of over 2000 pupils; the Yavne Academy, which is linked to the Colegio Moral y Luces, provides an Orthodox education and has approximately 120 pupils; the privately run Rambam School, which has 500 pupils over the entire school-age range; the Bilu School in Maracaibo whose 120 pupils include children from other communities.

The two Kehillot have also collaborated on the planning of the Institución Hebraica Asociación Civil which is proposed to take 1600 pupils of school-age.

Advanced Jewish education is provided by the Lubavitch Yeshiva Gedolah and the Higher Institute of Jewish Studies. Evening and part-time courses are held for both children and adults, and there are

187

other small groups supported by the World Zionist Organisation and Tel Aviv University. Venezuela's education system is supported by Jerusalem University under the Caracas-Jerusalem plan. About 93 per cent of Jewish youth go on to higher education.

Cultural Activities
The main social and cultural organisation is the Jewish Sports and Social Centre (Centro Social Deportivo Hebraica) which has a training centre attached to it. The Shalom Aleijem Cultural Centre also provides social activities. There is a specialist Jewish bookshop in Caracas.

Press
The principal paper is the weekly *Nuevo Mundo Israelita* which has a wide coverage of local and international Jewish news and Middle East affairs. Other publications include the annuals *Hatikvah* and *Haguesher* and reports by the Jewish Cultural and Information Centre, the Zionist Federation and the Human Rights Commission of the B'nai B'rith.

Welfare
The Jewish community's welfare service aims to ameliorate the conditions of individuals and family groups. The Family Institute of the B'nai B'rith helps individuals and family groups with psychological problems. Bikur Jolim (Ashkenazi) and Tsadaka Basseter (Sephardi) give aid to those in need.

Relations with Israel
The two countries have full diplomatic relations. The Venezuelan embassy moved from Jerusalem to Tel Aviv in 1982. While Venezuela remains neutral in Middle East affairs her relations with Israel are fairly cordial. There is a steady exchange between Israeli and Venezuelan scientists and artists and many Venezuelans study in Israel. Official visits of Venezuelan politicians and intellectuals are frequent. Many of the above activities are promoted by the Venezuelan-Israeli Cultural Institute.

Historical Sites
The cemetery at Coro is the oldest Jewish cemetery still in use on the South American mainland.

General Position
There is no active antisemitism in present-day Venezuela although the Venezuelan Committee of Solidarity with the Palestinian Arab People, with more than 100 000 supporters, assiduously promotes anti-Zionism. Some of these are extreme left-wing intellectuals but the majority are Venezuelans of Arab origin, many of them recent immigrants. The movement is also supported by the Syrian, Libyan and Iraqi embassies.

Christian-Jewish relations are promoted by the Committee for Relations Between Churches and Synagogues (CRISEV). Monthly meetings are held and leading personalities are invited to speak.

The Venezuelan Jewish community is unique in South America. Whereas other communities are declining the Venezuelan community is expanding. Its stability and increasing prosperity have drawn immigrants from all over the continent and it now boasts one of the most successful Jewish educational systems in the world.

VIRGIN ISLANDS (US)

Population: 99 000   Jewish population: 500

Jews have lived in the Virgin Islands since the middle of the seventeenth century. Under liberal Danish rule complete freedom of religion was granted to Catholics and Jews on St. Thomas Island in 1685. The community prospered with the rise of sugar plantations and shipping lines, increasing its numbers to 400. The Sephardi Synagogue at St. Thomas, built in the town of Charlotte Amalie in 1833, is the second oldest synagogue in the United States and its territories. The cemetery of that community is filled with Spanish and Portuguese names. Since 1917, when the islands of St. Thomas, St. Croix and St. John came under United States rule, there have been three Jewish governors.

Most Jews live on the island of St. Thomas, with just a few on St. Croix. The community consists of about 400 affiliated members with another 100 unaffiliated. The old families are mainly Sephardim, but most of the population are recent Ashkenazi immigrants, or their descendants who came from the USA after the Second World War. The Hebrew Congregation of St. Thomas is affiliated to the World Jewish Congress.

YEMEN, NORTH (Yemen Arab Republic)

Population: 9 274 000   Jewish population: 1000

Jews probably lived in Yemen in biblical days and there are actual records of Jewish settlement from the third century CE. In the fourth century the King of the Yemen, Abu Karib Asad (c.390–420), converted to Judaism, as did the fifth-century ruler, Dhu Nuwas, along with many of his subjects. Although the country subsequently came under Islamic rule it was not until the tenth century Shi'a regime that Muslim restrictive measures were enforced. In 1172, Maimonides wrote his famous letter to the Jews of Yemen, exhorting them to remain steadfast in their faith.

189

In the late seventeenth century the community produced the poet and cabbalist, Shalom Shabbazi, who lived in Taizz in the south and wrote in both Hebrew and Arabic.

Life remained difficult for Yemenite Jews up until the twentieth century. In 1905 the Yemeni ruler, Imam Yahya, reintroduced severe restrictions on Jews who were banned from riding astride an animal, acting in surety or as a guarantor and a height limit was placed on their homes. In 1921, a new law decreed forcible conversion of Jewish orphans under 13 even if the mother was still alive. Yemenite Jews began settling in Palestine from the fifteenth century onwards. A larger group settled in 1881–2, earlier even than the Bilu, and increasing numbers came from 1905 onwards. But in 1929, Jews were banned from emigrating to Palestine.

In 1948, Imam Yahya was succeeded by his less repressive son Imam Ahmed who subsequently abolished the ban on Jewish emigration. From May 1949 to September 1950, 48 818 Jews poured across the mountains of the Aden Protectorate to be airlifted to Israel on 430 flights in what came to be known as Operation Magic Carpet.

A few Jews remain in the north, in villages in and around the town of Saada, in Sa'ata province 55 miles south of the Saudi border and 110 miles north of Sana'a. Latest reports suggest that there is no longer any community left in the capital, Sana'a, but according to some sources there could be several thousand Jews still living in North Yemen.

The present Yemenite Jews are divided geographically into the Yahood Al-Maghrib (Western Jews) which includes the Saada area down to near Hajj (about 50 miles north-west of Sana'a) and the Yahood Al-Mashrag (Eastern Jews) to the east of Saada. Two synagogues may still be in existence in Saiqaya and in Amlah.

Under the present regime, Jews are relatively well treated and allowed to practise their religion but they still live as *dhimmis*. They are banned from politics, the army and civil service, and they cannot own land. Jews mainly work as artisans in gold and silver and as masons and small traders.

The Jewish community today is isolated and scattered and has great difficulty in obtaining religious books because of the ban on contact with world Jewry.

YEMEN, SOUTH (People's Democratic Republic of Yemen)

Population: 2 500 000   Jewish population: nil

Jewish settlement dates back to the Roman era and includes the Habani Jews, an exotic tribal community who lived in the Hadhramaut in the remote Eastern region. The modern community began with the British occupation of the country in 1839 and the subsequent establishment of a Jewish community in the port of Aden. The community grew and by 1946 numbered 7000 in Aden itself and a further 2000 Jews elsewhere in the Protectorate.

Its communal structures included a community council, a Beth Din and rabbi, four synagogues, a Jewish hospital and the Selim School, which had been established by the Anglo-Jewish Association.

In 1947 rioting against Jews led to 100 being killed. Continuing tension in the country was accompanied by steady emigration and on 5 June 1967, after further rioting at the outbreak of the Six-Day War, it was decided to evacuate the remaining 132 Jews from the country. They were flown out to Israel and Britain on 18 June 1967. There is no longer a community in South Yemen. About 70 per cent of the former community have settled in Israel.

YUGOSLAVIA

Population: 23 123 000   Jewish population: 5500

History

A Jewish settlement in what is today Yugoslavia was already known in Roman times. Later, medieval communities were established at Dubrovnik and Split on the Dalmatian coast. After 1492 refugees from Spain settled in the country and established centres at Belgrade and Sarajevo; under the Turks these communities owed allegiance to the Haham Bashi in Constantinople and spoke their hybrid language of Ladino into the twentieth century. Small communities of Ashkenazi Jews lived in Novi Sad, Subotica and Zagreb. The unsatisfactory situation of Jews in Serbia improved after the Treaty of Berlin in 1878. The Jewish community of Zagreb was founded in 1806, but Jews had only limited rights until their emancipation in 1873. With the formation of Yugoslavia after the First World War, Ashkenazi Jews from Austro-Hungarian territories augmented the Jewish population.

Yugoslavia was invaded by Germany on 6 April 1941. The Jews of Croatia were rounded up and by August of the same year about 6000 had been killed. On 1 October 1941 the Nazis established a large concentration camp at Jasenovac in central Croatia, where, by the Spring of 1942, the remaining 20 000 Croat Jews were imprisoned. From 1941 to 1943, the island of Rab, as part of Italian-occupied Dalmatia, was used as a large Jewish refugee camp. Though the majority of refugees managed to escape, some joining the partisans in 1943, about 300, mainly women and children, were deported to Auschwitz. Whilst 5000

Jews actively fought the Nazis their struggle was made harder by local support for Hitler. However, many Jews were helped to escape by the Yugoslavs or saved themselves by fighting with the partisans – some even reaching high ranks, such as Mosa Pijade, Vice-President and then President of the Yugoslav Federal Parliament until his death. By the end of the war 80 per cent of Yugoslav Jews, about 60 000 in number, had been killed in the Holocaust. Survivors numbered between 12 000 and 15 000. Between 1948 and 1951 some 9000 Jews emigrated to Israel.

Composition of the Community
The community, divided equally between Sephardi and Ashkenazi, comprises thirty-three separate communities. The three largest are Belgrade (1600), Zagreb (1100) and Sarajevo (1100). Most Jews are in the liberal professions, trade and the arts, and enjoy a relatively high standard of living.

Legal Status
The Federation of Jewish Communities is recognised by the government. The individual communities are voluntary associations. They have no right to levy taxes and are financed by voluntary donations. Only civil marriages are recognised. Laws against discrimination and incitement to racial and religious hatred are strictly enforced. Although Jews are formally recognised as a religion, they enjoy many of the rights available to national rather than religious groups.

Communal Organisation
Savez Jevrejskih Opština Jugoslavije (the Federation of Jewish Communities in Yugoslavia) in Belgrade has an executive council and a working executive committee, with a president, 4 vice-presidents and 3 deputy chairmen. The executive committee in Belgrade has 14 members and is in charge of day-to-day operations. Of the 4 vice-presidents, 3 are the presidents of the largest communities, Belgrade, Zagreb and Sarajevo. The governing body of the Federation, the Annual Conference, presides over questions of policy and finance. The Federation is affiliated to the World Jewish Congress. No separate Zionist organisations exist but there are fund-raising campaigns for Israel, in particular for KKL.

Religious Life
The only rabbi in Yugoslavia lives in Belgrade. In other parts of the country services are conducted by laymen. There are about twelve synagogues but no Beth Din. For the most part Jews concentrate on

their ethnic, rather than their religious identity. Communal seders on the eve of Passover are held regularly.

Education
No full-time Jewish schools exist but in both Zagreb and Belgrade weekly Hebrew evening classes are held and at two kindergartens, one in Belgrade and one in Zagreb, Jewish culture is taught.

Cultural Activities
Belgrade has a Jewish museum and the City Museum of Sarajevo has a Jewish section. The Federation has a good library of Judaica on its premises, and smaller libraries can be found elsewhere in Belgrade. The Jewish Museum in Belgrade has an archival collection as does Zagreb where there is also a small library of Judaica. The mixed Jewish choirs in Belgrade and Zagreb pay special attention to Jewish music.

A Jewish holiday resort at Pirovac provides cultural activities which are also attended by Jews from other European countries and from Israel. Twice yearly seminars are held for young people and several communities, notably Sarajevo, Skopje and Osijek, have youth clubs whose functions are well attended, as are the performances of the choirs on Chanukah and Purim. Community clubs meet weekly in Belgrade, Zagreb, Novi Sad and Subotica.

Press
The Federation publishes a bi-monthly, *Jevrejski Pregled* (Jewish Review), in Serbo-Croat with an English summary and a periodical for youth, *Kadima*. On a less regular basis it produces the scholarly *Jewish Studies*, and an annual *luah*.

Books on Jewish history and literature are published and foreign books are translated into Serbo-Croat. Two facsimile editions of the famous Sarajevo Haggada have been published.

Welfare
There is a home for the aged with 90 beds in Zagreb. There are Jewish welfare committees in different communities, eight of these are administered by women's groups.

Relations with Israel
Diplomatic relations were broken off in 1967, after the Six-Day War. However, trade relations between the two countries are good. About 11 000 Yugoslav Jews have settled in Israel and regular contacts are maintained between the Yugoslav community and the Israeli Yugoslav Immigrant Organisation (Hitachdut Olei Yugoslavia). Those wishing to emigrate to Israel are allowed to take any movable property with them.

193

Many young Jews go to summer camp in Israel and Israeli youth leaders are invited to the camps in Yugoslavia.

A Yugoslav section of the Martyrs' Forest in Israel has 60 000 trees commemorating the 60 000 Yugoslav Jews who perished in the Holocaust. Most of the money for this was raised in Yugoslavia by both Jews and non-Jews.

Historical Sites
The most important ancient synagogue is at Dubrovnik with others at Split, Novi Sad, Subotica, Rijeka and Sarajevo, the last having relics of the Spanish Inquisition. The Jewish Historical Museum in Belgrade houses a second-century pillar inscribed in Greek from a synagogue at Stobi near the Greek border.

Dubrovnik and Split have ancient cemeteries. There are about forty monuments to Jewish victims of the Holocaust, including those at the Mirogoj cemetery at Zagreb and at Novi Sad and on the public squares at Bitola, Orijek and Stip.

General Position
The population has remained relatively static for more than a decade. The community, though not religiously observant, is vigorous, with a strong sense of cultural identity. There is hardly any antisemitism and relations with the non-Jewish population are excellent with many Jews in prominent positions. The memory of Jewish involvement with the partisans is very much alive. There is a high level of intermarriage but non-Jewish spouses of mixed marriages have usually become active in the Jewish community.

ZAIRE

Population: 34 250 000   Jewish population: 200

In the early twentieth century a number of South African Jews settled in the former Belgian Congo. They were followed later by Sephardim from Rhodes (see under Zimbabwe, where others of the same group were referred to as 'Rhodeslies'). By 1959 the community numbered some 2500, with the largest settlement being in Elizabethville (later Lubumbashi) and a smaller one in Leopoldville (later Kinshasa).

Today Lubumbashi still has a synagogue and a chief rabbi, along with a main communal organisation, the Communauté Israelite du Shaba which is affiliated to the World Jewish Congress.

There are good relations between Zaire and Israel, which in the past trained Zairean military personnel. Zaire became one of the first African Countries to re-establish diplomatic relations with Israel in 1983 following the severing of relations by African states in 1973. Technical and agricultural aid from Israel to Zaire has begun again, and discussions have taken place regarding the strengthening of military co-operation.

ZAMBIA

Population: 6 420 000   Jewish population: 85

History
Jews came as cattle ranchers and traders and established the community's first congregation in Livingstone in 1905. By 1910 it had 38 members and by 1921 the total Jewish population had reached 110. Jews such as Sir Edmund Davis, Soly Joel and Sir Ernest Oppenheimer helped to develop the copper industry. Refugees from Germany came in the 1930s and post-war economic expansion brought the Jewish population to 1200 by the mid-1950s. When Northern Rhodesia became independent as Zambia in 1964, numbers declined, and by 1968 had fallen to 500. Up to 1978 Zambian Jewry came under the aegis of the Central African Jewish Board of Deputies, and the Central African Zionist Council, in Bulawayo, Zimbabwe.

Composition of the Community
The community is almost entirely Ashkenazi. There are Jews in Lusaka, and in the urban areas of the Copperbelt. Most are not Zambian citizens. The community is largely upper middle class.

Legal Status
The community is recognised as a private voluntary organisation, which has the right to levy taxes on its members. Both religious and civil marriages are recognised. *Shechita* is permitted.

Communal Organisation
The Council for Zambia Jewry Limited, founded in 1978, is the central body, and is based in Lusaka. The Trustees are appointed and serve on a voluntary basis. The Council is recognised by the whole community and represents Zambian Jewry in the World Jewish Congress. There are no separate Zionist women or youth organisations.

Religious Life
There is no rabbi, and laymen take the services. There is a synagogue in Lusaka and another at Ndola in the Copperbelt. Both synagogues have communal halls.

Press
Zambia possesses no Jewish press of its own, but the *Central African Zionist Digest* and the *Board* are sent individually to Zambian Jews from Zimbabwe.

Education and Welfare
The community does not possess any education or welfare institutions of its own.

Relations with Israel
Zambia and Israel do not have diplomatic relations. However, trade relations are expanding and a number of Israeli families work in the country on short-term contracts, attached to the Israeli construction company Solel Boneh.

General Position
Once a community with five separate congregations, Zambian Jewry has now gone into decline. The very small community left remains linked to the neighbouring larger community of Zimbabwe.

ZIMBABWE

Population: 8 300 000   Jewish population: 1200

History
Daniel Montague Kisch was the first Jew to live in the area that was to become Southern Rhodesia and later Zimbabwe. He traded in Matebeleland around 1870, where he became an adviser and secretary to King Lobengula of the Ndebele. The first congregations were established at Bulawayo in 1894, Salisbury (now Harare) in 1895, and Gwelo in 1901. Many of the early immigrants were from Lithuania and ran hotels and stores. The first mayor of Bulawayo was a Jew. In the 1920s and 1930s Sephardim arrived from Rhodes, and became known as Rhodeslies. By the time of the establishment of the Central African Federation in 1953, Jews had become part of the white elite of the colony, supplying several cabinet ministers and one prime minister, Sir Roy Welensky. With the failure of the Federation in 1963, Jews began to emigrate, and there has been a steady decline in the Jewish population since then.

Composition of the Community
The community is largely Ashkenazi with a significant Sephardi minority (the Rhodeslies). The population has fallen from a peak of around 7000 in the 1960s to less than 1200. It is divided between Bulawayo (474) and Harare (694), and a few families in other centres and consists mostly of well to do business and professional people.

Legal Status
The Central African Jewish Board of Deputies is recognised by the government and local authorities in Zimbabwe.

Communal Organisation
The Central African Jewish Board of Deputies, founded in 1943 as the Council of Rhodesian Jewry and changing its name to the present one in 1946, is the central body. Based in Harare, it is recognised by all sections of the community and is affiliated to the World Jewish Congress. The Central African Zionist Organisation is the Zionist umbrella body. The Zionist movement, which is very active, was established early in the area, and a Chovevei Zion 'Tent' was set up in Bulawayo as early as 1898 and is still functioning. Communal centres exist in both Harare and Bulawayo. There is also a Union of Jewish Women in Harare and the Women's Zionist Council of Central Africa is very active in Zimbabwe. The Hebrew Order of David has two Lodges: the Ashkelon Lodge in Bulawayo, and the Natanya Lodge in Harare. Youth organisations are mostly Zionist orientated.

Religious Life
Harare has three congregations, Ashkenazi, Sephardi and Progressive. Bulawayo has now only the one Orthodox Ashkenazi congregation; it recently absorbed the progressive congregation in the town. The Ashkenazi congregation in Bulawayo has a minister. There are also Chevrei Kadisha.

Education
The Jewish education system in Zimbabwe is very well developed. There are two Jewish schools: the Carmel School in Bulawayo and the Sharon School in Harare. However, with only 200 Jewish children of school-age there is now a large enrolment of African and Indian pupils, many of whom win the prizes for Hebrew.

Press
The Central African Board of Deputies publishes the *Board* and the Central African Zionist Organisation the *Central African Zionist Digest*.

Welfare
There is a home for the elderly in Bulawayo. There are also various benevolent and welfare committees.

Relations with Israel
Zimbabwe, which became independent in 1980, has never established diplomatic relations with Israel, and espouses Third World anti-Zionism. Large numbers of Zimbabwe Jews have settled in Israel and the emigration continues.

General Position
Many young people left the country between 1975 and 1980, and the community that remains is therefore ageing. While the community has declined numerically its institutions continue to function effectively. The schools have taken in large numbers of non-Jews, who are now in the majority. The outlying communities of Gwelo, KweKwe and Gatooma are now no longer viable.

TABLE OF WORLD JEWISH POPULATION IN DESCENDING ORDER

USA	5 835 000
Israel	3 590 000
USSR	1 810 876
France	535 000
UK	330 000
Canada	325 000
Argentina	228 000
Brazil	150 000
South Africa	120 000
Australia	90 000
Hungary	80 000
Uruguay	44 000
Mexico	35 000
Italy	34 500
Belgium	30 000
Federal Republic of Germany	28 000
Iran	25 000
Netherlands	25 000
Rumania	23 000
Turkey	23 000
Venezuela	20 000
Switzerland	18 300
Chile	17 000
Sweden	16 000
Ethiopia	15 000
Morocco	13 000
Austria	12 000
Czechoslovakia	12 000
Spain	12 000
Denmark	9000
Colombia	7000
Poland	6000
India	5600
Yugoslavia	5500

Bulgaria	5000
Peru	5000
Greece	4875
New Zealand	4800
Syria	4000
Panama	3800
Tunisia	3500
Costa Rica	2500
Puerto Rico	2000
Ireland	2000
Luxembourg	1200
Zimbabwe	1200
Finland	1200
Cuba	1000
Ecuador	1000
Monaco	1000
North Yemen	1000
Norway	950
Paraguay	900
Guatemala	800
Jamaica	800
Hong Kong	700
Japan	700
Algeria	600
Bolivia	600
Curaçao	600
Gibraltar	600
Virgin Islands (US)	500
German Democratic Republic	400
Surinam	350
Kenya	330
Portugal	300
Singapore	300
Egypt	240
Albania	200
Bahamas	200
Iraq	200
Thailand	200
Zaire	200
Dominican Republic	150
Haiti	150
Honduras	150
Philippines	150
Taiwan	150

Channel Islands	140
El Salvador	100
Lebanon	100
Zambia	85
Afghanistan	50
Barbados	50
Bermuda	50
Malta	50
South Korea	50
Aruba	30
Indonesia	30
Cyprus	25
Burma	20
Malaysia	10
Nicaragua	10
Trinidad and Tobago	10
Pakistan	5
People's Republic of China	5

GLOSSARY AND ABBREVIATIONS

H = Hebrew   lit. = literal meaning

Agudat Israel (H)   Orthodox religious movement, also the name of an Israeli political party.

AJDC   American (Jewish) Joint Distribution Committee

Aliya (H)   Jewish immigration to Israel.

Ashkenazi, pl. Ashkenazim (H)   Originally German Jews and their descendants in other countries. The term embraces Jews all over the world who share the Ashkenazi cultural legacy.

Av Beth Din (H)   Head of a Jewish ecclesiastical court.

Baghdadi (Arabic)   General term used to describe Jews from Iraq or of Iraqi origin.

Betar (H)   Revisionist Zionist youth movement.

Beth Din (H)   Jewish ecclesiastical court.

B'nai Akiva (H)   Religious Zionist youth movement.

B'nai B'rith (H)   International Jewish service organisation and fraternal society.

Brit Ivrit Olamit (H)   Organisation for the promotion of the Hebrew language.

Bundist   Member of Bund, the Jewish Socialist Party, founded in Russia in 1897 and devoted to Yiddish, autonomy and secular Jewish nationalism, and sharply opposed to Zionism.

Centro Deportivo (Spanish)	lit. Sports Centre. The central Jewish social and cultural institution in many Latin American communities.
Chazan (H)	Synagogue cantor.
Cheder (H)	School for the traditional religious instruction of young children.
Chevra Kadisha (H)	Burial society.
Chug Ivri (H)	Hebrew conversation group.
Dhimmi (Arabic)	lit. protected person; Islamic term for members of the Jewish or Christian religion who were given an inferior status.
Diaspora	Jews living outside Israel.
Dor Hemshech (H)	Youth organisation, often referred to as Young Leadership.
Dror (H)	Radical Zionist youth movement, merged with Habonim.
FEDECO	Federación de Comunidades Judias de Centro-america y Panama.
Firman (Turkish)	Oriental sovereign's edict; grant, permit.
Habonim (H)	Radical Zionist youth movement.
Hadassah (H)	Women's Zionist Organisation of America.
Haham (H)	Title given to rabbinic scholars. Sephardi Jews use the title for their local rabbis.
Hakoah (H)	Youth or sports club.
Hanoar Hatzioni (H)	Non-political Zionist youth movement.
Hashomer Hatzair (H)	Socialist Zionist youth movement.
Hassidism (H)	Popular Jewish religious movement which emerged in the second half of the eighteenth century.
Herut (H)	Right-wing Israeli political party.
HIAS	Hebrew Immigrant Aid Society.

Histadrut (H)	General Federation of Labour in Israel.
ICJW	International Council of Jewish Women.
JNF	Jewish National Fund.
JWB	Jewish Welfare Board.
Kashrut (H)	Jewish dietary laws.
Kehilla, pl. kehillot (H)	Traditional organised Jewish community, or communal body governing that community.
Keren Hayesod (H)	Subsidiary of the Jewish National Fund (KKL – see below).
KKL	Keren Kayement Le Yisrael – the Jewish National Fund.
Kosher (H)	Ritually correct, especially in relation to food.
Ladino or Judeo-Spanish	Hispanic language of Jews of Spanish origin.
Lag B'Omer (H)	Semi-holiday when the mourning customs of abstention are lifted.
Landsmanschaft (Yiddish)	An association of immigrants from the same country of origin.
Luah (H)	Calendar or year book.
Maccabi (H)	Non-political sports youth movement.
Machsike Hadass (H)	Ultra-Orthodox religious movement.
Madrich (H)	Group leader, usually in a youth movement.
Magbit (H)	General term for the major fundraising organisation for Israel.
Magen David Adom (H)	lit. Red Shield of David; the Israeli equivalent of the Red Cross.
Mapam (H)	United Workers Party, left-wing Israeli Labour Party.
Marrano, pl. Marranos (Spanish) or New Christians	Term applied to groups of Jewish converts to Christianity in the Iberian Peninsula and their descendants.

204

Matzah, pl. matzot (H)	Unleavened bread eaten at Passover.
Menorah (H)	Seven-branched candelabrum used in the Jewish ritual, also the official symbol of the State of Israel.
Mikveh (H)	Ritual bath.
Minyan, pl. minyanim (H)	The minimum number of ten men needed to form a quorum for a Jewish Orthodox service.
Mizrahi (H)	Religious Zionist movement.
Mohel, pl. mohelim (H)	Man who carries out the rite of circumcision according to Jewish law.
Oleh, pl. olim (H)	Immigrant to Israel.
Oneg Shabbat (H)	Friday evening ceremony welcoming the sabbath.
ORT	Organisation for Rehabilitation Through Training
OSE	Oeuvre de Secour aux Enfants – a worldwide organisation for child care, health and hygiene.
Poale Zion (H)	Socialist Zionist Movement.
Romaniot	Greek-speaking Jews of the Eastern Roman Empire, most of whom were gradually absorbed into the immigrant Sephardi communities after the fifteenth century.
Seder (H)	Passover meal and ceremony.
Sephardi, pl. Sephardim (H)	Descendants of Jews who lived in Spain or Portugal before the expulsion of 1492. The term is applied to Jewish communities sharing in the Sephardi religious and cultural heritage.
Shechita (H)	Killing of animals for food by the method laid down by Jewish dietary laws.
Shochet, pl. shochtim (H)	Man who kills animals for food according to the rules of Shechita.
Shtetl, pl. shtetlach (Yiddish)	Traditional Jewish township in Eastern Europe.

Shtibl, pl. shtiblach	Hassidic prayer room.
Sifrei Torah (H)	The scrolls of the Law.
UJA	United Jewish Appeal.
Ulpan (H)	School for teaching Hebrew (through the medium of Hebrew).
WIZO	Women's International Zionist Organisation.
WJC	World Jewish Congress.
Yeshiva, pl. yeshivot (H)	Traditional religious academy for rabbinical training and advanced study of the scriptures, particularly the Talmud.

Temple Israel

Minneapolis, Minnesota

IN HONOR OF
THE BAR MITZVAH OF
DANIEL LISZT
FROM
RICKY & CONNIE BUTWINICK